LIES, DAMNED LIES & ANGLERS

The One That Got Away and Other Fishy Tales

Also available by Bruce Sandison

ANGLING LINES

RIVERS & LOCHS OF SCOTLAND

Bruce Sandison

LIES, DAMNED LIES & ANGLERS

The One That Got Away
and Other Fishy Tales

BLACK & WHITE PUBLISHING

First published 2011
by Black & White Publishing Ltd
29 Ocean Drive, Edinburgh EH6 6JL

1 3 5 7 9 10 8 6 4 2   11 12 13 14

ISBN: 978 1 84502 341 6

Typeset by Ellipsis Digital Ltd, Glasgow
Printed and bound by MPG Books Ltd, Bodmin

Contents

	Foreword by Jim Seaton	xiii
1.	What Makes an Angler?	1
2.	Everything Under Control	3
3.	Play On, Give Me Excess of It	5
4.	Sandwood Bay	7
5.	Spring Into Action	10
6.	The White Heat of Angling Technology	12
7.	European Unions	14
8.	Are We There Yet?	17
9.	Poets' Pub	19
10.	Never a Cross Word	22
11.	The Ones That Got Away	24
12.	Fly-fishing with Yorkshire Terriers	27
13.	A Perfectly Good Boat of My Own	29
14.	The Annual General Meeting	31
15.	Loch Leven	35
16.	Dangerous Dancing	37
17.	The Tarmac Shuffle	39
18.	It Is All in the Boot	42
19.	A Stiff Brandy	45
20.	Magical Islands	47
21.	St Abbs	50
22.	Start Them Young	52
23.	Mountain Goat Salmon Fishing	55
24.	Sporting Gentleman	57
25.	The Secret of Angling Success	60
26.	Fishing and the Water of Life	62
27.	Hope Springs Eternal	65
28.	Bee Prepared	68
29.	Beavering About	70
30.	Canon William Greenwell	73
31.	Go Fly a Kite	74
32.	Pushing the Boat Out	77

CONTENTS

33.	When All Else Fails	79
34.	Two Caithness Gems	81
35.	UK's Fastest Flowing River	84
36.	Loch St Johns	86
37.	Bringing Up Anglers	88
38.	Finding Salmon Fishing	91
39.	Making an Angling Dream Come True	93
40.	A Wry Look at the Sporting Scene	95
41.	Highland River	98
42.	Go Wild for Real Salmon	100
43.	Scotland's Aquatic 'Wolf' from the Ice Age	103
44.	Summer Sun	106
45.	A Competitive Edge	109
46.	Fishing by the Short Loch	111
47.	Granddad	113
48.	The Best of Scotland	116
49.	Beginning	118
50.	Arkaig Treasure	121
51.	The Morning Rise	123
52.	A Cunning Plan	126
53.	The Rough Bounds	130
54.	Keep Your Hair On	133
55.	Ducked in the Don	136
56.	Ladies First	138
57.	The Happy Strath	140
58.	Leap Before You Look	143
59.	New Year's Day	145
60.	Big Alisdair's Loch	148
61.	First Loss	150
62.	Relaxing at Rhiconich	153
63.	Somebody's Got to Do It	155
64.	Caring for the Inner Angler	157
65.	Leith It to Me	160
66.	Catch and Release	162
67.	Fishing Robinson Crusoe-style	165
68.	Away From It All	168

CONTENTS

69.	I Want a Word With You . . .	170
70.	Birds of a Feather	172
71.	Hill Loch Fishing at Its Finest	175
72.	A Highland Half-hour	178
73.	Sparing the Rod	180
74.	Great Sport	182
75.	Where to Stay?	185
76.	The Silver Tay	187
77.	Auld Lang Syne	190

Acknowledgements

My thanks to the editors of the *John O'Groat Journal, The Inverness Courier, Fly-Fishing & Fly-Tying,* and the *Scottish Daily Mail* in whose pages some of these stories first saw the light of day.

For Ann, with all my love

Foreword

This book is a delightful collection of wonderfully eclectic essays about the joys of fishing in Scotland. It is suffused with humour and shot through with an intense love of the land. In places it is deeply moving: Bruce Sandison talks of the Naver as "a river of a thousand tears", a reference to the Clearances when Sutherland crofters were driven off the land to make more room for sheep. Crofters and their families were forced to take to emigrant ships bound for the New World, an incident the Scottish poet Alasdair Maclean likened to "a fox getting rid of its fleas".

I have been friends with Bruce Sandison for more than thirty years but he can still surprise me. The artist Jack Vettriano gave us the iconic painting *The Singing Butler*, a work believed to have sold more prints than any other; now Bruce has produced his own idiosyncratic (i.e. bonkers) take on the theme – *The Singing Angler*. It works like this: when the trout refuse every fly offered, lure them with music. The two offering the best guarantee, he claims, are Handel's "Messiah" and "Ho Ro My Nut Brown Maiden" (but the last in Gaelic only). I am surprised he did not give Schubert's "Trout Quintet" a try.

On the crucial question of whether this works only if you can carry a tune, he is diplomatically silent. But if, in a moment of desperation, you are forced to experiment with the Sandison sing-along, can I offer one caveat: watch out for the men in white coats carrying a long-sleeved canvas jacket that fastens at the back!

Every generation has had an impact on the environment. We have lost a whole range of species and others are teetering on the brink. Into this mix we may have to add the wild salmon and sea-trout in the lochs and rivers of the Western Highlands and Islands of Scotland. Many species have gone because of loss of habitat; our mighty *Salmo salar* is at risk because of an invasion of habitat – the proliferation of intensive salmon farming along the coastline.

Bruce Sandison has done more than anyone to highlight the threat to a fish the Picts once considered sacred. He is a passionate and unapologetic evangelist for Scotland and its wildlife. He reminds me very much of another great friend, the late David Stephen, a naturalist who believed that by looking after nature, people would be looking after themselves and the future. "Ours," wrote Stephen, "is the power but not very often the glory." He also argued that that which is ecologically bad or unsound cannot be ethically or morally correct. That strikes me as a litmus test for salmon farming.

This gentle and heart-warming collection embraces many disciplines: history, geography, climate, ecology and, of course, angling, but primarily it is a hymn to the wonders of wild angling in our glorious country. Like the man himself – and I speak from experience – it will make a wonderful companion on your angling trips to these magnificent waters. It is also the nearest thing to having Bruce as your gillie and that, I can assure you, is a privilege.

Just don't forget to pack the songbook!

Jim Seaton

Preface

I am indebted to my daughter, Jean, for the title of this volume. We had spent the day fishing Loch Heilen in Caithness – famous for the size and quality of its fish – none of which we had either hooked or seen during our visit. I tried to ignore Jean's comments about my choice of flies, but eventually, goaded beyond endurance, I reminded her that there was always an element of chance in fishing. "Yes, dad," she replied, "I know what you mean, lies, damned lies and anglers."

Nevertheless, every story in this book is true and some of the stories are even truer. You can depend upon that. After all, I am an angler and it is a well-known and widely acknowledged fact that we anglers never, ever, tell a lie; least of all when it comes to describing the size of the ones that got away. All anglers are paragons of probity. Believe me.

The stories in this book will adequately demonstrate this truth. I hope that they might also, once and for all, put to rest the calumny that has been so maliciously laid upon us by succeeding generations of non-anglers. We are cheerful and modest creatures, and we count amongst our fellows people of every culture, race and religion to be found anywhere in the world. Angling is and always has been an international pleasure.

Catching fish, however, is only a small part of being an angler. Yes, it does matter, but there are far more important facets of our art that constantly draw us back to river and loch; the sense of absolute peace and contentment that can only be found amongst the large religion of the hills; the call of curlew and golden plover; the majesty of a soaring golden eagle; the sound of loch water lapping the shores of our dreams. If this be error and upon me proved, I will eat my landing net.

Bruce Sandison
Hysbackie, Tongue, Sutherland

1.
What Makes an Angler?

I don't know how or why I became an angler. At least I don't think I know. Most children are introduced to the gentle art by a relative, grandfather, father or uncle. Some begin fishing because an older brother fishes or because they have friends that fish. But I can't remember anyone propelling me into my particular paradise.

None of my friends or family fished. Father was a golfer and though he tried to teach me to play golf, the attempt ended in disgrace and disaster. I lost so many balls that, by the age of twelve, father, in a rage, ordered me off the course he played at Swanston on the edge of the Pentland Hills near Edinburgh. I was sternly admonished never to darken its greens or fairways again until I had properly mastered the art of "keeping my eye" on the ball. Never did.

Much the same happened when dad tried to introduce me to the rudiments of billiards and snooker, to his great angst and the greater angst of the green baize, which I frequently ripped. Anything and anybody within ten feet of the table was at risk of being felled by an inexpertly struck ball, including valuable family heirlooms presumed safe on the mantelpiece.

I fared little better in trying to understand the card game, bridge. My bidding skills induced in my sire a state of near-fatal apoplexy that could have quite easily started World War Three. It was not just counting the cards that caused me difficulty, but the whole mysterious process of bidding. I never managed to master it, much to the anger of whoever is unlucky enough to draw me as their partner.

Rugby was also high on the paternalistic list of things for me to do. But I quickly discovered that lying in the mud at Jock's Lodge, Auld Reekie, on a lump of soggy leather whilst twenty-nine of my blood-crazed colleagues kicked the hell out me was a less than pleasant way of spending a Saturday morning. To this day I can still hear the voice of our semi-crazed sports master screaming, "Kill it, Sandison, kill it!"

I had a brief, slightly more confident flirtation with cricket, which I enjoyed. At least when I was required to participate, it was, more often than not, warm and interspersed with moments of calm during which I could survey the delights of nature. Which is why I invariably missed catches. I eventually hung up my cricket bat when my team mates began referring to me as "First-ball-gets-him Sandison".

I suppose it must have been around this time, by then being self-barred from most team activities, I stumbled into angling. Like many boys in those days, I collected birds' eggs and I deeply coveted a coot's egg from a nest in a mass of vegetation floating in the Water of Leith downstream from the Powderhall greyhound racing stadium. The nest was tantalisingly just out of reach from the riverbank.

Never did get the egg, but I did notice other things of interest in the water: sudden swirls, splashes and the occasional glimpse of brightly-spotted fish darting at flies which hovered above the surface. They fascinated me and I got closer to them at another of my favourite locations, also by the Water of Leith, near Canonmills, where I had a good friend, a tiny black-eyed robin.

There was a little park above the river accessed by a steep flight of steps where I could sit and watch the flow of the stream and its attendant wildlife, including my robin. There were blue tit, coal tit, chaffinch, blackbird, thrush, speckled starling, busy house sparrow, swallows and, clearly visible from the vantage point of my high perch, brown trout in the river.

I wanted them like a cat wants a bird – to touch them, hold them in my hand. But they were, like the coot's nest, beyond my reach. The nearest I came to catching a trout then was by dangling a bent pin wrapped with a fluff of red wool on a piece of string suspended from a garden cane. Trout circled round and grabbed at the wool, but I never managed to hook one. Perhaps that experience sealed my fate.

It certainly wrecked my father's peace of mind because from then on I nagged continuously about fishing, read copiously, talked about nothing else other than fishing and begged for a proper trout rod. It finally arrived, a twelve-foot-long greenheart salmon rod with a spike in the butt so that it could be positioned upright when not in use. A sage old rod well above sixty years of age.

As I write, I look up at the rod, now honourably retired, on the wall above my desk. It had a hard life and suffered many mishaps. Eventually, a rod-maker I knew whittled it down into a beautifully balanced six-foot brook rod. All my children learned to fish using it. I also taught one other person to fish with it – my father. He succumbed to the gentle art one evening when he had come down to collect me from the Flemington Pool on Lyne Water, a tributary of Tweed.

He sat in the parked car watching me fishing, then walked purposefully down to the river. I thought I was in trouble for being late. Instead, he said, "Here, give me a shot, Bruce." I handed the rod over. Dad rarely touched a golf club after that. Which was great news for me: transport to the river, new flies, reel and line and, eventually, a brand new split-cane fishing rod from Alex Martin's shop in Frederick Street, Edinburgh. Dad and I never looked back after that and the rest, as they say, is history.

2.
Everything Under Control

My wife, Ann, and I invariably have a day at the end of September fishing for sea-trout on Loch Hope in North Sutherland. Last year, however, it looked as though the wind was going to defeat us. Nevertheless, after a careful examination of the forward weather forecast, we decided to give it a go.

My first task on arrival at the mooring bay was to bail the boat. This took thirty minutes because the boat was full to the brim with storm water. I then returned to the car to pull on my waders. Which is when I discovered that I had brought Ann's (size 7) rather than my own (size 12). I somehow managed to heave them on and minced delicately down to the boat looking like an oversized, uncomfortable Japanese geisha girl.

I couldn't really complain. After all, I had organised our fishing gear and loaded the car. I thought that it would have been kinder, though, if my fishing partner had commiserated with me rather than falling about laughing at my predicament. Her only, I thought, less than supportive comment, was, "Don't worry, dear, I am sure that you will be up and about again on all fours by tomorrow morning."

Task two was to get the boat to the water. Easier said than done. The recent gales had blown it almost into the small birch wood that borders the shore of the loch. But Ann was brilliant. Not so much because she is physically strong, although she is, but because she is very determined and a wonderful director of operations which was great news for my newly acquired hernia.

Having eventually got the boat afloat, I set up the electric outboard and returned to the car to collect the battery. This was the first time that I had encountered the wretched brute and, believe me, it weighed a ton. I staggered back to the water, arriving breathless and bent double. Thus, with everything ship-shape, sort of, we eventually made it across the loch to Beat 2 at the mouth of the Strathmore River where we began to fish.

Well, to be absolutely precise, I did start to fish, but only briefly; I had to stop and attend to my partner's cast. The naughty old wind had tangled it into a bird's nest, a not infrequent occurrence when we are fishing together. I generally find that it is easier and quicker to tie up a new cast, rather than waste good fishing opportunities trying to perform miracles.

By the time I had sorted it out, it was time to return to the top of the beat to begin another drift. Once there, I turned the boat broadside on to the wind, chucked out the drogue, made a first cast for my partner and handed her the rod. Unfortunately, however, I had forgotten to secure the drogue rope inboard and had to row furiously, upwind, landing net poised, in hot pursuit of the billowing parachute.

With all in order again, I picked up my rod to start fishing, which is when I noticed that Ann's cast was, once more, in complete disarray. Smiling as brightly as I could, I took her rod and began the process of tying up another cast. But as I did so, we were being driven onshore and I pondered my options: bring in the drogue, raise the outboard motor to avoid damage to the propeller on rocks, abandon Ann's tangled cast – which by this time had also caught me – row like hell to keep the boat offshore, or just pray?

I decided to abandon ship and, at the appropriate moment, in the shallows, threw myself over the side, collecting two bootfuls of icy water in the process. I grabbed the bow and heaved the boat safely onto terra firma. I was soaking, my own line was snagged somewhere under the boat and my feet were killing me. "Well, done," said the Manager, "a perfect place for lunch."

Did I mention that Ann had brought Hareton, her wretched Yorkshire terrier, with her? No, I didn't, sorry. I managed to free him from the soggy drogue, and the landing net, and carried him ashore. He recovered his customary ill humour after wolfing down a boiled egg, and my finger will be better soon after he bit the hand that fed it to him.

In the afternoon, the wind got really worked up and we decided to head for home. If we hadn't had the electric outboard we would never have made it across the storm-tossed loch. Even using the motor, I had to row the boat like a galley slave to help it along, whilst Ann cheered me on from the bow. With the boat secure, I humped the dread battery back to the car.

But in spite of everything, it was a wonderful day and we did manage to catch four sea-trout, all taken on a size 12 Ke-He. Ann caught four of them and I caught the rest. Mind you, if my feet hadn't been clamped in a vice and my body chilled to the marrow, it might have been an entirely different story. Well, I think so.

3.
Play On, Give Me Excess of It

Music is an angler's best friend. Not many people know that, but, honestly, it is true. I discovered this fact as a youth when fishing Tweed downstream from Manor Bridge. The river here tumbles into a deep pool, pounding a rocky outcrop on the far bank before sweeping on into the gentle glides below Neidpath Castle.

Trout were rising constantly but persuading them to take my flies was beyond my skill, which was probably because, at that stage in my angling life, I was as skilful with a rod and line as I was with a golf club. Green-keepers used to shudder in horror when they saw me coming, which was one of the reasons why I took up fishing.

It was raining, hard, and I fished on automatically and without much hope. I began to hum an aria from George Frederic Handel's "Messiah" – a work I had recently discovered and enjoyed. Nobody was about, so I burst into song: "He shall feed his flock, like a shepherd . . ." It suddenly occurred to me that, given the number of fish I was catching, I wouldn't be able to feed anybody, let alone a whole flock.

This was when the trout "took". Delighted, I began to concentrate, seriously. The trout stopped rising. I thought that I had just been lucky. I began singing again. Another trout rose and took the middle fly, a March Brown. This seemed to be too much of a coincidence, so I sang again, loudly. As long as I did, fish rose to my flies. With six in the basket I retired happy.

Years later, I gained a degree of notoriety when I used this technique whilst filming a TV show with Paul Young. We were running out of time and the fish were refusing to cooperate. In desperation, I decided to give them a bit of Handel's "Messiah". I strode over to the producer. "Set up the camera and I will catch a trout," I said.

"Are you sure, Bruce?"

"Yup, when I start singing, you start rolling."

He gave me a strange look. "Are you feeling all right?"

With the camera in action, I cast and sang, "He shall feed his flock . . ." The moment flies landed, a trout rose, was hooked, played, and released. In truth, I was surprised, but not half as much as the producer was.

That is exactly how it happened, neither more nor less. Nothing was "fixed". To this day I still meet anglers who don't believe it, but it is surprising how many times I hear the dulcet tones of my companions having a bit of a tune when I am fishing.

Is it a load of nonsense? Well, I agree that it does sound far-fetched, but perhaps by singing we relax, and perhaps when we relax we become better anglers, less fractious and less anxious to catch fish. Sometimes the technique works, and sometimes it doesn't, but it generally does for me.

And not only me. When I was researching a book about Scottish gillies, I interviewed a wonderful man on the island of South Uist. We sat before the peat fire in his living room at Lochboisdale and shared a dram whilst we talked. He told me that he and a friend had been out one day on Loch Bornish when the fish were "down", so, to pass the time, this gentleman turned on a tape recorder to listen to songs sung by Callum Kennedy.

Towards the end of the tape, a trout rose and was hooked, a fish of about 2lb. They played the tape again and, towards the end, another trout rose and was caught. When this happened for a third time, they looked at each other in amazement. Had they stumbled on the secret of angling success? Quickly, they ran the tape forward until the same tune was playing and, again, caught another trout.

During the course of an hour or so, every time the tune was played they had sport. No other tune produced results. I poured another dram and said, "That's a very strange story. Can you tell me the name of your gentleman so that I can speak to him about it?" He did, and soon afterwards I got in touch with him, Iain Christie, a solicitor in Portree on the Isle of Skye.

Iain confirmed all the details and told me that he had designed a fly to commemorate the event and named it after his friend and gillie, Charlie MacLean. Iain sent me a copy of the fly, and three other patterns which he had invented: the Solicitor, designed for sea-trout fishing on Loch Lomond, the Holy Willie, named after one of his fishing companions who was a minister on North Uist, and Wee Peter, after another one of his angling friends.

When Iain shuffled off to that great trout loch in the sky, fly-dresser extraordinaire, Robbie Danabie, sent me examples of these four patterns tied using material from Iain's own box and I have them framed and hanging proudly on my work room wall as I write.

Most of us probably could rustle up a few bars from "Messiah", if needs must, and in all fairness, I should tell you the name of the tune that was used to catch the Loch Bornish trout. It is "Ho Ro My Nut-brown Maiden", well known and most of us have probably sung it at one time or another. The bad news, however, is that it has to be sung in the Gaelic, "Mo Nighean Donn Bhoidheach". Now, there's a challenge for winter's fishless months.

4.

Sandwood Bay

The great fleet sailed south from Cape Wrath. There were 100 warships, their sides sparkling with long lines of shields, powered by fierce, merciless men. Their leader was old in a time when survival was chance and old age remarkable.

King Haakon of Norway surveyed his force with eagle eyes: 8,000 battle-hardened men.

But this was to be Haakon's last battle. Within a few weeks, many of these ships would lie wrecked off the coast at Largs, destroyed by September gales and the cunning of the twenty-two-year-old Scottish monarch, Alexander III. Viking power in Scotland was broken and Haakon died in Orkney whilst shepherding the shattered remnants of his fleet home.

When I walk the hills and cliffs of the Parph Peninsula in North West Sutherland, I imagine I see this mighty fleet sailing past Sandwood Bay to meet its fate. Parph means 'turning point' and in August 1263, the year of the Battle of Largs, the Vikings sailed past Sandwood and rested in Loch Inchard, close to where the busy fishing port of Kinlochbervie stands today.

Sandwood Bay is the most beautiful bay in Scotland – two miles of golden sand washed clean by long, wind-fringed, blue-green Atlantic breakers born a thousand miles away. Rocky outcrops and black, sea-sprayed promontories strut aggressively into the middle of the bay, challenging the elements in an endless battle of surf and thunder.

Northwards, the sands mingle with emerald slopes that stride in an amazing array of jagged stark cliffs, marching towards Cape Wrath. To the south, the slim stack of Am Buachaille, 'the herdsman', breaks the waves in their rush to greet the cliffs of Druim na Buainn. Behind the dunes, Sandwood Loch sparkles in summer sunlight, surrounded by green fields specked white with grazing sheep.

The Sandwood Estate is owned by the John Muir Trust, a charity dedicated to conserving wild places for nature and people. Their policy is to welcome unrestricted responsible pedestrian access to the estate. They make angling permits available locally, but do not actively promote their availability. Fishing on some of the lochs is discouraged to prevent disturbance to sensitive wildlife.

The road from Laxford Bridge, the A838, turns and twists north through desolate heather moorlands. It climbs to Rhiconich at the head of Loch Inchard and the turn-off to Kinlochbervie and the road out to Oldshoremore and Sandwood. Just after Blairmore, a notice points the way to the bay.

From the high point of this track, the white speck of Cape Wrath Lighthouse blinks above green-brown hills. Reay Forest mountains uncompromisingly climb to meet billowy clouds dominated by the razor-edge of Foinaven and the grey shoulder of Arkle. Suddenly, the bay lies before you, bounded by lime-rich pastures, blushing with wild flowers and the breathtaking sweep of the golden bay.

This is where a local shepherd, Sandy Gunn, said he saw a mermaid, sitting on a rocky ledge gazing wistfully out to sea. My wife, Ann, and I were resting on these same rocks on a warm autumn afternoon when a movement in the surf caught our eye. It seemed to be human and I fumbled for my camera, anticipating the photograph of the century.

A young seal was playing in the breakers, surfing to the shore and then swimming out again to repeat the ride, clearly enjoying a moment of most un-seal-like irresponsibility. We watched, transfixed, as the graceful creature tumbled in the foam.

A large wave washed the seal onto the sands and, unaware of our presence, he flapped ashore in a series of ungainly shuffles. We could see the whiskered face and bright, black eyes as he settled on the sands to while away a comforting moment in the sun.

After a while, we put the dogs onto their leads and walked towards the sleeping seal. From about twenty-five yards away he saw us and decided that the sea was a safer place. We waited as he struggled afloat. A moment later, a dark head appeared above the foam and we responded with a cherry wave, thankful for the pleasure he had given us.

Find Sandwood on OS Map 9, Cape Wrath, Second Series, Scale 1:50,000 at Grid reference 227640. Park at Blairmore (198601) and walk north to reach the loch in about two hours. Visit Sandwood as part of a round tour, fishing Loch na Gainimh (204614), Lochain nan Sac (198625), Loch a'Mhuilinn (207630), Loch Meadhonach (210635) and Loch Clais nan Coinneal (213639) on the way out and then, after Sandwood, the Shinary River (240620) and Loch Mor a'Chraisg (9/230602) on the way home.

You will find good stocks of modest brown trout. There are larger specimens, but they keep to the depths and are rarely caught. Sandwood is joined to the sea and in high tides and spate conditions there might be a chance of salmon and sea-trout as well, particularly in June and then in August and September. Whatever, and almost regardless of fishing, Sandwood Bay is one of the special places on Planet Earth. Get there if you can and discover all that is finest about this wonderful country we call home.

5.
Spring Into Action

Spring is late this year. Lingering Icelandic whooper swans still graze stubble fields and few northern trout anglers consider an outing before these graceful birds depart. Even then a sudden storm, rushing wildly in from the Arctic, can leave you frozen and gasping. In the North we get "constructed" rather than dressed, prior to early fishing expeditions.

Bank-fishing frequently brings best results. I have had marvellous sport stalking the shore during April snow showers. Loch Stemster, adjacent to the A9 in Caithness, is a super early loch where fish are always in excellent condition. Some years ago, fishing Loch Swannay in Orkney during an Easter holiday, I had two fine fish each weighing about 1lb 14oz from near Scruit in a blizzard.

But my best spring trout was caught one 1 April from Loch Stilligarry on South Uist in the Outer Hebrides. My son, Blair, was secretary of the South Uist angling club for a number of years and he and his wife Barbara had arranged a day out to celebrate the opening of the season.

After several hours of frozen fingers and no fish, the rest of the party, my wife Ann, Blair, our son Charles and young daughter Jean, retired hurt to investigate the picnic and warm their chilled bodies.

I persevered. The sound of the car boot opening and the flash of Blair's hip-flask eventually brought me to my senses. But as I turned to leave, a trout rose just outwith my casting range. I waded in, feeling ice-cold water seeping through my socks, shoes and trousers.

I cast over the widening rings and the fish took: a magnificent trout of 2lb 4oz. Every time I mention this incident, which is frequently, my family remind me that it is not only anglers who are fools on 1 April. But I know better. Sheer skill, I call it.

Nevertheless, I sometimes wonder – about skill. Did I take that 4lb 10oz trout from Loch Heilen, or did it take me? I was looking the other way at the time. Or that 3lb 1oz fish from Watten? My flies were dangling in the water when it grabbed. Or the monster I lost on a tiny Sutherland loch? I was wading back to the bank, trailing the cast when it slashed at my tail-fly. Skill or luck?

I believe that confidence is half the battle, the sure and certain knowledge that if there are fish about, then you are going to catch them. But to maintain the required level of enthusiasm, anglers must possess at least a semblance of technical proficiency. Not, I hasten to add, because it may necessarily encourage the fish, but rather because it is essential encouragement for the man wielding the rod.

Mastering the practicalities is not difficult, provided that you have basic casting skills. By that, I do not mean lashing out a mile-long line, or stumbling about in chest waders. From the bank, simply presenting a few, neat, well-controlled yards will suffice. Indeed, wading is perhaps one of the first signs of inexperience when fishing our northern hill-lochs from the shore. Most trout are caught in shallow water. Stay well back, always.

My wife Ann is an expert at this technique. In all the years we have fished together, I have never once seen her wading a hill-loch, and she invariably catches more fish than I do. Where the bank overhangs the loch, Ann keeps well back, often crouching down below the skyline. A short line snakes out and is danced shoreward. The rest, as I know to my cost, is history.

Fishing from a boat requires a different approach and, again, casting a short line is the key to success. Never stand up. Apart from being downright dangerous and scaring the fish, it is unnecessary. Stay seated at all times. The fish will come to you, eventually. Hooking them is much easier as well, given that you are constantly in touch with your flies.

I often meet visitors from the south who have little knowledge of fishing Scottish lochs and, consequently, leave with a poor impression of our wild brown trout fisheries. I once met a couple in Halkirk who showed me the leaders that they had made up: eight feet long with two flies, two feet apart, tied to seven-inch droppers. "Why do we keep getting tangled?" they asked.

My ideal leader for both boat and bank fishing is about twelve feet long, with three flies. The bob-fly, nearest to the line, should be placed five feet down the leader, the middle fly, four feet on, followed by the tail-fly. Droppers should be approximately three inches long. This balance allows you to work the bob-fly over the surface for a longer period, which attracts fish mightily.

Cast about four or five yards of line in front of the boat. The moment the flies alight, raise the rod point, at the same time drawing down the line by hand. These actions – raising the rod and drawing down the line – should be one continuous movement. Keep the bob-fly dancing over the waves, right to the side of the boat. Pause momentarily before casting again, as trout follow the flies and often take at the very last moment. Give them the chance to do so.

Another common complaint I hear from southern visitors is that Highland trout are too small, and frequently too difficult to catch. What fun is there, they ask, in catching 8–10oz trout, when they are accustomed to hooking stocked rainbows that average over 2lb in weight? My response is to remind them that there is far more to fishing than size, weight or numbers caught; that fishing for wild trout is a great gift, bestowed by the gods for the pleasure of men and women. Have a good season.

6.
The White Heat of Angling Technology

My friend Jim was in the stern, I was at the sharp end. Murdo Sutherland, our gillie, was poised to launch us afloat on Loch Hope. "Murdo," said my companion, "before we begin, I must warn you that you are going out with a novice. A man who barely knows one end of a fishing rod from the other."

Murdo smiled. "Now don't you bother about that, I'll take good care of you."

"It's not me I'm talking about!" Jim replied, smugly. "It's him," he said, pointing at me.

"Nice one, Jim," I muttered through gritted teeth. "Wish I had thought of that."

"You will, Bruce, you will," came the sharp rejoinder.

Having a sense of humour is as important as having a fishing rod when angling in the far north. A sense of humour, and a rhinoceros-thick skin, are essential if you hope to survive for half a microsecond with some of my angling friends. I wish it no other way. Banter and backchat is far more important than catching fish. Some of the most memorable days I have spent have been fishless, but unforgettably packed with incident and laughter. Tales and stories of ones that got away and of a few that didn't. Happy evenings spent with like-minded companions.

However, when the talk turns to the relative merits of fast-sinking, high-density fishing lines, Dog Nobblers and bite indicators, I turn off, completely. Technical innovation in angling leaves me cold. It may ding tackle-shop cash registers, but in my view, it is of little real value to man's proper function in life, which is the removal of trout from their natural habitat. The bottom line is a bent pin and a garden cane. All else is window-dressing, a device for extracting cash from punters. Well, I think that it is.

My first clash with white-heat technology was on the shores of Loch Watten in Caithness. I was out with a rather smart couple, both ex air-force officers, and, being a decent sort, I put up the lady's rod. I was carefully threading the line through the rings and had discovered some sort of plastic sleeve at the end. Grunting a bit about people who don't tidy their gear properly at the end of the day, I bit it off. She howled, "What have you done? That was my cast connector!" Cast connector? I had never heard of such a thing, let alone seen one. I make a loop in a piece of nylon, to begin constructing my cast, then tie it directly on to the end of the line using a figure-of-eight knot. I grovelled in the car park, searching for the missing vital plastic sliver.

Fishing rods have become status symbols. Some makes cost upwards of £800 a throw, although many of those who buy them can barely throw a line across the room. Then, of course, there is the "man who has everything". You know who I mean. Mention dapping, and at the drop of a half hitch he is proudly advancing across the lawn with his pride and joy, a "proper" dapping rod, at least twenty-five feet long. Avoid talking about anything piscatorially antique to them. These people invariably have several cabinets full of the stuff and they just know you would love to see it.

They arrive at a river or loch looking like the angling version of the famous *Punch* cartoon, which shows how the military outfitter thinks a World War

One officer should appear, equipped and dressed for the trenches. I know anglers who regularly lug along everything bar the kitchen sink. Boat rod, boat seat, single-handed and double-handed rods, dapping rod. A phalanx of reels fitted out with various lines for various occasions. Neoprene body-waders, thigh boots as well, hats ridiculous, full-length jacket and short-version wading jacket. Landing net, wading staff and life jacket. And that's just the start. There then follows a dozen fly boxes containing several million flies, assorted pre-tied casts in assorted breaking strain strengths of nylon.

Dry-fly floatant, pliers, scissors, priest, trusty all-purpose knife, suntan lotion, insect repellent, Polaroid glasses, camera, lenses and film, binoculars, and, once, even an altimeter. And, of course, lunch, both liquid and the other. By the time they get themselves sorted out, the day is generally half gone and very few that I meet have the faintest idea of how to use half their tackle. For them, buying the product seems to be enough. Having done so, having spent the cash, they imagine they will be automatically and miraculously transformed into better anglers.

Sorry, but it just doesn't work like that.

7.
European Unions

Matters European are rarely off front-pages or television news these days. Politicians go at it hammer and tongs, banging away endlessly about euros, the Common Agricultural Policy, or lack of it, and how we must all learn to snuggle up together, or not, depending upon your point of view. I don't know how I will cast my vote if a referendum ever comes, but I do know we have to accept that people are different.

This was exemplified to me when I spent a week fishing in the company of two Spanish, two German and two French anglers. They represented three European fishing magazines, *Der Fliegenfischer*, *La Pêche* and *Trofeo*, a journalist and photographer from each. I arranged the visit and acted as their host and guide. The week was illuminating, incident-packed and great fun precisely because of their different national characteristics.

The Frenchmen arrived minus their fishing rods and half their luggage, a not unusual Inverness airport occurrence in my experience. Apparently, the missing baggage was on its way to Rome. They were less than pleased and expressed this displeasure, loudly, to the duty staff at the BA desk. After a lot of Gallic shrugging and Gauloises, the problem was resolved. I would lend them tackle until theirs could be located and returned.

The Germans, however, had everything neatly to hand, plus collapsible mini-trolleys for the transportation thereof. They checked their baggage, heel-clicked hello, then marched purposefully and in good order to where the car was parked. Here, everything was meticulously checked again prior to being loaded into the boot. I was impressed.

On the other hand, the Spaniards, who were accompanied by their wives, wandered round the airport for half an hour, buying souvenirs, smiling, cheerful and carefree. By the time I had them all gaggled together and loaded and ready for the off, my German and French friends were distinctly edgy.

We spent our first day together salmon fishing on a North West Sutherland stream. The water level was perfect and fish were showing almost continuously. By lunchtime, there were four fresh-run salmon on the bank: two to the Germans and two to the Spaniards. My French companions said nothing, but were seriously glum. I sensed an international incident brewing. Happily, the afternoon proved to be kind to the French, albeit with only one fish between them. But honour had been satisfied.

I had asked them to be back at the car for 5.30pm, leaving plenty of time to relax and freshen up before dinner. As I waited patiently to collect my little flock, I watched them coming down the riverbank. The track they had to follow divided just before a fishing hut. One branch, the correct route home, angled away from the river, round a small hillock to a bridge across the stream. The other branch led to a dead end and a precipitous drop into a deep pool.

At 5.25pm the Germans hove into view, their fish slung on designer ropes fitted with wooden carrying handles. At the junction, they unhesitatingly followed the correct path and arrived at my side at 5.30pm precisely. At 5.45pm, the Spaniards appeared, talking earnestly together, looking at the river, pausing to inspect pools and to point at splashing salmon. Their fish were slung casually over their backs. At the junction, they started down the wrong track, then, realising their mistake, they retraced their steps and rounded the hillock.

By 6.00pm the Frenchmen had yet to appear and the Germans were agitated, worrying about dinner. "We must go. We will be late. Leave them a note saying you will come back for them." We heard the Frenchmen before we saw them, when they were some distance off, talking at the tops of their voices. Then we saw them, gesticulating down the track, arms flying, the air blue with tobacco smoke. Without pause, they took the wrong turning and arrived at the side of the river.

Their salmon fell to the ground, almost into the stream. After a heated argument about what to do next, they walked back to the junction and continued the debate over another cigarette. I roared across the river and waved directions. Eventually, they found the route and tramped over the bridge to where we were waiting, full of courteous apologies for being late. "It is so beautiful," they said, "we just forgot about the time." I walked back across the river to retrieve their salmon, which, in the white heat of argument, they had forgotten to pick up.

There were language difficulties, mostly on my part, but between us we managed. The Germans spoke reasonable English and French. The Spaniards had good English and some French and the French spoke excellent English and German. However, one thing we all had in common was a love of fishing and that joy solved most problems.

Which I suppose is what makes fishing such an international blessing? Regardless of race, class, colour or creed, or language spoken, most anglers identify with similar things: a shared concern for the environment and for the well-being and future of our well-loved quarry, be it salmon, trout or sea-trout.

At dinner on the last night, the Germans, by way of a "thank you", gave me a book. For the first time since leaving home, I reached for my spectacles. I put them on and gasped in fright. I had suddenly gone blind in one eye. Then I remembered my son and daughter being particularly solicitous before I left: "Here, dad, you almost forgot your glasses." The blighters had pasted a black patch over the port lens.

I peeled off the patch, much to the amusement of the assembled company, and grabbed the cloth from inside the case to wipe the lens clean. As I did so, I exposed a neatly printed note, stuck firmly in place, upon which was written

Basil Fawlty's classic line: "Don't mention the war!" Maybe if our political leaders spent more time fishing and less time gabbing, they would get on better and perhaps make the world a happier place?

8.
Are We There Yet?

During service for Queen and Country, I used to lead convoys of vehicles through rebel-infested mountains in southern Arabia with unerring accuracy. This does not, however, qualify me for map-reading duties in the north of Scotland. At least, not according to the Manager, my wife, Ann.

Just because once, well, maybe twice, I made minor map-reading errors, she now always insists that I follow, silently, at a respectful distance in the rear, whilst she trail-blazes. I am told, unkindly in my opinion, that if map-reading were left to me we would spend most of the day going round and round in ever decreasing circles, and who wants that on a fishing expedition?

Which is why I found myself resting thankfully in Coigach in Wester Ross whilst Ann plotted our route ahead. Our objective was Loch Doire na h-Airbhe, a small loch to the south of Loch Sionascaig in the Inverpolly National Nature Reserve and I was happy to pause for a moment to regain my breath. Not that I proposed to admit it, though.

Coigach and Inverpolly are very special, they make up a magical wilderness, magnificent, lonely and desolate. In all our journeys there we have never once met another soul. Mountains crowd every horizon: jagged Stac Pollaidh (613m), Cul Beag (769m) and grey Cul Mor (849m); the dramatic peaks of Suilven (713m), the Vikings' "Pillar Mountain"; and the long, comfortable shoulder of Canisp (864m).

"Where are we?" I asked, aggressively.

"Be quiet. I'm looking at the map."

"I can see that," I replied crossly, "but whilst you are doing so, trout are rising and we are not there to catch them. Are you sure you know where the loch is?"

Ann stood up, shouldered her pack and marched off down the side of a steep hill. "Are you sure this is the way?" I ventured. No answer. So I followed, lamblike and trusting.

Earlier that morning we had parked the car near Loch Dail, the lower of the Polly Lochs, and, gallant to the last, I piggybacked Ann across the little river before we set off eastwards up the hill. Now, after about three-quarters of an hour of serious grunting, I tramped after her into Gleann na Gaoithe, "the glen of the wind". Sunlight warmed our backs and the burn running through the glen bubbled urgently over weed-fringed boulders on its way to greet the sea.

This was the outlet burn of Loch Doire na h-Airbhe and with journey's end in sight we quickened our step. The loch is one mile long by quarter of a mile wide and the name means "the loch of the oak grove". A wide variety of native trees – oak, birch, rowan and alder – cluster unexpectedly along the south shore, providing welcome shelter when cold winds blow.

However, that morning, the weather was perfect and the first thing we did on our arrival was to cool off with a splash in the shallow margins at the west end of the loch. This area produces an endless stream of small, well-shaped trout, which give great sport. Wading is comfortable and safe and it is possible to cover a large area of water. Well, relatively speaking for me, given my casting skill.

As you progress eastwards, the water deepens and the bank becomes steeper. Sooner, rather than later, you find yourself in mountain goat country, casting from high above the surface of the loch. Taxing fishing. By the time you have reacted to a swirl, the fish has long since gone. But concentrate, because all the way along this steep bank is good fishing water: from the start, round to the point and down to the hazel tree, which overhangs the water.

We had constant sport here and kept three beautifully marked trout, each fish weighing just under 1lb. Landing them was "interesting" and really requires a long-handled net. Otherwise, get your partner to hold onto your heels whilst you dreep down to try to secure your catch. Another reason for maintaining friendly relations with your fishing partner.

The east end of Loch Doire na h-Airbhe is easier to fish and every bit as exciting. You will find a rock shelf here above moderately shallow water where excellent trout lurk. Eastwards again, the hillside is tree-clad and idyllic. We had lunch and dozed in the warm afternoon sun. When we wakened, a wasted fishing hour later, it was time to head homewards.

We hiked round the north shore of the loch and into the surrounding hills. There are a number of lochs and lochans here, unnamed on the Ordnance Survey map (Sheet 15, Loch Assynt) and we stopped for a cast or three in each. Here again, the trout were plentiful and hard fighting, averaging in the order of three to the pound. You will find Loch Doire na h-Airbhe at Grid reference: 15/105126.

The walk back to the Polly Lochs was hard, wet, soggy and tiring. This time, we arrived at the Upper Polly loch, near to where it flows out from vast Loch Sionascaig. Further downstream, we managed to cross dry shod, although it involved some minor mountaineering and delicate footwork over fences and a ragged "bridge".

We made it, safe and sound, and, as always, I complimented Ann on her nifty map reading. Pays to keep her happy, otherwise I suspect that she would simply run away and leave me stranded in the middle of some desolate moor. Wildflowers bobbed in the shade as we passed through another delightful small wood. We reached the car in good order at the end of a splendid day, and a micro-second before the midges came out to play.

Permission to fish Loch Doire na h-Airbhe should be obtained from Inverpolly Estates prior to fishing. Tel: 01854 622452. The estate has a self-catering property, which is let, along with fishing, on a number of other estate waters.

9.
Poets' Pub

St Mary's Loch in the Borders is a magical place. Wizards and fairies still haunt the surrounding hills and moor lands where curlew call and lark sing. And, on a narrow spit of land separating St Mary's Loch from its neighbour, Loch of the Lowes, is one of Scotland's most famous inns: Tibbie Shiels, which had its beginnings in the early years of the nineteenth century.

The Scottish poet, writer and angler, James Hogg (1770–1835), the "Ettrick Shepherd", was a regular visitor, as was his friend, the novelist Sir Walter Scott

(1771–1832). Another of Hogg's friends and fishing companions was Thomas Tod Stoddart (1810–80), angler and author of the first book on Scottish fishing, *The Art of Angling as Practised in Scotland*, published in 1835 and later republished as *The Angler's Companion to the Rivers and Lakes of Scotland*.

This is the heartland of the Borders, peopled by a pragmatic race that has survived the slings and arrows of outrageous fortune for thousands of years. However, the only battles that rage now by St Mary's Loch are between fish and anglers, and the Tibbie Shiels Inn has been caring for anglers for nearly 200 years. The loch, which is the largest body of freshwater in the Borders, is three miles long by up to half a mile wide and there is something here for every angler, coarse fisherman and trout fisherman alike.

Stoddart and Hogg were expert anglers and fished together many times on St Mary's. One of their most notable days was 4 May 1833, when they shared a boat, catching seventy-nine trout weighing 36lb. No doubt they celebrated their victory over a dram or two with Tibbie. Isabella "Tibbie" Shiel, the first owner of the inn, was born near Ettrick in 1783. In 1806, she married Robert Richardson who was employed as a mole catcher on the Thirlestane Estate of Lord Napier. When her husband died suddenly in 1824, Tibbie was left almost destitute with a family of six children, so she decided to set up in business as an innkeeper to provide for her family.

Tibbie Shiels Inn was much used by anglers who came to fish St Mary's Loch, but because of its association with James Hogg, Thomas Tod Stoddart, Sir Walter Scott, Robert Louis Stevenson, Thomas Carlyle and other literary figures, it soon became a gathering place for poets and writers as well as for fishermen. In his excellent booklet, *Tibbie Shiel*, published in 1986, Michael Robson recounts an early visitor's impressions of the inn:

> The old-fashioned kitchen of Tibbie Shiels Inn was the model of what a kitchen ought to be; it had such an air of cosy warmth and welcoming hospitality. In the vast open fireplace were glowing peat embers, the kettle sang on the hob, the white-faced grandfather's clock ticked beside the "bink", and was there ever anything so quaintly picturesque as the box beds with their sliding doors? But best of all was Tibbie's spinning wheel on one side of the hearth, and Sir Walter Scott's armchair on the other.

Another patron of Tibbie's, and friend of Scott's group, was Professor John Wilson, lawyer and Professor of Moral Philosophy at Edinburgh University in 1820. Wilson described Tibbie as being "a shrewd, kindly, comely woman". John Wilson was a well-known sportsman and keen angler. He bestowed upon himself such titles as MA, Master of Angling, and FRS, Fisherman Royal of Scotland, but he is best remembered for his column in *Blackwood's Magazine*. The articles were written under his pen name "Christopher North" and describe the adventures and exploits of himself (North), James Hogg (the Shepherd) and John Gibson Lockhart (Tickler), who married Sophia, Sir Walter Scott's elder daughter.

North's *Noctes Ambrosiane* and later *Recreations of Christopher North* lampooned polite Edinburgh society and were instantly popular. They included frequent references to the great angling exploits of the Shepherd, as in one of the finest angling "put-downs" that I have ever read, when the Shepherd tops one of North's fishing tales:

> *Shepherd:* Poo, that was nae day's fishin' ava, man, in comparison to ane o' mine on St Mary's Loch. To say naething about the countless sma' anes, twa hunder about half a pun', ae hunder about a haill pun', fifty about twa pun', five-and-twenty about fowre pun', and the lave rinnin' frae half a stane up to a stane and a half, except about half a dizzen, aboon a' weicht that put Geordie Gudefallow and Huntly Gordon to their mettle to carry them pechin to Mount Benger on a haunbarrow.

It was rumoured that Tibbie Shiel had a "soft spot" for James Hogg and towards the end of her life she is reported as saying: "Yon Hogg, the Shepherd, ye ken, was an awfu' fine man. He should hae ta'en me, for he cam coortin' for years, but he just gaed away and took another." Tibbie outlived most of her more famous customers and died in July 1878 at the age of ninety-six, but the memory of the charm of the innkeeper by St Mary's Loch and her famous customers lives on. Tibbie Shiels and St Mary's Loch are still places of pilgrimage for anglers and travellers today.

For details of fishing on St Mary's Loch and Loch of the Lowes, log on to the St Mary's Angling Club comprehensive website at: http://sites.google.

com/site/stmarysloch/. You may also email: stmarysloch@gmail.com (mobile tel: 07980 350031). The Loch Keeper is Peter Kokot, tel: 01750 423290 (mobile tel: 07907 531605) or email Peter at lochkeeper@progressiveorange. com. The largest brown trout caught in recent years (2009) weighed 8lb 6oz; the largest pike (2008) weighed 24lb 13oz.

10.
Never a Cross Word

I blame the wind, otherwise we would never argue. Indeed, my wife, Ann, and I rarely exchange a cross word, apart, that is, from when we are afloat in the wind. You see, I have this absolute conviction that I know far more than she does about handling small boats in difficult conditions. Unfortunately, she thinks otherwise. In our case, when the storm rages, it's not a question of a danger shared. By the time we have done shouting and arguing, it frequently becomes a danger doubled.

Having been swept mercilessly on to some rocky shore, we clamber out of the water-filled boat and continue the fight with renewed vigour in the shelter of the nearest tree. It is generally at this point that we notice the boat drifting off round the headland and the fight flares anew over who should have secured it and why it wasn't done.

Our first real brush with the elements occurred on Gladhouse Reservoir, near Edinburgh, more years ago than I care to remember. In those days, the loch was controlled by the "City Fathers" and fishing on it was subject to a ballot system. In theory, the names of all the anglers wishing to fish this excellent water on any given day were put into a hat or box, and first out got the boat.

In practice, it never seemed to work for us. Far be it for me to criticise such an august body, but after several fruitless attempts, I eventually had a word with a friend who was employed by the council, and, lo and behold, we obtained a booking. But that was the start of the problem, because, being anxious to make full use of this heaven-sent opportunity, in spite of a howling gale, we launched the boat.

Within seconds we were in the grip of the wind and being whisked down the loch like a kamikaze mayfly. Outboards are not allowed on Gladhouse and it was all I could do to keep the boat stern on, so to speak, let alone turn her into the wind. Our rods lay untouched in the bottom of the boat as we were buffeted, white-faced, down the loch.

I aimed in the general direction of a grassy bay and kept my fingers crossed. As soon as the boat touched bottom, I leapt out and heaved it to safety. Ann staggered ashore with the gear, and, for once, we were almost speechless. I was horrified at my stupidity in launching the boat, particularly as Ann was only three months from giving birth to our second child.

As soon as we had sufficient breath back to start arguing about whose fault it had been, we moved into the shelter of a large, neat hedge in order to fight in more comfort. From directly above our heads came a polite cough. We stopped talking and looked up. Smiling down at us was a gardener. He seemed to be standing on a pair of step-ladders, cutting the hedge.

"Had a bit trouble, then?" he enquired solicitously.

"Oh, no. It's all right really," I replied rather shamefacedly.

"Can I give you a hand?" he asked.

Expecting him to descend the steps, I nodded and indicated that he should come round and join us. Without more ado, the gardener moved to his left and walked round the corner of the hedge.

He was the largest man that I have ever seen, and I'm 6ft 4in. "You should have used a sea-anchor to slow the drift," he said. Bending down, with one hand, he picked up a massive chunk of concrete. It had a ring embedded in the top and he held it for a moment or two to make sure that I got the point.

I examined the stone and, believe me, I could hardly raise it an inch from the ground. As we had been talking, I had been worrying about how I was going to get the boat back to the mooring point. I had vivid images of being flogged up Edinburgh's Royal Mile to be hanged, drawn and quartered at the Market Cross in the High Street for damaging City property. Could our new-found friend provide the answer?

"You wouldn't like to help me row the boat back to the mooring bay, by any chance, would you?"

"Surely," he replied, "glad to lend a hand and the wind's dropped a bit now."

The wind had dropped slightly but even so it was still blowing hard. The memory of that mad row over heaving, dipping Gladhouse Reservoir will remain with me until the day I die. And at the time, the prospect seemed imminent. Taking an oar each, we struggled on. Well, to be truthful, I struggled.

My companion simply sat back and stroked the passing waves as though he were paddling round the local boating pond on a hot summer's day. Once he realised that we were, in fact, going round in circles, and that I could not match his strength, he smiled and gestured that I should sit in the stern and let him have both oars.

Moments later, as dusk was falling, we tied up and I staggered ashore, shattered. After I had secured the mooring rope, I turned to thank my Good Samaritan for saving me from a fate worse than death. He gave me a cheery wave and ambled off into the gathering gloom, a never-to-be-forgotten moment.

The passing years have brought us caution with regards to bobbing about in boats in gales. Nowadays, if in doubt, we don't. When the wind is raging down the loch, churning the water to foam, you will find Ann and me tucked away in some quiet corner or sheltered bay. We fish safely and happily from the bank, separated by several, mishap-free yards, calling occasional words of encouragement and good-humoured advice to each other – and never argue at all.

11.
The Ones That Got Away

If I had a penny for every fish that I have lost I would be a rich man. And every glass case of my angling dreams would be filled to overflowing with mighty trout. Unforgettable, magnificent wild fish of up to and over 8lb in weight. Yes, indeed, all the "ones that got away".

My consolation is that I know where they live. I know to the exact inch where it was on loch or river that they grabbed my fly. The precise location where I encountered them even if it was for only a brief, exciting moment: the heart-stopping tug, the scream of an angry reel, the agony of the moment when the fly came loose.

These instances mark an angler for life. Things are never the same again. Each succeeding cast awakens the memory of those moments, rekindles the hope that this cast might be the one which consummates the marriage for which all piscators pray: a trout so large that, in telling of it afterwards, we never need to lie.

My first great loss happened above New Water on the River Tweed near Innerleithen. I had been stumbling about, fording the river and getting two bootfuls of ice-cold water in the process, and decided to have a passing cast downstream. The instant the flies landed on the surface, a huge fish grabbed, almost pulling the rod out of my hand. Then, as quickly, it was gone. I can only guess at the size of the fish, perhaps it was a salmon, but most certainly it would have been "worth the hauding".

The next came whilst I was fishing a tiny lochan in Caithness. I saw the trout clearly and it was definitely over 5lb in weight. The fish had taken my tail fly, a small Silver Butcher, as it dangled in the water whilst I struggled to untangle the other two flies on the cast from my landing net. The huge fish was unconcerned. I don't think it realised it was hooked. But I was in shock at the prospect of landing such a monster.

I knew the best chance of securing this prize was to act quickly. Which is how I acquired a life-long loathing of landing nets. I got the wretched thing loose, but it wouldn't flick open, no matter how hard I flicked. After a minute, the big trout turned lazily and headed off for the middle. My "bob" fly snagged on the disgusting net and the cast broke.

However, not only do I manage to lose my own specimen trout, but I also manage to lose other people's, even after I have efficiently dispatched them with a well-aimed blow to the back of the neck. Ann once caught a hefty trout whilst we were fishing a small loch to the north of Helmsdale. She had been stalking the margins, well back from the water's edge, fishing with barely a couple of yards of line. It was the largest trout Ann had ever hooked.

After I netted the fish for her, tapped it over the head and congratulated its captor, I placed the trout in a polythene bag staked to a post in the shallows in order to keep it in good condition. Half an hour later, on examining the bag, I found to my abject horror that it was empty. The fish had recovered and swum off to fight another day. Which was more than could be said for me. I have never been allowed to forget that incident.

The largest trout I have lost was in a lochan near our home in Tongue, Sutherland. The first time I visited the water I thought it was fishless: dark, difficult of access, lying at the centre of a midge-ridden peat bog. But on my second visit, I hooked a veritable leviathan that tore the line from my reel faster than any fish had ever done before. It ran three times, taking me down to the backing, leaping spectacularly at the end of each run.

Eventually, it tired and I managed to work it back towards the net, which, this time, had opened, responsibly, at first flick. I could see this was, at last, the trout of my dreams: beautifully shaped, deep body, small head and wondrously marked. It was at least 6lb. I pictured the fish in pride of place above the mantelpiece. I saw myself modestly recounting the event to admiring friends on cold winter evenings.

As I slipped the net below its huge frame, the trout, in a final display of power, dashed between my legs. I tried to lift my leg over the line and, in doing so, toppled backwards into the loch, during which process the fish escaped. If you are an angler, you will understand the depths of my despair. If not, take my word for it, at that moment I wanted to die.

Nevertheless, at other times, fate has been kinder. Although nothing as large as the Tongue peat-pool trout has come my way since, I have had a few luckier moments. I remember with pleasure a 2lb 8oz trout from Paradise Wood on the River Don. A superb 3lb 8oz fish from Loch Caladail, one of the famous Durness limestone lochs. A fish of 4lb 8oz from one of the finest trout lochs in Scotland, Loch Heilen in Caithness.

I can't pretend these creatures were caught due to my angling prowess. Fishermen are basically truthful and honest. Mostly, I was looking the other way when these fish rose to my fly – fiddling with my cast, drinking coffee, watching a black-throated diver ... The Heilen trout took when my rod rested crossways on the boat, flies unattended, lying supine on the surface. In fact, this is a technique I have since developed into a fine art and it is surprising just how often it brings results. Who knows, it might provide the same service for you. Try it. After all, you have nothing to lose other than a monster trout.

12.
Fly-fishing with Yorkshire Terriers

I can't remember not having a dog, always one and sometimes two, and always golden retrievers. They were decent, friendly, biddable creatures and wonderful companions. Training them was easy because they were endlessly anxious to please and to learn. They were trustworthy and well-behaved under all circumstances and loved the water. However, this was never a problem when fishing. The trout did not seem to mind. One of my dogs, Breac, the Gaelic name for trout, used to swim parallel to me when I bank-fished and I have caught trout casting a fly almost in front of his nose.

Then I got involved with Heathcliff, a thug of a Yorkshire terrier and one of the worst angling mistakes that I have ever made. I fished with him for thirteen years. Where I went, he went. Or rather, wherever his mistress, my wife Ann, went, I followed them both. Heathcliff featured large in my piscatorial affairs, more often than not in derogatory terms – "dogoratory" might be more appropriate. He mightily enlivened the days we spent together amidst moorland and mountain and not always for entirely laudable reasons, the least of which was his tendency to chase anything that moved and his feigned deafness when I attempted to call him to heel. But he was a character, for all his faults, and Ann loved him dearly.

His "Sunday" name was Cantalon Aristocrat and he was born in Edinburgh on 16 October 1983. When I first met him I was looking for an additional companion, other than myself, for my wife. Don't ask me why we men do such things, these matters are complicated enough as it is. His breeder had shown me a litter of puppies and for some reason I hesitated. The breeder then opened a door and stood back. Heathcliff bustled in, gloriously black and gold, his tiny white teeth glinting, looking for trouble. He rushed at my feet, lay on his back, legs kicking, and began chewing the hell out of my left shin. I jumped about a bit, shaking my trouser leg, but to no avail. A few moments later, he and I were in the car heading for the north of Scotland.

I had the good fortune to marry a Yorkshire lass, a devoted Brontë fan, hence Cantalon Aristocrat's family name, Heathcliff. Ann is also a keen hillwalker and angler and far more competent in both matters than I will ever be. Thus, Heathcliff landed on his feet. Not for him the silk cushion and fashionable red bow. He was destined for higher things: Stac Pollaidh (612m), Canisp (847m), Hope (927m), Loyal (763m), Klibreck (961m), Stack (721m), Mhor (620m) and Hecla (606m) in South Uist, Baosbheinn (883m) and Beinn an Eoin (854m) in the Flowerdale Forest and miles of intermediate moorland and urban sniffs in-between.

Our first fishing expedition was to Lochain Doimhian near Scourie in North West Sutherland, a soggy, vigorous, eight-mile round trip and hard going for a much larger dog, let alone for a modest Yorkshire terrier. Heathcliff was six months old at the time and he ended the walk, shivering, tucked into the poachers-pocket of my jacket. The principal reason for his state was due to an altercation he had with a mallard. He rose the bird, which was tending a family of chicks, as we passed by the "Murder Loch". The mother flapped off water-wards, pretending a broken wing, whilst the chicks hid in the heather. Heathcliff followed mum into the loch. A moment later he was drifting out to the middle, drowning. My son, Blair, stripped off and waded to the rescue.

On our return home, Ann set about making Heathcliff a waterproof fishing jacket to ward off the cold, complete with landing-net ring and wool fly patch. I never saw him use a landing net; he was made of sterner stuff and adopted a more direct approach to the retrieval of trout: he used his teeth. Like most anglers, Heathcliff enjoyed meeting like-minded people, particularly if they happened to be female and on heat. His ability to scent the possibility of an intimate, special relationship was legendary. My ability to find him once he had set off in pursuit of conjugal bliss was less so, although I admit that I lost pounds of unnecessary flab in the process. I have also lost count of the number of times when I have had to explain, red-faced with embarrassment: "He is a Yorkshire terrier. I'm sorry, it's just the way they are."

You get to know someone well, really well, when you go fishing with them, even better when you sleep with them every night for thirteen years. But what's a little midnight grooming between friends? Only a minor deflection from a good night's sleep and of small consequence. So what if your fishing companion regularly bites the hand that feeds him, or any other portion of your body that his teeth can reach? After all, we live in a democracy, do we not? Friendship and constancy are more important than intermittent favours and everyone has their little foibles.

Heathcliff died in Assynt not long after climbing Sutherland's great Ben and I miss his little foibles more than I ever imagined possible: his fixed, hideous grin as I landed a trout that he instantly grabbed and buried, far from my ken. I miss his presence, neatly equidistant between my forward foot and the heel of his mistress as we descended from some God-forsaken height. Fishing will never be the same. Until Hareton, Heathcliff's grandnephew, arrived. I took him to where Heathcliff lies and explained the rules: no yapping, no running away, no gratuitous screwing and, most important of all, no stealing your master's fish, got it?

13.
A Perfectly Good Boat of My Own

When the Good Lord decided that His world needed a wash, he advised Noah to start sawing cubits. He also instructed Noah to pass the word to The Macneil of Barra, warning him of the impending flood, and to keep a place in the Ark for The Macneil and his family.

Noah sent a messenger to Macneil telling him that a main deck cabin with all mod cons had been reserved for his use. Macneil responded with typical Gaelic courtesy, thanking Noah for the invitation, but assuring him that he had a perfectly good boat of his own.

I first visited the island at the end of a journey from the Butt of Lewis in the north to Barra in the south, whilst researching my book *The Heather Isles*. I arrived at Castlebay on the birth of a cold, misty, morning with dawn sunlight just beginning to slant over the grey shoulder of Heaval (383m) and I instantly fell in love with Barra.

However, unlike Noah, my principal concern was not for Clan Macneil, but for Fred, the 8lb salmon I had caught the previous day on East Loch Ollay whilst fishing with John Kennedy, the South Uist Estate Fishery Manager. Fred lay in the ship's galley, wrapped in a mountain of newspaper, and I had to get him quickly to his next resting-place, the Castlebay Hotel freezer.

That task completed, I set off round the island in search of adventure and, hopefully, a successful encounter with some unsuspecting Barra wild brown trout to keep Fred company on his cold journey back to my home in Sutherland. My first call was on an old friend, Compton Mackenzie, who lies at rest in the graveyard at Cille Bharra.

Compton Mackenzie's most famous book, *Whisky Galore*, was made into a film in which Mackenzie himself played a part. The subject of the book, the wreck of the SS *Politician* and the 'liberation' of a large part of its cargo of whisky by local people, has an enduring fascination. Not so long ago, a consortium was formed to 'liberate' anything else still trapped in the wreck. Sadly, this only produced about a dozen bottles.

Barra is stunningly beautiful, surrounded by emerald green seas, flecked with white-fringed, 3,000-mile-old, blue Atlantic waves. The view from the summit of Heaval is breathtaking. Northwards, across the Sound of Barra and Eriskay, tower the mountains of South Uist, Beinn Mhor, Corodale and graceful Hecla. To the east lies a distant prospect of Cuillin on Skye and the Torridon peaks on mainland Scotland. South is a dream-like carpet of small isles, Vatersay, Sandray, Pabbay and Mingulay.

Pleased with my day and all that I had seen, I returned to Castlebay and, after dinner, had the good fortune to fall in with the secretary of the Barra Angling Club, a local teacher. "How many members do you have?" I inquired. He paused, mentally counting, and, after a moment said, "About seven, I think, but then, of course, not all of them are as keen anglers as I am."

According to the Ordnance Survey Sheet No. 31, Barra appears to have few game fishing opportunities and, I suppose, that is why so few people bother to visit Barra for an angling holiday. But the island has some quite outstanding trout fishing that would be difficult to better anywhere in Scotland. Also, it is the perfect location for a family holiday where the bucket-and-spade brigade will find white, empty beaches washed clean by the warm waters of the Gulf Stream.

Loch an Duin in the north of Barra is the local water supply and it contains hard-fighting wild brown trout which average 8oz in weight, with the odd much larger fish, as well as occasional sea-trout. Ruleos, Loch nam Faoileann and Loch nic Ruaidhe, to the east, can all be fished in a day, making for a wonderful walk combined with great sport with bright little trout.

High on Heaval, below Beinn na Moine, is Cadha Mor, a magnificent place to fish and full of lovely trout that average half a pound. Visit Cadha as much for the view as for fishing. But the real 'gem' of Barra is Loch Tangusdale, also known as Loch St Clair, an easy walk down the hill from the road at Kinloch. If I were ever asked to design a trout loch, then it would probably look very much like Tangusdale: not too big, with both shallows and deeps, easy wading and shelter, and excellent feeding for fish.

Tangusdale has all this and more, being dominated by the ruins of a small castle perched on a tiny island by the south shore. I had been told that Tangusdale trout averaged 2lb in weight but had greeted this news with a certain degree of scepticism. After half an hour with neither sight nor sound of a fin, I was beginning to wonder if I was wasting my time.

I inched down the east shoreline, sometimes fishing from the bank, sometimes edging a few yards out, concentrating furiously. A golden eagle circled overhead. As I stared heavenward, a trout grabbed with such force that it almost pulled the rod from my hand. I hung on grimly as the reel screamed in anger. The fish leapt spectacularly, a golden bar in afternoon sunlight.

Cautiously, I played him ever closer to the shore and then triumphantly beached the trout. The fish was dark in colour, with clearly defined, bright-red spots, deep-bodied, with a small head and in perfect condition. My prize weighed 2lb 12oz and it had given me some of the best angling moments of my life.

I walked over to Loch na Doirlinn, close to Halaman Bay. This is a weedy loch with barely enough weed-free space for half a dozen casts. It can produce trout of over 5lb in weight, but not for me. The following morning, with my salmon and his new friend in the ferry freezer, whipped by the tail end of a mad hurricane but well content, we bucketed back across the Minch to Oban.

14.
The Annual General Meeting

I was digging around recently in my memories of seasons past when I came across the minutes of an angling association meeting held more than three decades ago. I sat down to read:

The Annual General Meeting of the Sandison Family Fishing Association was held in the Dining Room, Mossbank, Louisburgh Street, Wick, Caithness at 8.00pm on 23 October 1977.

Present: Mr Bruce Sandison (Chairman); Mrs Ann Sandison (Secretary); Mr Blair Sandison (Treasurer); Miss Lewis-Ann Sandison (Social Affairs Secretary); Mr Charles Sandison (Catering Clerk); Miss Jean Sandison and Associate Member, Horace Cat.

The minutes of the last meeting were approved and the Chairman welcomed the newest member, Miss Jean Sandison, aged two-and-a-half. He hoped Miss Sandison would enjoy her time with the Association and asked the Secretary to restrain her from eating agenda papers.

The Chairman reported that the catch for the year showed a significant increase on previous years due to his untiring efforts. He commented that perhaps other members should try harder.

Ms Lewis-Ann Sandison said that if other members fished as often as the Chairman, the figures would have been considerably higher. However, someone had to wash dishes, do the ironing, cook meals and look after the house, she said.

The Secretary thanked Ms Lewis-Ann Sandison for her kind remarks.

Ms Lewis-Ann Sandison replied that she was talking about herself, not the Secretary, who had been fishing much more often than some other members of the Association.

Mr Blair Sandison raised the question of "missed fish" and asked what action the Chairman proposed to take to improve his casting technique?

The Chairman said he was more concerned by the difficulty some members had using a landing net, particularly whilst landing the Chairman's trout.

Mr Blair Sandison commented that if members were expected to work with second-rate equipment, accidents would happen. Whilst he regretted losing the Chairman's 1lb trout, he felt bound to add it was unreasonable to expect members to hang out of boats in force-five gales as the Chairman allowed a small fish to run rings round him.

The Chairman said the trout in question had weighed at least 4lb and that Mr Blair Sandison's failure to land the fish was, to say the least, suspicious. It was agreed the Secretary investigate the purchase of a new net for next season.

Miss Jean Sandison said she wanted to go fishing. The Secretary explained it was dark and that all the fish had gone to their beds. Miss Jean Sandison began to cry.

Mr Charles Sandison proposed a short adjournment for lemonade, warm sweet tea, chocolate biscuits or anything else that happened to be going.

The Chairman said he would prefer a large whisky with a little water and Mr Blair Sandison said he would too.

The meeting adjourned to the kitchen for refreshments.

Due to the rising cost of electricity and the expense of keeping the dining room fire going, the chairman proposed the meeting be continued in the kitchen. Ms Lewis-Ann Sandison said it was only because some people wanted to be nearer the drinks cabinet.

Upon being put to the vote the motion was carried and the meeting continued in the kitchen.

Mr Charles Sandison reminded the meeting that there were only fifty-one shopping days left until Christmas and could he have a fishing rod of his own. Miss Jean Sandison said that she wanted one too.

The Secretary was instructed to raise the matter with Mr Claus but the Chairman told the meeting that funds were limited as his rod would require to be refurbished after falling into Loch Watten.

Mr Blair Sandison said that whilst he sympathised with the Chairman's predicament, this expense should be borne by the Chairman alone since it had been due to the Chairman's own stupidity that the rod had been lost.

Whilst agreeing with Mr Blair Sandison, the Chairman pointed out that the cost of hiring a frogman for the day had been not inconsiderable. He hoped the Association might agree to help with these costs.

Ms Lewis-Ann Sandison said she agreed with Mr Blair Sandison and that people should pay for their own silliness.

The Secretary reminded members it was customary to be polite and asked Miss Lewis-Ann Sandison and Mr Blair Sandison to withdraw their remarks and apologise to the Chairman.

The Secretary said the cost of recovering and repairing the Chairman's rod was far cheaper than buying a new rod and that members should be glad the Chairman's rod had been found.

It was agreed the Association pay 50% of the cost of having the Chairman's rod refurbished if he agreed to stop hiding his fly boxes.

At this point Horace Cat left the meeting to attend to urgent business in the garden.

The following year's holiday was discussed. It was proposed by Ms Lewis-Ann Sandison and seconded by Mr Blair Sandison that the Chairman and Secretary curtail smoking and drinking in order to defray costs and thus provide better equipment with the money saved.

The Chairman and Secretary suggested a subcommittee be appointed to investigate this possibility, reporting back to the Association at their next Annual General Meeting.

Ms Lewis-Ann Sandison demanded a named vote. Three members, Mr Blair Sandison, Ms Lewis-Ann Sandison and Mr Charles Sandison opposed the motion. Mr Bruce Sandison, Mrs Ann Sandison and Miss Jean Sandison supported the motion.

The Chairman used his casting vote to decide the issue in favour of a sub-committee report, reminding Miss Lewis-Ann Sandison that this was an excellent example of the democratic process in action.

The Sandison Cup for the heaviest trout of the season was awarded to the Chairman. There was some desultory clapping and Miss Jean Sandison said she wanted one too.

It was unanimously agreed that the Chairman and Secretary be reappointed for the following year. The Chairman thanked the members of the Association for their continued support and said that he felt privileged to belong to one of the best angling clubs in the world.

Miss Jean Sandison having fallen asleep and there being no further business, the meeting ended at 11.00pm.

As I finished reading, I wondered what the now-scattered members of the Sandison Family Fishing Association, and their children, were doing to celebrate the start of the new season? What unforgettable memories they have given me. But I can still catch more trout than the lot of them put together, so there.

15.
Loch Leven

Loch Leven was the first trout loch that I ever fished, in, well, not exactly yesterday. I was a boy at the time and my fishing mentors, Tom and Mrs Kelly (I never knew Mrs Kelly's first name) ran a busy newsagent's shop down Annandale Street in Edinburgh, where I was frequently sent to collect the evening paper and assorted shopping.

Somehow or other, they discovered that I was an angler, albeit embryonic. From then on they encouraged my interest, showing me how to tie fail-safe knots that I still use to this day, describing different flies and how and when to use them, offering casting lessons and the loan of magical books on the subject. Even although the shop was busy, Tom always had time to spare to answer my questions or to give me few flies.

They regularly fished Loch Leven, during a two-week-long June holiday, and, one year, I was invited to spend a day with them on the loch. They provided the train ticket – Waverley to Kinross return – and when I arrived at Kinross station, there was a taxi waiting to take me to the pier. I can't remember feeling anything other than extreme excitement as we went afloat: Mr and Mrs Kelly, our two boatmen, Big Eck and his son, and me.

It was a wonderful day and I managed to catch a fish. Nor will I ever forget the amazing site of the whole surface of the loch alive with the sound and sight of eagerly rising trout. We had lunch on Castle Island, in the castle, when it was still an undeveloped ruin. As I returned to Edinburgh, my mind was filled with the events of an unforgettable day and the kindness of my hosts.

After that, I often fished the loch during the 1960s, with and without success, but I fell in love with Loch Leven and was devastated when things began to go seriously wrong and water quality deteriorated to such a degree that the loch was declared a public health hazard and closed to fishing: "Scum Sunday", June 1992. Ann and I visited the loch soon afterwards and were horrified, standing at the pier, to see the loch bright green with white scum fringing the shoreline.

In its glory days, Loch Leven could produce upwards of 80,000 fish during a single season (86,000 trout were caught in 1960) and Loch Leven progeny have been used to stock fisheries all over the world: New Zealand, Australia, Tasmania, India, South Africa, Kenya, Chile, Argentina, the Falkland Islands and many other areas. When I was in the army, I caught Loch Leven trout in Kenya, in the River Rupengazi, a tributary of the mighty River Tana. In Chile, in the 1990s, I caught Loch Leven trout in Lago Yelcho and its adjacent lagoons in Chile's X Region. The sea-trout for which the Falklands and Tierra del Fuego are famous originated from Loch Leven stock.

Until 1830, the loch was considerably larger than it is today, being some four miles long by three miles wide. Indeed, water lapped at the foot of the tower on Castle Island where sad Mary, Queen of Scots, was imprisoned after her defeat at the Battle of Carberry (1567). There were only four islands in the loch then, not seven: St Serf's, Castle Island, Reed Bower and Roy's Folly. However, in 1830, a drainage scheme was completed to improve surrounding agricultural land and, in consequence, the level of the loch fell by more than five feet, reducing Leven to its present shape and size, about three-and-a-half miles across and covering an area of 4,300 acres.

Loch Leven's history, in spite of its recent chequered years, still makes it one of the most significant trout fisheries in the world and I am sure that, in due course, it will fully regain that status. Maybe not in my lifetime but, believe me, it will. It is also, quite simply, a wonderful place to fish. Indeed, it has more environmental and conservation designations than any other loch in Europe and is noted for its variety of wildlife habitats and, in particular, its outstanding number of overwintering birds. Much of this is explained at the Royal Society for the Protection of Birds' wonderful Vane Farm Visitor Centre on the south shore.

The loch is guarded to the west by the graceful Lomond Hills (522m), north and east by the lower skirts of the Ochills, and south by the stark ridge of

Benarty Hill (356m). After living in the far north for the past thirty years, Ann and I are looking forward to fishing Loch Leven again. It holds dear memories for us both and, fishless or otherwise, just being there will be pleasure enough.

Find Loch Leven on OS Map 58, Perth & Kinross, Scale 1:50,000, Gd Ref: 122018 (boat mooring bay and car park); Castle Island: Gd Ref: 138018; St Serf's Island: Gd Ref: 160005; Vane Farm RSPB Nature Reserve: Gd Ref: 160990; West Lomand Hill: Gd Ref: 197066. Boat bookings may be made by contacting: tel: 01577 863407; charges: day, from 10am to 6pm, three anglers, outboard engine: £39.00; single angler: £24.00; part day (4 hours): £12.00. Evening session prices are similar. There are also early morning sessions on Saturdays and Sundays, from 5.00am until 10am.

16.
Dangerous Dancing

I blame the dancing, not the drink. Uisge beatha had nothing whatsoever to do with it, honest. And, after all, it was New Year's Eve. What better time can there be for a reel, a jig and a few neat steps? Which is how I came to find myself, at 1am, strapped to a trolley in the Royal Infirmary in Edinburgh being treated for a badly strained ankle. Utter ignominy – struck down by a couple of drams and the Glasgow Highlanders' setting step.

The following morning, bandaged and walking-sticked, vigorously protesting my alcoholic innocence, I sat in the little woodland by the north-east shore of Portmore Loch, twenty minutes' drive south from Edinburgh. The corporate plan that day had been to welcome in the New Year on top of Dundreich (622m), one of the splendid Moorfoot Corbets, with summits of over 2,000 feet in height.

I sulked in solitary splendour as my companions set off round the leaden-grey margins of the loch and disappeared up the hill. Still, it was one of these brisk, sparkling, finger-tip-tingling, good-to-be-alive mornings. I was warm and, apart from my self-inflicted injury, fit and happy and looking forward to the bright, new, opportunity-packed angling season that lay ahead.

Walkers and anglers often ignore the Moorfoot Hills. They forget that Peeblesshire, in terms of altitude, has a higher average height above sea level than any other Scottish county. Therefore, for hillwalkers and fisherfolk, the Moorfoots offer endless miles of wonderful, high-plateau walks and secret streams set amidst dramatic scenery "far from the madding crowd".

But I have to declare an interest. I was almost brought up in the Moorfoot Hills and they are an essential part of my childhood memories, recollections of a time when each hour seemed to have 120 minutes and each day forty-eight hours. A time when spring burst upon the sleeping earth with an almost messianic force and when summer months were endless.

As boys, my friends and I used to haunt these hills, guddling for trout in tiny, crystal-clear burns, poking about under steep, heather-clad banks for small, bright, red-spotted fish. Many of the little Lothian streams still offer these same pleasures today, from the silver Tyne and its tributaries, including Humble Water, Birns Water, Gifford Water and Fala Dam Burn.

They may not contain monster trout, but their fish are of the highest quality, circumspect and challenging to catch. Much of the bankside is overgrown and presenting a fly requires a high degree of skill. One of my fondest memories is of taking a 1lb 2oz trout on a size 16 Greenwell's Glory, insinuated through the tangled branches of an alder tree whilst sitting on the parapet of the bridge in the village of Fala Dam.

Lyne Water, near Romano Bridge, was another favoured fishing location. I committed all the early sins of my angling life in that stream: hooking the back of my neck, filling Wellington boots with ice-cold water, breaking the tip of my antique greenheart rod, falling face first into shallow pools and the never-to-be-forgotten moment when I landed my first wild brown trout – all of four inches in length, whisked from the river on a Silver Butcher on a vigorous back cast.

Also, unbeknown to me then was the fact that my future wife was fishing Lyne Water two miles upstream. When we did meet, seven years later, we had a lot to talk about, mostly of fishing, and we have been doing so ever since; nice to start married life in the way in which one hopes to continue. Although, being a far more adventurous angler than I am, my wife fished Lyne Water using a worm, our only recurring bone of contention when it comes to addressing the task of removing trout from tiny, fast-flowing streams or when fishing in spate conditions.

We became Portmore Loch regulars in 1960. It was about a twenty-minute cross-county drive from our cottage at Fala Dam and ideal for an evening's sport, or so we thought. However, in those days, obtaining permission to fish, paying the required amount, collecting the key for the boat and bailing out said boat could take at least an hour.

Neither was the loch productive. Indeed, in all the times we fished Portmore I can only once remember seeing a fish rise. But I can honestly declare that I never lost a fish – simply because I never had the chance to do so. Our total score was one small, educationally subnormal perch. However, the reason we kept returning was because Portmore was such a wonderful place to fish.

Although man-made, by the construction of a dam wall in the 1880s, Portmore has an entirely natural feel about it and the surrounding scenery and wildlife is quite outstanding. There was the possibility, albeit remote, that we might, eventually, from the depths, land that ever-elusive "one for the glass case", but we never did.

Although we now live in the far north of Scotland, surrounded by some of the most exciting wild trout fishing in the world, I still have fond memories of my fishing days in the Lothians. A small part of my angling mind will always be with Portmore Loch.

Whenever I return south I attempt to devise ways and means of extending my stay so that I can revisit Portmore. Perhaps the next time I'm down I should wear the kilt and have a dram and a dance for auld lang syne? After all, a gammy foot shouldn't stop one from fishing.

17.
The Tarmac Shuffle

I used to travel by air between Newcastle and London. At that time we were living in Northumberland, near Hexham, in an old house overlooking the River South Tyne, then one of the finest brown trout streams in Europe. The

HQ of the company I worked for was in Ealing. Door-to-door took an hour and a half. But ever since being caught in an electrical storm over darkest Africa, and landing sideways in Arabia, I have never liked flying.

It was during my flying period that I first became aware of the similarity between airline passengers and anglers. You might imagine the connection is tenuous, but hang on a moment and I will explain. For prospective high-altitude tinned sardines, flying has all to do with the seats next to the emergency exit at the rear of the plane, at least it was in those days, in the Tridents that used to ply the route. Possession of one of these seats was the ultimate prize.

I used to wonder what the unseemly rush was all about. But I soon grasped the fact that the seats at the rear offered a greater degree of comfort with regard to additional legroom. I am an untidy 6ft 4in. According to those "in the know", those seats were also the safest place to be in the event of an accident. Retrospectively, that last claim was a bit fragile. Still, I suppose it would have been nice to be able to cross and uncross one's legs in that final descent from 20,000ft.

The trick lay in obtaining possession of them without making a spectacle of oneself in the process. This became known to me as doing the "tarmac-shuffle". At the crack of dawn, approximately 100 bleary-eyed, dark-suited, slightly-used-briefcase-carrying business executives would foregather in the departure lounge in a manner befitting burgeoning bulwarks of industry. But as soon as the flight was called, we heeled-and-toed it across the tarmac with complete disregard for anything other than hitting the steps to the rear entrance ahead of all comers.

As we stumbled into the plane, the glint of battle still in our eyes, stewardesses with long service and good conduct medals would shrink aside. But oh, the sweet smell of success I used to scent settling into those precious few more comfortable, safer inches. Later, with seat belts unfastened and breakfast served, sanity would return. People relaxed and regained their composure. It was just the undignified pre-take-off scramble that exposed, momentarily, the baser self.

Anglers frequently show the same disregard for their fellows when it comes to getting to river or loch. The popular picture of the pipe-sucking gentleman, sauntering reflectively to the waterside, is a myth. He exists only in the imagination of romantic novelists and filmmakers. Then, the angler usually appears as Lachlan, Sandy, Iain or Donald, "clean-limbed, strong and handsome". Lachlan, Sandy, Iain or Donald is invariably portrayed kilted, reflectively studying the "rowan-fringed" depths of Lochan Gulp an t-Choke, which invariably nestles below the heather-clad rugged grandeur of Beinn something unpronounceable or other.

Which reminds me of Lew Gardner, a TV presenter I once met on the shores of Loch Awe in Argyll. I had been introducing him to the intricacies of the gentle art, whilst he rabbited on about minor issues, like the Arab/Israeli War and what he said to Harold Wilson during a famous interview. He paid scant attention to my pearls of wisdom. Nevertheless, he managed to catch a few small trout. I suggested that a visit to some of the remote hill lochs in the area would be even more stimulating. A look of horror crossed his face as he gazed up towards the summit of Ben Cruachan, towering 3,000 feet above the north shore. "If you think for one moment that I am going anywhere near the top of Mount Cracken, then you are off your tiny Scottish mind!" he gasped.

Anyway, as I was saying, the only Lachlans, Sandys, Iains and Donalds I know have never paused to study anything reflectively – other than the glint of evening sunlight on a large lochside dram – and then only briefly. As for consideration of others, when it comes to getting to the river first, it is generally the deil tak the hindmost. Two senior anglers of my acquaintance provide a perfect example of what I mean. For many years they fished the Thurso in Caithness. On Beat 3 there is a salmon lie that invariably produces a "take" to the first fly of the day fished through it.

I have watched them putting up their rods, pretending to be in no hurry but seething inwardly with the desire to be "first" over that lie. On one occasion, I swear, I saw one of them "accidentally" drop his companion's spool of nylon into a clump of rushes. The line on reels becomes inexplicably tangled. Fly boxes mysteriously disappear. "Well, John, since you are not ready yet, I'll just wander over and give it a throw. You don't mind, do you?" In spite of everything, they remained firm friends and fished together all their lives.

Don't be fooled for a moment, either, by solicitous offers of assistance to get tackled up. What is really meant is: "For goodness' sake, get a move on. We are wasting good fishing time. I'm off, see you there." By the time you struggle over the ankle-breaking bog, with outboard motor and petrol, he will be dancing lightly along the shore playing his tenth trout. "Oh, there your are!" he will announce as you collapse to the ground, red-faced and breathless. "I was beginning to worry. Thought you might have fallen into a peat-hag. What have I been doing? Oh, just warming up. Look, the boat's over there. No, no, not in the water! Fifty yards up the bank . . . Damn it, missed one. With you in a jiffy." He never is.

Once settled, with the first trout safely in the bag, an astonishing transformation takes place in the angler's character. It is dramatic and inexplicable. From being perfectly capable of stooping to the lowest depths of animal cunning, he suddenly metamorphoses into a being of sweet reasonableness.

He becomes the creature non-anglers know and love – steadfast, rock-like, dependable, courteous and considerate. So, there you have it, the connection between airline passengers hot-footing it over the tarmac and fishermen. I used to sympathise with these poor, struggling business travellers in their distress – usually from the comfort of "that" seat. Being an experienced angler, I invariably made it first.

18.
It Is All in the Boot

I have in my possession a photograph of a well-known fisherman's boot. Not, you understand, his left or right wader, but the boot of his car. The reason this photograph is remarkable is because it substantiates a theory that I have long held: that the angler is an inherently untidy and forgetful beast, completely incapable of keeping his tackle and equipment in any semblance of order from one fishing trip to the next.

"How on earth," I exclaimed, "do you ever manage to find anything amongst that heap?"

"What heap?" he replied, unperturbed.

I pointed, "The mountain of reels, rods, baskets, waders, rugs and cameras in the back of your car."

"Oh, that heap! Well, Bruce, it might seem like a heap to you, but to me it is a highly-organised pile. I know exactly where everything is."

"All right, I'll take your word for it, but since we're using my car, what about untangling a few bits and pieces and transferring them? We're wasting good fishing time." A few minutes later, we were off to the hills.

Now you might imagine that the precise nature of the art of fly-fishing would indicate an equally precise attitude concerning accoutrements. When you list the essential requirements for a day out – rod, spare rod, two reels, nylon, fly-boxes, bag, net, waders, priest, scales, wet-weather gear, spare socks and so on – it would seem sensible to ensure that they are easily accessible in order that nothing is forgotten.

If you have tramped six miles over a peat bog to fish a remote loch, and on arrival find that you have left your favourite fly-box behind, apart from loud cursing, there is not much you can do about it. The wise angler, therefore, guards against this contingency by keeping his kit in well-ordered readiness and repair.

My eldest son, Blair, is a meticulous man. All his work shows the attention to detail and thoroughness of a well-ordered mind. However, the number of occasions I have had to "whisk" huge trout into a boat because he has forgotten the landing net are too numerous to mention.

"Oh, well done, dad!" he will exclaim as a 1lb 8oz trout comes flying inboard on a size 14 hook and 3lb breaking-strain nylon. "Jolly good!"

"Blair, would you please pass the priest?" I request, through gritted teeth, exercising great restraint. There follows a hurried scrambling in the fishing bag. He looks up.

"Didn't you bring it, then?" he asks.

Nowadays, I do my own packing. It's safer. Struggling round a rock-strewn shore in two left waders, one of which is leaking, is not my idea of fun. Another very good reason I have for caution, and doubling-up on equipment, is my youngest son, Charles. I don't want to be unkind, but teaching him to fish was a difficult and expensive experience.

Rods seemed to collapse the moment he looked at them. Spools fell out of reels, always overboard and always into the deepest part of the loch. A moment's loss of concentration invariably meant a half-hour, one-oared paddle round the loch looking for the other oar, which he had "accidentally" bumped out of the boat. A day in a boat, no, a few hours in a boat with Charles could knock up a bill for damages that would make a whole barrack-room quake. The worst part is that he generally catches more fish that I do as well.

By now you must be convinced that I am either a neatness freak or at least efficiency personified. Well, I am neither. I am, if anything, more untidy and forgetful than the rest of the family put together. In my own defence, however, I must say that I do not pretend to be otherwise, unlike some whom I could mention but will not do so for fear of embarrassing certain members of Clan Sandison.

I have no illusions and confess freely to being one of the most untidy creatures on God's earth. But I try to improve, all the time I try, and it does pay off. Now, I rarely forget any really important items of tackle ("Like the hip-flask," my wife interjects unkindly), but accidents still do happen. How was I to know she hadn't packed her rod?

At the end of every season I resolve to be better. I promise to hang up my line to dry, varnish my rod, repair that broken top ring, sharpen the hooks, you know the sort of thing. Somehow, come the following season, it all has still to be done. Worse, most of my tackle has completely disappeared under mounds of old newspapers and all those terribly useful Christmas boxes and empty bottles which you have promised to do something clever with but never will.

My worst habit, I think (and anyone who has ever been unfortunate enough to borrow a jacket of mine will instantly agree), is biting off flies and stuffing them into all sorts of pockets. During the course of a day, when changing casts – I never get "fankled" – and at the end of the day, I can't be bothered to undo things in an orderly fashion. So I just bite casts off and stuff them into the most convenient pocket.

My rationale for this is that, due to the number of fish I catch, the nylon wears out faster and as far as the line is concerned, at one-eighth of an inch per outing, twenty-five yards lasts me years. My teeth tend to tingle a bit now and then, but when the day is done, or when it is wet, cold and windy, that's exactly how I dismantle my tackle. By the end of the season, my fly-boxes are empty and my pockets dangerously full.

There is, nevertheless, one consolation about coming to terms with incipient forgetfulness and an untidy nature: you will be in good company. Do you remember that "well-known angler" I mentioned at the beginning of this piece and his unorganised heap in the car boot? When we eventually arrived at our distant loch, I noticed him scrabbling frantically in his bag.

"Anything wrong?" I enquired politely.

"Oh, no," he replied, "It's just that I seem to have mislaid my nylon." Then, anxiously: "You've got plenty, haven't you . . . ?"

"Yes," I replied smugly. "It comes from being well-organised, don't you know."

19.
A Stiff Brandy

It is a long time since I first visited Loch Brandy, but I will never forget it. Not just because of the excitement of discovery, but also because of the effort involved in getting there. The loch lies at a height of 2,000 feet and the climb up is unrelenting.

There were seven of us, parked by the banks of the River South Esk at the head of Glen Clova: my wife, Ann and her constant companion – not me, but that rag-haired, black-snubbed, bad-tempered thug of a Yorkshire terrier called Heathcliff – eldest son Blair and his wife, Barbara, second son Charles and small daughter Jean, and me.

I looked at the open door of the Clova Hotel. "Boots on, Bruce, I know what you are thinking and the answer is no."

"Have you got my jam doughnuts?" inquired Jean. My youngest can only be tempted uphill by promise of reward at the top. In this case jam doughnuts – which I was expected to carry.

There were numerous notices at the foot of the hill warning walkers to keep proper control of their dogs. One such notice explained that keepers had instruction to shoot stray dogs on sight. Glancing at Heathcliff, I was reassured to see that he was safely on the lead.

Sunlight warmed our backs as we fell into line behind Ann, who is the only one who can read a map – at least that's what she says. Making our way past the little school, we followed the narrow track, climbing steeply between Ben Reid and Rough Crag. Grouse-shooting country, dogs too.

Early July heather begged to bloom, covering the hill in a dark-green, purple-specked carpet, and twin streams chortled busily by – a good-to-be-alive day. Then I remembered my camera. I had left it on the roof of the car. By this time, the fitter members of Clan Sandison had disappeared over the first ridge. I was bringing up the rear, to "encourage" Jean.

I instructed Jean to wait and, fingers crossed, set off back down the hill hoping that the camera would still be there. Thankfully, it was. I hastened back up, anxious that my little charge hadn't come to any harm. She hadn't, but was deeply resentful when I suggested we continue up the track.

We found the others having a coffee break and I noticed that Heathcliff had managed to persuade Ann to slip his lead. Just as I opened my mouth to complain, a hare broke cover and bounded over the moor. Heathcliff gave a joyful yelp and set off in pursuit.

I had a vision of a dozen twelve-bore shotguns being raised to twelve tweed-clad shoulders. Throwing down my coffee cup, I sprinted after the brute, screaming at him to stop. It was like talking to the wind, or to a Member of Parliament, a complete waste of breath.

The dog had vanished. I stopped, panting, covered in sweat. In the distance, a small group of black-faced sheep grazed peacefully. Heathcliff couldn't be anywhere near them. I wandered over the hill, calling, "Heathcliff! Heathcliff!" like some hirsute Cathy in search of her Yorkshire lover. Had he gone back to the car? By this time I was half way down anyway, so I went to look. No luck. No dog.

Wearily, I started up the hill, for the third time. All I had wanted was a quite midsummer stroll amidst the peaceful glens of Angus. Suddenly, the sound of voices raised my eyes heavenwards. Blair, with Heathcliff clutched in his grasp, was waving.

I increased pace, planning what I would do when I laid hands, feet and anything else I could find lying about on his misshapen body and fog-filled head. But Ann had also increased pace and she and her dog were way ahead, her theory being that by the time I caught them I would be too exhausted to do anything, which was true.

With lunch spread out, as if by some devilish command, clouds suddenly filled the corrie. Rain mixed with sleet drove in horizontally as we huddled, sheltering from the storm. Ann pulled Jean closer. "Now then, Jean, isn't this fun?" she announced brightly. "What about my jam doughnuts?" came the angry reply. I had the answer. They were still in the car, where I had unintentionally left them, nor did I offer to dash back and get them.

But it was a wonderful day. The storm passed and we tackled up and addressed the task, hopefully, of the removal of a few resident trout for breakfast. Brandy is deep and the water is crystal clear. I was fishing with size 16 wet flies, Black Pennell on the bob, March Brown in the middle and Silver Butcher on the tail, and I fished from the east shore.

An hour later, the deed was done and I had four beautiful trout in my basket, marvellously marked and each weighing about 8oz. On the way back down the hill, line astern, Barbara produced her recorder and we sang appropriate Scottish airs, the morning's tribulations forgotten. Ahead, the welcoming embrace of the Clova Hotel.

Find Loch Brandy on OS Map 44, Ballater, Scale: 1:50,000. Loch Brandy, Gd Ref: 339755; start point and parking, Gd Ref: 326731. No charge is made to fish the loch, but anglers must obtain advance permission before setting out because the area is used for stalking. For further information, contact Rottal Lodge Cottage, Glen Clova, tel: 01575 550230 or Airlie Estate Office, Cortachy, Kirriemuir, tel: 01575 540222.

20.
Magical Islands

At the southern end of the Outer Hebrides lie three magical islands: North Uist, Benbecula and South Uist. The western edge of these Atlantic gems is fringed by wonderful, white, shell-sand beaches, backed by flower-bright, fertile machair fields. The east coast is rugged and inhospitable, bounding a trackless land confronting mainland Scotland over the stormy water of the Minch.

But the most remarkable aspect of the Uists and Benbecula is the number of freshwater lochs. To believe it, you must go there and see for yourself. I did for the first time in 1979 when we spent a family fishing holiday in the Hebrides. All of our family fish. The Chinese call it brainwashing. I call it common sense. From earliest years, each of our four children was introduced to the gentle art and they are still anglers today.

Driving south from Lochmaddy brought instant joy. Everywhere we looked, around every corner, over every rise, a seemingly endless array of lochs and lochans. Moorland, mountains and hills crowded every side, the sea shimmered azure, emerald, green, and blue in August sunlight and the scent of peat smoke filled the air.

For two blissful weeks we explored the islands: wandering over the moors to distant trout lochs and seaweed-fringed pools. Buzzard, golden eagle and harrier shadowed our way; curlew piped from sphagnum tussocks; soft, seemingly endless sunny summer days amidst a peaceful, glorious world.

North Uist is circled by a convenient road within which lie a series of superb brown trout and sea-trout lochs: Scadavay, with shores that meander round the moor for a distance of more than fifty miles, full of fishy points and promontories, is reputed to contain 365 islands, one for every day of the year, with many of these islands hosting small lochs of their own.

A single track divides North Uist from north to south, built in 1845 to provide employment during the terrible potato famine that ravaged the Highlands in the mid-nineteenth century. To the west of this road are the principal sea-trout waters: Struban, Dusary, Trosavat and Hosta. But the most exciting sea-trout fishing is to be found in distant sea-pools around the coastline. One morning, my son Blair and I walked south from the A867 to the Oban Sponish sea-pools on the north shore of Loch Eport; a hard hike, tramping for two hours over wet moorlands round Scadavay's ragged shores.

Oban Sponish is a long, narrow, tide-marked inlet, guarded from the sea by a rock bar. When the tide rises, cold waters flood in, bringing with them hard-fighting sea-trout which dash through the brackish waters, sending waves swirling and anglers' hearts racing; outstanding sport amidst outstanding scenery.

My favourite Benbecula loch is Ba Alasdair, at the south end of the island. It lies to the north of a narrow track that leads north and then eastwards from the B891. This is a brackish loch into which sea-trout charge when the tide is right. Linked to Ba Alasdair by a feeder stream, just north over the hill at the head of the loch, is a classic trout water, known locally as Bluebell Loch. In spring and early summer some of the little islands here are a stunning mass of bluebells.

Blair worked on the islands for a number of years, eventually becoming the secretary of the South Uist Angling Club, an appointment which was mightily welcomed by me; thus we had expert advice whenever we visited. Blair once took me to where he had landed his best sea-trout, in the sea-pool between Clett headland and Rubha Gias over the golden sands at Geireann. At low tide, the sands are exposed and it is possible to walk out to the sea-pool. Travel carefully, though, because there are quicksands and you should check tide times before setting out.

When we arrived at the pool, Atlantic waves were breaking over a rock bar, surging in with each swell through a narrow channel. The sea was emerald green, crested snow-white, and the water was myriad-coloured, reflecting the golden sandy shallows with shades from green hills and blue skies shimmering across the surface. The pool was busy with salmon and sea-trout, tearing round like mad things, splashing and leaping, throwing themselves out of the water in spectacular displays. In spite of all my best efforts, they remained in their domain, although Blair caught two; but just seeing them, and just being there, was reward enough.

Stilligarry is my favourite South Uist loch, a shallow straggle of bays and corners where good fish lurk. One Easter, whilst visiting Benbecula, my thoughtful daughter-in-law, Barbara, suggested a fishing picnic to Stilligarry. Early April in the Hebrides can be wild, but we always go, regardless of weather conditions. That morning was particularly wet and windy, with a mantle of mist shrouding the slopes of Hecla and Beinn Mhor. The mist also shrouded the fish and we thrashed away mightily to no avail.

One by one, the members of Clan Sandison retired hurt. Left alone in solitary splendour, I could see them crouched behind the car, the flash of a hip flask indicating that inner man and inner woman were being warmed. I fished on, more as an act of defiance than in the hope of catching anything. As I was about to surrender, a fish rose beyond my reach. Not expecting much action,

I hadn't bothered to put on boots, let alone waders, but I was determined to land a fly over that trout's nose so I waded out, regardless of the freezing water, soaked to the knees.

The moment my fly touched the surface, the fish grabbed. I stumbled shore-wards, praying the hook would hold and, after a considerable struggle, managed to beach a fine trout of just under 2lb in weight. Triumphantly, I carried it to the car. "Fair weather anglers, the lot of you," I announced, demanding immediate refreshment for my efforts.

21.
St Abbs

The first light of a grey dawn touched the night sky. We were wide awake and waiting, my brother and I, in the bedroom of a small fisherman's cottage in a row of brightly-painted houses overlooking St Abbs harbour in Berwickshire. Stones rattled against our window and we rushed to look. Jake Nisbet, dressed in a huge white jersey, a jaunty black cap on his head and trousers tucked into black boots, was beckoning. A few moments later we proudly followed him down to the harbour and boarded his boat.

Jake had a small, inshore boat and he used to take us fishing in it below the red, ragged Berwickshire cliffs. But he also had a share in a much larger sea-going vessel and he had invited us to spend the day at sea, sleeping onboard overnight, returning to harbour the following evening. As a boy, I can't remember ever being so excited about anything and I will never forget the experience.

Jake was a wonderful man, full of tales and stories about his whaling days in the South Atlantic. He had an amazing collection of whale bones that he had carved into shapes and figures, and I believed every word that he said. He was one of those people to whom things happened. Many years later, when I read that a St Abbs fisherman had hauled in his nets and landed a complete suit of sixteenth-century armour, I knew instantly who that fisherman would be; I was right, it was Jake Nisbet.

The days I spent with Jake and his crew settled in me my love of the sea and of fishing, a love that has remained with me to this day. Most of my fishing now is for wild brown trout, sea-trout and, occasionally, for salmon, but I still regard the sea as my spiritual home. All of human life owes its existence to the sea and I believe that anything that damages the sea and the creatures therein, damages us all.

But our seas are in trouble, from over-fishing and pollution, and nowhere more so than in the North Sea. When I was a young man, friends who had been ditched by girlfriends were told not to worry because there were "plenty more fish in the sea", that they would soon find another woman upon which to lavish their affection. Today it ain't necessarily so. There may well be plenty of girls left for men to woo, but our seas are being ruthlessly denuded of their fish.

It would be easy to blame our political masters for this ecological nightmare. So I will, because that is exactly where the blame lies. Since 1992, the International Council for the Exploration of the seas (ICES), which advises governments on the status of fish stocks, has warned of the impending collapse of North Sea cod stocks because of over-fishing. ICES reported, as far back as 2003, that the numbers of young fish boosting cod populations in the North Sea were the lowest they had been in twenty years and advised, yet again, all cod fisheries be closed to allow stocks to recover.

When our granddaughter Jessica was a toddler and had created a shambles somewhere in the house, she would announce in a sombre voice, "Mess, granny." The only words that I can think of that describe the present state of UK fisheries policy echo this cry, "Mess, granny." In the 1990s, one of the world's greatest cod fisheries, the Grand Banks fishery in Newfoundland, collapsed. In spite of all recovery plans, it is still in a ruinous state. That is what is happening to cod stocks in the North Sea.

Fish farming is offered as an answer to dwindling wild fish stocks, particularly the farming of Atlantic salmon, but, in its present form, fish farming does not protect wild stocks from over-exploitation. Farmed fish are fed on a diet rich in oil and fat, and this oil and fat is sourced from small fish at the base of the food chain, species such as sandeels, pout, capelin and anchovies. In Scotland, best estimates suggest that it takes three tonnes of these small fish to produce one tonne of farmed salmon.

In the 1950s, when we had a family holiday in Orkney, I discovered the miracle sea-pools left behind by the falling tide. From under every stone, sea-creatures scurried; killing or being killed by the smaller or larger inhabitants trapped with them in their temporary prison. The shores were coloured brown, blue and gold with rank, sweet-smelling seaweed. The air resounded with seabird cry. The cliffs where the birds nested were busy tenements, bustling with life.

Revisiting the islands today exposes the full extent of the impact that the mismanagement of our seas has had upon our environment. My rock pools are virtually devoid of life, barren and bare, and many of the cliff nesting sites where I marvelled at clouds of seabirds are often deserted. What, I wonder, would my childhood friend, Jake Nisbet from St Abbs, make of the state of our seas today? I don't know, because he has long since departed this life to fish in another place, but I know other fishermen who still make a living in and around our coastal waters.

As long as they continue to do so, then perhaps future generations of children will be able to stand at their bedroom windows, as my brother and I did so many years ago, waiting excitedly for the arrival of a kindly fisherman to take them on an adventure that will change their lives forever. I am sure that Jake Nisbet would approve.

22.
Start Them Young

Michael Finnegan, it is alleged, had whiskers on his chinigan, some of which "grew out and then grew in again". Distressing for poor old Michael because, according to contemporary reports, it appears he always had to begin again. I don't think Michael was an angler but, standing beside a loch many years ago, preparing to introduce my first grandson, Brodie, to the gentle art of fly-fishing, I knew exactly how Michael must have felt.

I seem to have spent nearly half my life introducing little ones to fly-fishing: our four children, nephews and nieces, the offspring of friends various, and some not so little ones, such as my father, mother and two brothers. On family fishing expeditions I rarely got the chance to cast a line. I was always far too busy tying up other people's casts, sorting out fankles, rescuing snagged flies and trying to keep the peace when disputes arose about who was to fish where and for how long.

As I pondered these matters, I glimpsed Blair, Brodie's father, striding off to the far side of the loch: "Hoy, just a minute!" I yelled. "Where do you think you are going?" He waved derisively, stripping off line and casting over a rising trout. The fish grabbed.

"Granddad," urged Brodie, "can we catch a fish?" I looked down at the excited child by my side. Resigned, I began, yet again.

Brodie Sandison was only three years old at the time, and yet he was already infected with the urge to fish. Unlike other little boys, whose first adventures into diction involve words such as Mummy, Daddy, train, dog or cat, Brodie's vocabulary was dominated by more important verbal concepts like: fishing rod, reel, fly-box and trout; his favourite phrase, which he articulated perfectly, was, "Going fishing with Granddad."

Again, some may call it brainwashing, but I prefer to call it common sense. Giving children a love of fishing is far more important than putting money in the bank for them; money comes and goes, but a love of fishing stays forever. It worked with our four offspring, who are all expert anglers – at least, that is what they tell me – and I suppose, to be truthful, I was delighted at being given the honour of helping Brodie to catch his first trout. "All right, Brodie, Granddad will catch you a fish." I said a silent prayer, crossed my fingers, and cast into the loch.

Finding the right place for that first outing is vital. There has to be an absolute certainty that fish will be caught. Nothing is more calculated to depress little spirits (and big ones) than the lack of the sound of rising trout. Choosing the right day is also essential: torrential rain and a force-eight gale are unlikely to persuade children to persevere. Pack a special picnic with their favourite food, which in Brodie's case was not too difficult: a couple of silver-wrapped chocolate biscuits.

Loch Rangag in Caithness is the perfect place to introduce beginners, young or old, to the gentle art of fly-fishing: close by the road and not too far to stumble to the water, a tumbling stream and sheltered picnic spot; shallow margins with banks free from bushes and other obstructions; and full of hard fighting, breakfast-sized trout that even on a bad day rise readily to the fly.

Close to Rangag is another excellent Caithness trout loch, Stemster, which contains larger fish and is also a suitable venue for beginners. Less exposed than Rangag, and less public, on any reasonable day, Stemster generally produces fish. Charles, my second son, once had a super trout of just over 2lb and I once caught, on the same cast, two fish each weighing 1lb. It is possible to drive almost to the shore of the loch and there is a good boat available, although we usually fish from the bank.

If the wind is howling, then head for Stemster, rather than Rangag. The loch is generally circular and, consequently, it is always possible to find a sheltered area from which to fish. And bank fishing is every bit as productive, if not more so, than fishing from the boat. At the south end of Stemster, long fingers of rock poke out into the loch. They are easy to wade and allow you to effectively cover a wide area of water.

On Loch Rangag, my first choice of flies would be a Ke-He on the "bob", March Brown in the middle, and a Silver Butcher on the tail. In truth, however, Rangag trout are not in the least fussy and rise readily to almost any pattern. On Stemster, I would begin with the same cast, and then try also Black Pennell, Soldier Palmer, Greenwell's Glory and Peter Ross.

"Granddad, look!" shouted Brodie. I returned to the present just in time to see the tail of a fish disappearing into the depths. I cast again. Missed. Missed again. I sensed my halo slipping. Missed again. Clearly I would have to do something pretty damn quick, otherwise I would be in big trouble when Brodie's dad arrived back on the scene. Then I hooked one. "Come on, Brodie, take the rod." I crouched by Brodie's side and helped him reel in, the fish splashing and fighting all the way.

Brodie's face was bright with excitement. "Look, Brodie, your first trout! Won't daddy be pleased?" I heard a noise behind me. "Thank you, father," said Blair, as he put his camera away. "Glad to see that you are on form this morning. What about missing a few dozen more, just for the record?"

For further information about Rangag and Semster, and indeed all you want to know about fishing in Caithness, contact Hugo Ross, Fishing Tackle shop, 54 High Street, Wick, Caithness, tel: 01955 604200.

23.
Mountain Goat Salmon Fishing

For me, the upper beat of the River Kirkaig on the Sutherland/Wester Ross border is "the salmon river from hell". It is beyond compare. I don't think that anybody has the right to call themselves a salmon angler until they have tackled this part of the river. It is pure mountain-goat country, from Falls Pool at the top to Arrow Pool at the end.

It is fished from the Inver Lodge Hotel (tel: 01571 844496) and Falls Pool reached after a hike of about forty minutes from Inverkirkaig. The pool is accessed via a descent down a steep cliff face to a casting platform. Even when the water is flowing gently over the sixty-feet-high falls, you are drenched in spray. Afterwards, it is back up the cliff and then, immediately, down again to fish Lower Falls Pool.

Now climb the cliff once more to find the ankle-breaking track that runs along the hillside. This leads to a series of narrow pools where the slightest casting error has your flies tangled irretrievably in a tree on the opposite bank, or snagged in the bracken behind you.

One of the finest pools is Little Falls Pool. It is reached from the main track, but, even then, it is a serious stumble down through the undergrowth. Salmon lie close to the far bank. Getting a fly to them is a work of art in itself, given the limited places from which to cast. Hooking one and holding it in within the pool is just as challenging.

My favourite pool is Otter Pool, so hard to find that sometimes I have passed it by. The last time I fished it, on the way down through the trees, my companion slipped, inches from a twelve-foot drop into the pool. He grabbed the branches of a silver birch with one hand, whilst I caught hold of his other hand and pulled him to safety. During the process, his fishing bag came loose. The last we saw of it was when it hit the water and disappeared downstream.

You will not be able to park your car by the side of the Upper Kirkaig. It is just you, the river and the salmon. However, having spent a few days stumbling along the Kirkaig's steep-sided banks, the Inver Lodge can also offer guests a less taxing day out on the River Inver, a few miles north from the Kirkaig.

The hotel has fishing on the Upper Inver and the Lower Middle Inver, both beats being more sedate than the Kirkaig, but nonetheless attractive and just as much fun to fish. There are three principal pools on the Upper Inver, Loch na Garbhe Uidhe, where the flow from Loch Assynt tumbles in, Lochan an-Iasgaich, which is a wide extension of the main river, and Turn Pool, downstream from Lochan an-Iasgaich.

Lower Middle Inver is separated from the Upper Inver by a long, private stretch, and it has three principal pools, Mackenzie's Stream, Brachloch Pool and the Minister's Pool. Having said this, the runs between all these pools, given the right water conditions, can produce fish and deserve a few casts as you pass by.

Lochan an-Iasgaich is a wonderful pool: wide, with a substantial flow rushing in, even in low water conditions. It is easily accessible and wading is safe and comfortable. It is possible to ford the river at the neck, but received wisdom advises you not to do so, because of the possibility of disturbing any salmon lying in, or moving up through the well-oxygenated water.

However, I have to confess that I have often waded the neck because reaching the south bank would otherwise involve a tiresome hike upstream to access a footbridge. This may account for the fact that, in spite of my best efforts, I have rarely prevented the residents of the pool from going about their lawful business.

But there can be few more scenic places in which not to catch salmon. The pool is overlooked by one of my favourite Scottish mountains, Quinag (808m), and the whole graceful ridge, from Spidean Coinich in the south to Sail Gorm overlooking Unapool and Kyle Strome in the north, dominates the horizon.

Turn Pool, where Allt an Tiaghaich Burn bustles in, has been kinder to me. I remember one September evening, as I was weighing up the relative merits of a few more casts or a retreat to a refreshing pint in the hotel, when my fly stopped in midstream. I tightened into a fish, a salmon of about 6lb in weight and spawning-red, so I carefully unhooked the fish and returned it to the stream.

A few moments later a much larger fish took and after a considerable struggle I managed to bring him to the bank. I did not weigh him because he, too, was returned, but I estimated the salmon to be in the order of 14lb/15lb.

I wish I could say that I returned him without a moment's hesitation, but that would be telling less than the whole truth.

Still, good behaviour brings its deserved rewards. A few weeks later, a side of beautifully smoked salmon arrived unexpectedly at Castle Sandison, courtesy of a friend with whom I had been sharing the beat. "That's nice," said my wife, Ann. "Why don't we send it to Blair? He won't often get the chance of wild smoked salmon in China, will he?"

Dutifully, I did the deed and posted off my prize to my son. I didn't actually tell him that I hadn't caught the fish, but rather hoped that he might just assume that I had.

24.
Sporting Gentleman

The gillie is the backbone of Scottish salmon fishing. These are people who invariably spend their whole life fishing a single stream, whose knowledge of their river is second to none. For visiting anglers, the gillie is the key to salmon fishing success and the vast majority of Scottish gillies work hard to ensure that their guests have the best possible chance of sport.

Nevertheless, gillies are often undervalued and in some cases even insulted by rods who employ them. Aggressiveness seems to be in the nature of some of the salmon fishers who now venture north of Mr Hadrian's Wall in search of sport – over-dressed, over-loud and over here; intolerant and rarely prepared to take advice proffered; dismissive of the gillie's experience, until something goes wrong.

Like not catching fish. Then it is the fault of the gillie. He has put the angler in the wrong place at the wrong time, recommended the wrong pattern of fly, the wrong type of line. Failure to catch fish has nothing whatsoever to do with the guest's general lack of angling ability, it is entirely the fault of his gillie: "Damn man had me fishing with a floating line. Didn't touch a fish. Didn't even see a fish."

I remember, less than happily, being in the Lochmaddy Hotel in North

Uist one evening and listening to a group of visitors complaining about the local gillie. Apparently, he had been less than accommodating with information when they tackled him about fishing locations at the bar prior to dinner. "Typical!" complained one. "That's the sort of man who gives fishing a bad name."

I went over and spoke to them. "Do you mind me asking what you do for a living?" I said.

"I'm in investment, in the City" he replied.

"And you?" I said to his companion.

"I'm a lawyer, why?"

"Would either of you give advice and information to total strangers, completely free of charge?" I inquired.

"Of course not!" they laughed.

"Well, in future, think about that the next time you expect a free ride from a gillie. He is as much deserving of a fee for his knowledge as you are."

Nothing is more certain in angling than the uncertainty of salmon fishing, particularly given the sad state of Scotland's salmon stocks – fewer fish than before; ever increasing numbers of anglers trying to catch them. Which makes it all the more important to listen to the advice of your gillie. More than anyone, he is most able to direct your effort to best effect. Ignore his advice and you might as well stay at home.

I remember one Tweed gillie telling me of a typical incident: "The river was high, but we had four salmon. At the end of the day, he turned to me, in a conspiratorial sort of way, and said: 'You see that yellow tree on the far bank? Well, Wallace, the next time the river is in this condition, take your guest there. That's where the fish lie.' I had been seeing the tree for damn near thirty years, but I just smiled and thanked him for his advice."

The finest anglers I know are gillies, not only because of their superb fishing technique or knowledge of their river, but also because of their love of and commitment to the environment and the flora and fauna it supports. Show me a gillie and I will show you a conservationist.

Willie Matheson is one such man, the fourth generation of Mathesons to have worked on the River Beauly in Inverness-shire. I met Willie a few years back and, after half an hour, asked him if he would fish down the pool while

I watched. His casting technique was a miracle of perfection, controlled, seemingly effortless, a work of art. Worth every inch of the 100-mile journey I had made to the river, just to witness it.

The late Gordon Dagger, erstwhile Fishery Manager on the little River Forss in Caithness, was another. Gordon could place a fly, millimetre-perfect, yard by yard down Falls Pool, by every stone, under every overhanging branch, faultlessly.

Johnny Hardy, on the Helmsdale in Sutherland, is a superb angler and wonderful fishing companion. Johnny Hardy can make fishing in the midst of a nail-biting March snowstorm as pleasurable and exciting as fishing on the mildest May day.

Colin Leslie, on the River Tay at Cargill, combined an amazing casting ability with an encyclopaedic mind of tales of ones that got away and a few that didn't. He was full of endless stories about those who tried to catch them, including an account of the tip he received from the financier, J. D. Rockefeller, 10s/6d (52p), and the day General Francis De Guingand, Montgomery's Chief of Staff in North Africa during World War Two, took a severe ducking in the river just up from the Cargill fishing hut.

My favourite story, however, is about the tip that never was. A London angler was fishing in the Highlands many years ago and, at the end of the week, told his gillie he was not going to give him a tip. Instead, the guest said: "Give me whatever savings you can afford and I will invest them for you, along with a similar amount of my own. Each year, when I come fishing, we will do the same."

The financier made a great friend and fishing companion. From time to time, the gillie would visit London to "inspect" his investment. He was always greeted with the greatest possible courtesy and hurried to the chairman's office. After thirty years, the gillie retired with a more than substantial investment fund, financially secure and easily able to afford to build himself a new house by the river. Our gillies are our finest angling asset and deserve our fullest respect.

25.
The Secret of Angling Success

The secret of angling success is to be in the right place at the right time. Regardless of whether the quarry is salmon, trout or sea-trout, this is a central fact of angling life. Personal skill, technique, tackle and equipment all play a part, but the over-riding common denominator lies in placing your fly where there is a fish that is in the mood to take it. If I am wrong, I will eat my landing net, and yours too.

Neither is it just a question of weather conditions or water height. It can often mean only the distance of a few feet, from one end of a boat to the other. My wife, Ann, would be delighted to confirm this theory. I once spent a whole day fishless in the bow, whilst she caught half a dozen perfect wild brown trout from the stern. And we were using exactly the same patterns of artificial flies at the time.

I remember sharing a boat on Loch Hope in Sutherland with Andy Walker of the Pitlochry Freshwater Fishery Research Laboratory and one of his colleagues who was a complete novice, barely able to get a fly line out in any semblance of casting proficiency. Andy is one of Scotland's most experienced and competent anglers, but by the end of the day, if Andy and I had caught two more fish between us we would have had a brace. The novice caught four.

The Fionn Loch in Wester Ross is a duffers' paradise, packed with suicidal small trout that swim around waving white handkerchiefs, begging to be caught. Even on a bad day you should go home with breakfast. The last time I fished Fionn, with my wife, Ann, and John Corbin of the Gairloch Angling Club, we caught twelve trout: Ann caught six, John caught six, and I caught the rest.

Salmon fishing is even nicer. The late Willie Merrilees, a famous Leith policeman, went salmon fishing for the first time and caught, if I remember correctly, six fish. I caught five salmon one day on the River Thurso in Caithness when I wasn't really looking, and never caught another one for ten years, although I was looking really hard all the time.

Is there a salmon angler alive who hasn't suffered the torture of fishing a pool where salmon are leaping about madly in all directions and yet refusing to look at the flies you are so artfully offering them – large, small, red, yellow, blue and black – fast, slow, on the surface, fished deep, backed-up – standing on your head and screaming at the top of your voice in frustration?

I live and work in the far north of Scotland, near Tongue in Sutherland, surrounded by some of the finest game fishing in the world. Rivers such as the Naver, Brogie, Dionard and the delightful little Polla are a few minutes' drive away. Super trout lochs – Lanlish, Loyal, Hakel, Haluim, and Craggie – are on my front door. I can be fishing the wonderful waters of Caithness within an hour: Watten, Heilen, St John's and Calder.

The benefit of this is that I can improve my chance of success by choosing the best time to fish, when conditions are most advantageous. My rod is always tackled up, ready and waiting in the garage, and with the first whiff of a fond south-west breeze, I can be up and at 'em. However, others are not so fortunate and for many, their annual holiday is the only time that they have to concentrate on the removal of fish from their natural habitat.

In Sutherland, they could do no better than seek the advice of the Tongue and District Angling Club through the Benloyal Hotel (tel: 01847 611216) who have excellent boats with outboard engines on a number of productive lochs, and good sea-trout fishing in the Kyle of Sutherland. The hotel also has a boat for sea-trout fishing on South End Loch Hope, now the best sea-trout loch in Scotland.

In Caithness, visitors should seek advice in arranging these matters from the Wick tackle shop of Hugo Ross (tel: 01955 604200), known in local angling circles as Mr Fixit. Hugo can't arrange the weather, but he can arrange just about everything else: accommodation, boats, engines, permits, flies and tackle, and thus give the visiting angler the best possible chance of enjoying good sport.

A couple of years back, on a blistering June day, I fished Loch Watten from Hugo's Oldhall site. There is a comfortable little lunch hut here, with a well-marked, duck-boarded track to the mooring bay and two first-class boats. Getting afloat was a pleasure, none of the customary heaving and gut-bursting boat-shoving one usually associates with north of Scotland angling. Step in, push off, fish.

My companions that day, father and son, were expert anglers (at least that is what they keep telling me) but I won't mention any names for fear of embarrassing James and Jeremy Paterson, and I have to confess that I also fondly imagine that I am no slouch either in the piscatorial stakes.

We lashed the water to foam to no avail. Yes, trout rose and splashed at our flies, but hooking them was beyond us. At the day's end, sunburned, fishless and frustrated, we retired hurt, muttering dire threats about breaking rods and taking up golf.

"Come on then, Bruce," James complained, "you are supposed to be the know-all guru, what's your explanation?"

I summoned up a brave smile: "Simple," I replied, "we were in the wrong place at the wrong time. But wait until tomorrow, James, believe me, that's when the big fish will be moving, honest."

He responded with that unique Scottish phrase that manages to be both double positive and double negative at one and the same time: "Aye, right."

26.
Fishing and the Water of Life

Fishing and whisky are inextricably linked. The rivers and lochs that nurture the salmon and trout we love also nurture the peat and barley used to make uisge beatha, the water of life. In Scotland, you can match a malt to where you are fishing and these notes will help you to do so.

The rivers and lochs of Edinburgh and the Lothians are splendid, as is the pre-eminent lowland whisky Glenkinchie, elegant smooth and smoky. The distillery lies south of Edinburgh and draws its water from Kinchie Burn, a tributary of Humbie Water, which flows into the River Tyne. The Tyne was famous as a sea-trout stream and whilst these fish are still caught, the river is fished mostly for brown trout today.

For sport afloat, head for Gladhouse Reservoir, 400 acres in extent and my favourite Lothian water. This is really a hill loch as it lies on the skirts of the Moorfoot Hills at an altitude of 900ft. Outboard motors are not allowed so be prepared for heavy oar work or pack a strong friend and sufficient Glenkinchie to keep him encouraged. Trout average 12oz in weight and fish of over 3lb are taken most seasons. Tempt them with Black Pennell, Grouse & Claret, and Cinnamon & Gold.

North from Glasgow are Loch Lomond and the Trossachs, the "bristling country". Wonderful single malts are shaped at the Loch Lomond Distillery at Alexandria. The Loch Lomond malt is light and graceful, whilst Inchmurrin and Inchmoan are named after islands in the loch. But the prize here has to be Auchentoshan, distilled by Morrison Bowmore. Its aroma is achieved by a unique triple distillation, a process that creates a dream-like malt.

Loch Lomond is also dream-like. The system produces 1,000 salmon and 1,500 sea-trout most seasons. Salmon average 8lb in weight, sea-trout 2lb 8oz. Boat fishing brings best results and the most popular fly-fishing drifts are at the shallow, south end; out from Balloch, where the River Leven leaves the loch on its journey to the Firth of Clyde; and from Balmaha, on the south-east shore.

The greatest concentration of Scottish single malt distilleries is in Speyside and Moray. This area also offers some of the finest game fishing: the fast-flowing Spey, the Rivers Findhorn and Deveron, and, for brown trout, historic Lochindorb on desolate Dava Moor, the ideal place to introduce beginners to the gentle art of fly-fishing.

A focal point for fishing and distilling is Ballindalloch estate. Here you'll find superb angling on the Spey and its longest tributary, the River Avon, and two best-loved malts, Cragganmore and the world-renowned Glenfarclas distillations. Cragganmore has a floral fragrance and a malty taste. All the Glenfarclas distillations are magnificent, from the straw-gold of the ten-year-old, to the stunning thirty-year-old ABV malt.

In 1892, William Grant built a new distillery at Balvenie on the banks of the Fiddich. There are five "partners" in the Balvenie box and it is hard to choose which to try. The Balvenie Single Barrel is drawn from a single cask of a single distillation. No more than 350 hand-numbered bottles are produced. The Balvenie Vintage Cask is exceptional.

Also guaranteed to please is the Macallan, described by whisky expert Michael Jackson as the "Rolls-Royce of single malts". The Macallan is distilled at Craigellachie, close to where the River Fiddich flows into the Spey. The company has an excellent salmon beat. Offer the salmon Silver Stoat's Tail, Garry Dog and Willie Gunn. For sea-trout, try Black Pennell, Peter Ross, and Mallard & Claret.

In Skye you will find the wettest rain in Scotland and Talisker, one of Caledonia's most distinctive malts. Drinking Talisker is always a pleasure, but pleasure with Skye salmon comes only after heavy rain. A number of streams can provide sport. The most productive is the River Snizort, a narrow river where light tackle and flies fished "fine and far off" bring results. Try Green Highlander, Kate McLaren and Garry Dog.

The best of Skye is to be found amidst its trout lochs. The principal water, the Storr Loch to the north of Portree, contains some super-large specimens. North again will bring you to little Loch Mealt, notable for its unique strain of Arctic char, descendants of fish which have survived there since the end of the last Ice Age. Bushy patterns of fly work best: Ke-He, Soldier Palmer, Black Zulu and Blue Zulu.

Two fine malts welcome you to the Island of Mull: Tobermory and Ledaig. Tobermory is lightly peated and medium dry while Ledaig is more intense, with a peppery kick. The island's fishing "wares" include the chance of salmon in the Lussan and Forsa Rivers, and trout fishing on the Mishnish Lochs and Loch Frisa.

On Islay, there is whisky and fishing enough to last several lifetimes. The isle has eight distilleries, all of which produce spectacular malts. When trout fishing on Loch Gorm in the north-west, or on Loch Finlaggan near Ballygrant, fill your flask with magical Bowmore. Sir Harry Lauder, the Scottish comedian, celebrated here with a "decent dram" in 1930 when he landed the only salmon ever taken from the loch.

For me, the most splendid Scottish malt is Lagavulin, distilled in the south-east of Islay near the ruins of Dunyveg Castle. This is a majestic malt, bottled when sixteen years old, redolent with the taste of peat smoke, salt-tinged, robust and wonderful. The final step of our journey takes us over the Sound of Islay to Jura, "the island of the deer", where you will find myriad trout lochs amid some of Scotland's most dramatic scenery. The Isle of Jura malt, an extraordinary whisky, will help you catch them, and add miles to your casting distance.

Neil M. Gunn (1891–1973), a Scottish author who knew more about whisky and fishing than most, must have the last word. The opening chapter of his book, *Highland River*, describes a small boy catching a huge salmon in a narrow stream.

No angling writer I have read matches the power of Gunn's prose. He was equally eloquent about whisky, "embodying in it the tempest of thunder and the sweetness of innocence, a work of art which is always repeated yet always unique". *Slàinte, sonas agus beartas.*

27.
Hope Springs Eternal

Amidst the doom and gloom of the decline in Scottish West Highland and Islands sea-trout stocks, one loch still holds the promise of outstanding action with this most graceful of all sporting fish: Loch Hope in North West Sutherland. Upwards of 500 fish are taken most seasons and in order to preserve and enhance Loch Hope sea-trout stocks, all fish of under 1lb 5oz must be returned to the water to fight another day.

The loch lies amidst spectacular scenery and is approximately six miles north/south by up to one mile wide, dropping to a depth of over 180 feet in Middle Bay. The west shoreline is trackless and may only be reached by boat, whilst the east shore is margined by a narrow, twisting, single track road from Altnaharra in the south to Hope in the north.

The fishing on South End Loch Hope is divided into four areas: Beat 1, Beat 2, Beat 3 and Middle Bay. Outboard motors are not used on South End because, to reach Beat 2 and Beat 3, boats have to cross Beat 1. It is considered that the disturbance created by an outboard engine passing overhead might put flighty sea-trout "down" on Beat 1. Therefore, unless you have the services of a gillie, pack a strong, unsuspecting young friend to bend his mind to the oars whilst you get on with the business of removing fish from their natural habitat.

The no-outboard rule creates problems in less than calm weather. If you are fishing on Beat 2, or the far end of Beat 3, and the wind rises, then there can be very real problems in returning to the mooring bay at the south-east end of Beat 1. Sudden storms are not entirely unknown in these airts and safety should be of paramount importance. Always wear a life jacket. Never stand up whilst fishing. If in doubt, don't go out. If you are caught on the west side of the loch, then getting back to the mooring bay involves a huge walk, up the Strathmore River, hauling the boat along the rocky shore as you go.

I have been blown off Loch Hope more times than I have been blown off any other loch in Scotland. The most memorable occasion happened a couple of years ago when, after one drift on Beat 1 during which we moved more than a dozen fish, the wind rose and we were forced to row for the shore. We spent the next three hours sitting on the bank, fingers crossed, praying for the wind to drop, musing on the best day's fishing we never had. Savage entertainment. The wind didn't drop and we abandoned Hope for a sheltered trout loch.

Each of the South End beats has its own, distinctive character and Loch Hope regulars have their own favourites. The truth is, however, that all the beats can be wonderfully productive in their own right, although Middle Bay perhaps less so towards the back end of the season. Beat 1 is relatively shallow, with an average depth of 15ft, and fish may be taken from almost anywhere on the beat, from the margins to the middle. The long, finger-like, south extension of Beat 1 is not fished, being a nursery area for small trout.

Beat 2 includes the mouth of the Strathmore River and is always exciting to fish. You just know the fish are there, smelling the fresh water flowing down from Glen Golly and the north face of Meall Garbh (752m). The outlet of the river is very shallow and over the years, silt and sand have been washed into the loch, forming a considerable shelf. Sea-trout and salmon congregate here, and in the bay to the west of Eilean Mor, where half a dozen small streams rush in from craggy Meall Glas (300m). However, as on Beat 1, salmon and sea-trout may be encountered almost anywhere on the beat, so cast with supreme confidence.

Beat 3 takes in the narrowing neck of South End, prior to where the loch opens up into Middle Bay. Both banks, east and west, are included, although most rods concentrate on the west shore. The beat begins where an old wall comes down the hill to the water and the best drift is along this shore, about ten to fifteen yards out from the bank. It is virtually essential to have someone on the oars all the time, holding the boat in position. Too far in or too far out is just not good enough. You must hold the right line, always, to have the best possible chance of sport. Fish the drift right down to the sandbar at the entrance to Middle Bay.

Middle Bay itself is a vast affair, two miles north/south by up to one mile wide. Most rods begin fishing on the west side, in a large, semi-sheltered wide sweep of a bay which extends from Creag Bhreaig (100m) in the north to a point of land half a mile south. Close to this point is the feature known as "The Castle" – an underwater stack around which sea-trout shoal. Finding the location of "The Castle" requires a deal of experience. Draw an imaginary line from the top of Creag Bhreaig south down the loch. Look to your right and you will see a "notch" which breaks the horizon line of the hills. Draw a line from there to intersect the first line. Where the lines cross is the location of "The Castle". Or should be.

The east shore of Middle Bay is tree-lined and looks very fishy, an endless delight of points and corners, shingle banks and weed patches. But I have never had much success fishing there, although I once saw Andy Walker take an 11lb salmon at the north end, and the largest sea-trout ever landed from Loch Hope was caught at the Black Rock on this shore – a magnificent fish of 17lb 2oz, caught on 4 August 1959 by legendary Altnaharra Hotel gillie, Hugh Sutherland.

The remainder of Loch Hope, North End, is fished from Ian McDonald's cottage close to where the A838 Tongue/Durness road crosses the River Hope on its brief journey to the sea in Loch Eriboll. North End is not as productive as the South End, but still produces excellent numbers of sea-trout most seasons. Ian McDonald is the keeper and boats, with outboard engines, are available on a daily or weekly basis at a very reasonable cost.

On North End, the wooded west shoreline is a good place to begin, drifting south to the cairn and stream mouth near Arnaboll Cottage. On the east bank, arrange a drift in the vicinity of where the Allt a'Mhuilinn enters the loch and south again into the next bay, down to the mouth of the Allt Braesgill burn. Keep the boat near the shore, approximately 10m out, and, again, it is best to have a third person constantly on the oars in order to do so. North End also retains the right to fish one boat each day on Middle Bay, although it is a long haul up the loch to reach it. Make sure that you have spare fuel for the outboard.

As for the flies to use, I tend to stick to the same patterns, year after year, for both brown trout and sea-trout, and for salmon: Ke-He, Soldier Palmer, Black Pennel, Grouse & Claret, Greenwell's Glory, March Brown, Dunkeld, Silver Invicta, Silver Butcher. However, dapping is perhaps the most popular fishing method on Loch Hope and, I am told, most fish are taken "on the dap", almost always using a Daddy Long Legs.

Bookings: South End: Altnaharra Hotel, Altnaharra, tel: 01549 411222; Ben Loyal Hotel, Tongue, by Lairg, Sutherland, tel: 01847 611216, website: www.benloyal.co.uk; Mrs Heather Gow, Pitscandy, Forfar, Angus, tel: 01307 462437, website: www.gowsport.co.uk. North End: Ian McDonald, the Old Keeper's cottage, Hope, by Lairg, Sutherland 1V27 4UJ, tel: 01847 601272.

28.
Bee Prepared

One of the largest trout I never caught came when I was standing on the bank of a loch untangling the top dropper and middle fly of my cast from the folds of my entirely useless landing net. Whilst doing so, my tail fly was dangling an inch above the water. A trout, which I estimate to have been at least 5lb in weight, took the fly and set off like a steam train for the middle of the loch breaking my cast and my heart in the process.

Most trout lie in shallow water and wading only scares them out into the deep. I suppose that we all have to learn these things the hard way and there is no harder way of doing so than by losing a large wild brown trout. Never ignore the margins of the loch. This dictum of carefully fishing the shallows also applies when boat fishing. Don't end the drift prematurely, fish right into the shallow water.

East Loch Bee on South Uist perfectly illustrates this point. I have never caught a decent trout there but I know someone who has – my son, Blair, who was Secretary of the South Uist Angling Club for a number of years in the

1980s. He and his fishing partner, Dr Iain Jack, used to play a sort of East Bee roulette by seeing who would give up first whilst casting into a foot or so of water. They caught some marvellous trout whilst doing so.

East Bee is easily accessible and lies at the north end of the island adjacent to the A865 road. Use OS Map 22, Benbecula, Second Series, Scale 1:50,000 to find your way round. There is a parking place close to where the boats are moored at Gd ref 783433. This is a large, peat-stained, shallow loch, which is rarely more than six feet deep and it extends eastwards from the road for a distance of almost one mile.

It is also a very lovely loch and invariably graced by large flocks of mute swans. The southern horizon is lined with the South Uist mountains, Hecla, Ben Corrodale and Beinn Mhor and golden eagle, buzzard and hen harrier are frequent visitors. You often share your fishing with a curious otter. Wild flowers abound, particularly on the main island, which is the perfect place for lunch.

A narrow, weedy channel leads from the main body of water to reach a fifty-acre extension of East Bee, unnamed on the OS map but known locally as the Shell Loch (Gd ref: 806417). In low water conditions, it is sometimes necessary to haul the boat through parts of the narrows but it is worth the effort involved in doing so because the Shell Loch can offer exciting sport.

North from Shell Loch is little Loch na Lice Baine (Gd ref: 810423), whilst in the hills to the south, on the east shoulder of Rueval, there are three more excellent lochs, Loch Clach an Duilisg (Gd ref: 789395), Loch Rueval (Gd ref: 786399) and Loch an Uisge-ghil (Gd ref: 791401).

These lochs drain north into East Loch Bee through Bagh nam Fiadh (Gd ref: 789414), a southern "leg" of the main loch. To the east of Bagh nam Fiadh is Loch nan Sgeireag (22/800407), which is also worth a visit.

Another channel at the south-east end of Bee takes you to a one-mile-long extension centred on Gd ref 805413, whilst further sport may be had in the small lochs to the north of East Loch Bee, Loch Dubh an Ionaire (Gd ref: 790438) and Loch Druim an Iasgair (Gd ref: 803434).

East Bee is best fished from the boat and the most productive drift is probably from the main island in a direct line to the south shore. On the west shore, by the causeway, a deep channel connects East Bee to West Bee. This can be a highly productive fishing area although you could, unless you are careful, hook more passing cars on the causeway than trout. East Bee brown trout are of outstanding quality and their average weight is in the order of 10oz, but fish of up to and over 4lb are by no means uncommon.

When high winds make it impossible to launch the boat on East Bee, head for the hills to explore the surrounding waters. However, the narrow, weed-fringed channel to Shell Loch offers good bank fishing whilst the south-east arm, towards the Flood Gate, holds some really serious trout, although few anglers make the effort to tramp out there.

West Loch Bee covers an area approximately two square miles and is linked to the sea at Clachan (22/769465) at the north. Indeed, only the Flood Gate at the south-east end of East Loch Bee stops the whole system from being a separate island in its own right. The loch is very shallow and fishing, from the bank, is restricted primarily to the north-west in the vicinity of the small islands and in the narrows at Gd ref: 764456. The principal pool lies between the shore and the largest of these islands.

Favourite flies include: Black Pennell, Ke-He, Soldier Palmer, March Brown, Greenwell's Glory, Grouse & Claret, Silver Butcher, Kingfisher Butcher and Teal, Blue & Silver. There is a lifetime's fishing here, amidst some of the most dramatic scenery in Scotland. For excellent accommodation and advice, contact Billy Felton at the Angler's Retreat (tel: 01870 610325).

29.
Beavering About

Black, grizzly or otherwise, bears scare the hell out of me. I am reliably informed that the key point to remember, should you ever be confronted by a bear whilst fishing, is not to run. Apparently this only encourages the beast to chase after you and that inevitably leads to a catastrophic rearrangement of irreplaceable body parts.

Two American friends of mine panicked and ran when they came face to face with a bear when salmon fishing in Alaska. The bear, true to form, set off after them in hot anticipatory pursuit. After a few hundred breathless yards, one of the intrepid duo stopped to retie a shoelace that had come undone.

His companion screamed at him in terror: "Good God Jim! What do you think you are doing? Never mind your shoelace – run faster!"

His friend smiled and replied, "No hurry, Hank. I don't have to run faster than the bear. All I have to do is run faster than you – and I have been able to do that for years."

This story may be apocryphal but it always springs to my mind when talk turns to reintroducing species that have become extinct in Scotland, particularly large, predatory carnivores such as bears and wolves. I agree in principle that they could, and probably should, be reintroduced, but I question the practicability of doing so.

It certainly would be one way of reducing Scotland's massive red deer population. A couple of hundred ravenous wolves and bears roaming our hills would sharply rearrange their numbers. The problems would begin when this readily available supply of venison dried up, or, to be more accurate, was eaten up.

Bears and wolves, no doubt by then thriving mightily, would turn to other available sources of food like sheep, cows, hens and anything else that happened along – including, and no one can deny the possibility, the odd, unsuspecting angler.

But the presence of these animals would greatly add to the excitement of a day out in the hills and records from countries where these beasts live naturally suggest that they pose minimal risk to human life or to farm stock. In any case, landowners would quickly persuade their friends in government to pay compensation and grants to reimburse them for any alleged loss. Your average Highland laird can spot a grant-aid opportunity quicker than a golden eagle spots a wounded hare in the heather.

There is, however, one animal, the European beaver, that was once native to Scotland, which could be reintroduced without cause for alarm and, personally, I support Scottish Natural Heritage's (SNH) desire to do so. Beavers would enhance our freshwater habitats. The dams they build store organic matter and this is recycled in rivers, bestowing benefits upon all creatures that depend upon that habitat for survival, including trout and salmon.

However, according to SNH statistics, more than 80% of Scottish anglers are opposed to the reintroduction. But be they ever so cuddly – beavers that is, not Scottish anglers – fishermen seem to think that beavers might threaten the survival of wild salmon, sea-trout and brown trout. If that is indeed the case, then beavers don't stand a chance. Anglers will be the people most likely to come into contact with beavers and if they think that beavers are a danger to wild fish, then beavers will suffer.

Anglers might also reasonably ask why SNH has spent upwards of a million pounds of public money researching the implications of reintroducing a species that became extinct in Scotland 400 years ago, and yet has done precious little to protect and preserve species that are currently in danger of becoming extinct: West Highlands and Islands wild sea-trout and salmon, whose numbers are diminishing because of the impact of disease and pollution from fish farms.

Factory fish-farming in coastal waters and freshwater lochs has decimated wild stocks that have survived in Scotland virtually genetically intact since the end of the last Ice Age 8,000 years ago. Sea lice from fish farms kill migrating smolts; millions of farm fish escape from their cages and compete with wild fish for a finite source of food; farm fish interbreed with wild fish and degrade their genetic integrity; fish farms are food-magnets not only for sea lice, but also for seals, which prey upon both wild and farmed salmon alike.

It is more than a decade now since SNH brought forward their beaver proposals, introduced at a press conference held on 19 March 1998 at Battleby near Perth. Since then, even more money has been spent upon determining where the first reintroduction should take place (Argyllshire) and in preparing public opinion for the event. But in spite of SNH's best efforts, successive Scottish ministers have delayed giving the go-ahead, and it is increasingly uncertain whether they ever will.

However, nature, as always, seems to have taken a hand. Recent reports from Perthshire confirm that up to half a dozen European beavers have escaped from captivity and are now busily engaged in doing what beavers do best: cutting down trees and building dams. Good luck to them and I hope that they survive and prosper. Perhaps SNH could now concentrate their efforts on saving our wild salmonids?

30.
Canon William Greenwell

One of the most famous canons in history is neither weapon, music nor verse; it is human, Canon William Greenwell of Durham. More than 150 years ago, the reverend gentleman devised a pattern of artificial fly that is still a primary weapon in the trout angler's armoury today.

Canon Greenwell asked James Wright of Sprouston, near Kelso, to dress the pattern in 1856. He intended it to imitate Tweed's natural olives. Since then, the fame of the Greenwell's Glory has encompassed the angling world. The Canon fished the fly for the remainder of his life and was still taking trout with it shortly before he died at the age of ninety-seven in 1918.

Others have notched up a place in angling history by giving names to outstanding flies. One of the best known is the Soldier Palmer, allegedly designed to represent a small insect brought back to this country on palm leaves carried by knights returning from the Holy Land Crusades. The knights were known as "palmers".

The Silver Butcher is another standard pattern, designed by G. S. Dewhurst of Tunbridge. Dewhurst was also responsible for a salmon fly called the Baker, although there is no record of him ever having produced a Candlestick-maker. That honour fell to a Mr Holbrow.

Another butcher, Peter Ross of Killin, Perthshire, gave his name to a successful brown trout and sea-trout pattern. Ross was not an angler, he simply enjoyed tying flies.

Then there is the March Brown, without which any early-season trout angler must be presumed naked, first mentioned in angling literature by Charles Cotton and James Chetham in the late seventeenth century.

This tradition of fly-tying is alive and well today. Each season a flood of new patterns arrives on the market. Luminaries such as Oliver Edwards, Malcolm Greenhalgh and Stan Headly work at the cutting edge of the art, constantly devising ever-more realistic patterns of artificial fly.

When I started trout fishing, the flies I used most often were H. Cholmondeley's Black Pennell, Canon William's Greenwell's Glory and Mr

Dewhurst's Silver Butcher. I have changed in recent years because of the kindness of fly-tying friends, notably the late Ian Christie of Portree, James Paterson from Kelso and Adrian Latimer in Paris.

Each has given me an unparalleled pattern and I rarely fish with any other flies. The first is Ian Christie's amazingly versatile Charlie Maclean, named in honour of a wonderful South Uist gillie who died a few years ago. The second is the Willie Ross. Willie worked as a gillie at Altnaharra by Loch Naver and I discovered his fly when I met his widow. James Paterson tied it up for me.

The last fly, devised by Adrian Latimer, has a special place in my angling "id". Whether or not it will rise in fame to match the giddy heights reached by the Greenwell's Glory remains to be seen. But if doesn't, then it won't be through any lack of effort on my part. Adrian named it "The Bruce" – a clarion call to piscatorial action if ever I needed one.

31.
Go Fly a Kite

Chile is considered to be one of the world's most exotic and exclusive trout-fishing locations; a country where outstanding sport is assured; a land where your wildest angling dreams can come true; a place where catching a double-figure fish is almost a certainty. Well, I have to tell you that it ain't necessarily so. Like those of other nations, Chilean trout have their off days and it is just your bad luck if you happen to arrive when the fish have decided to be uncooperative.

I speak from personal experience, having spent nearly a year of my life fishing in Chilean Patagonia, through two consecutive seasons, October until March, exploring the X Region which is relatively unknown to the general angling public. This region boasts ice-blue rivers, lakes and small lagoons, which are home to North American rainbow trout, brown trout of Scottish and German ancestry and Canadian brook trout, all of which were introduced in the later years of the nineteenth century.

There were wonderful days when trout rose constantly to surface insects, fish that averaged 3lb in weight with some of up to and over 10lb. But there were times when, in spite of every effort, not a dimple disturbed the surface and you would swear that the place was fishless. I remember one such day, fishing with an American friend, Jimmy Molchun, on a small lagoon, which I knew was packed with fish that invariably rose to even a less than expertly cast fly. After a couple of hours, when I was beginning to despair, Jimmy turned to me and said with a wry smile, "Hey, Bruce, are you the guy who called the witch doctor a son of a bitch?"

But no matter where you fish – be it in Chile, Alaska, Russia, New Zealand or your local water, wherever – the gods of angling hover constantly, dishing out a fish or two to him, nothing to another, perhaps a couple of heart-stopping rises to someone else and, on special occasions, when you have been very, very good, a basketful. I remember once spending a day on Loch Watten in Caithness with David Street, author of that marvellous book, *Fishing in Wild Places*. Neither of us touched a trout, although I had fished the loch for twenty years and David was certainly no slouch when it came to the removal of trout from their natural habitat.

Two of our companions, new to the loch, fished Watten the following day, covering exactly the same drifts that David and I had so fruitlessly lashed and using the same patterns of artificial flies that we had used. They came home with a basket of ten trout weighing 18lb. I wish that I could pretend that fishing conditions were better when they launched their assault than when we launched ours, but that would be less than the truth and it is a well-known and established fact that we anglers never tell a lie – well, not often.

If anyone can explain this phenomenon to me, then I would be delighted to listen, but I honestly believe that fishing has more to do with "unseen forces" than it has to do with skill, knowledge or experience. Being in the right place at the right time, it seems to me, is the only, all-important rule for angling success. If your name comes up, then you will catch fish regardless of what you chuck at them. If not, then you might just as well go fly a kite for all the fish you will catch.

Which I have, in fact, done once – fly a kite that is – when lack of trout drove me to agree to extreme measures. The name of the pilot of the kite will remain secret as will the name of the loch where we used it. Yes, it was his idea, but I concurred and even laid out the line and managed the machine prior to take-off. We had attached a length of nylon to the tail, at the end of which was a particularly large and inviting Loch Ordie. The rest, as they say, is history: a trout of 1lb 3oz unceremoniously hoisted aloft after dapping the fly across the surface for barely five minutes.

I honestly confess that we were more surprised than the unsuspecting fish and, shamefacedly, returned it to the loch to fight another day whilst hurriedly dismantling our devilish contraption before someone caught us in the act.

I am older now and, hopefully, wiser but when first infected with the fever of angling I admit to at times resorting to less than normal tactics in the pursuit of trout, as when, many years ago, my wife, Ann, and I were fishing a hill loch in North Sutherland. Most of the waters we fished held excellent stocks of modestly-sized trout. However, a few contained specimen fish of prodigious size.

One morning, we arrived at a lochan that was said to hold the largest trout in the area. He was infrequently seen, rarely hooked and allegedly lived below the branches of a ragged rowan that overhung the water, making it virtually impossible to get a fly to his lair.

To my everlasting regret, I resorted to devious means in order to have a chance at the fish. Whilst standing at the west end of the loch, I persuaded Ann, against her better judgement, to take the cast and, as I paid out line for my reel, walk round the loch with it to the east end. Once she was in position, I called out, "Let go!" and she dropped the cast into the loch. Slowly, I wound the flies in, past the rowan where the trout lay. I was utterly convinced that the fish would take my fly, and utterly dejected when it did not.

Today, I am far more sanguine about our gentle art. If I manage to catch a brace, that's fine, if not, then there is always tomorrow. Just being there is sufficient unto itself and more than enough for me.

32.
Pushing the Boat Out

Pushing the boat out on well-managed southern fisheries is rarely a problem. However, up here in the far north of Scotland, it is often a case of first finding the boat before you can even begin to think about giving it a shove. I speak from fifty years' experience in these matters.

One of the most memorable occasions involved a death-trap punt on Loch Garbh in Caithness. Reaching the loch involved a bumpy thirteen-mile ride over a deeply rutted track, then a fifteen-minute hike across the heather. The Manager and I examined the craft carefully before lugging it to the water. Everything seemed satisfactory.

The fish were rising, so we loaded up and pushed off. It had a shallow draft and was easy to get afloat, but rowing the beast was a nightmare, not much helped by the fact that the oars were of different lengths and almost impossible to keep in the rowlocks. We zig-zagged out to the middle where most of the action seemed to be.

Casting required co-ordination and caution. If we both cast at the same time, the vessel tipped violently. So we alternated effort. Moving, even an inch, caused further stability problems and it was during one of these episodes that I noticed that we were also sinking. I pointed this out to my better half and suggested we row for the shore, pretty damn quick.

We made it, just in time, and arrived on terra firma soaked to the waist with as much water in the punt as there was outside of it. I am happy to say that, shortly thereafter, a great storm came and blew the punt to smithereens.

Just across the hill from Garbh lay Loch Caol, another of our favourite waters, which also had a boat. But not in the water. It was lying upside down about 100 yards from the edge. It took us an hour to manhandle the hulk to the loch, by which time our tempers and muscles were distinctly frayed.

Once we had the boat in the loch, we collapsed in a heap over coffee and sandwiches. Thus refreshed, I wandered over to the boat. It was half full of water. I bailed it out and tried to find the problem. There was a hole at the bottom of the transom. I searched for something to plug the hole. Eventually, in desperation, I used my underpants. To no avail. I tried my vest, then my shirt. It had started to rain. Ann, sheltering in the boathouse, watched my antics with growing alarm. "Bruce," she called, "why don't we just bank fish?"

However, one of the most dreadful boats I have ever suffered in was a model called the Green Highlander, designed, I am certain, by an engineer having a bad hair day at the office. This entirely useless lump of misbegotten plastic used to lurk on the shore of the Plantation Loch, near Altnaharra in Sutherland. It was narrow, pointed at both ends, about twelve feet in length, and had a cleverly designed box running from stem to stem for stowing the oars.

I fished from it once, with my friend, the late David Aird. It was so heavy and deep-keeled that David had to walk several hundred yards before it floated, encouraged by myself from the middle of the boat. As he tried to leap in, the boat almost capsized and I found myself sitting in the loch up to my neck in freezing water.

The only way in was over the pointed end, one at a time, which we finally managed to achieve. And the only way to fish was by sitting astride the oar box, knees pressed tightly against our chins, casting alternately. I don't know what happened to the boat. Thankfully, it wasn't there on our next visit. I expect some crazed angler took an axe to the thing. Well, I hope so.

In fairness to those who provide boats in the Highlands, it is true to say that they come in for a lot of hammering – the boats that is, not the providers. Many anglers simply don't know how to handle boats and even those who purport to be experienced sailors can come to grief, as I know all too well to my cost, in this case to the extent of £250.

I bought a boat for Loch Toftingall in Caithness and lived, barely, to regret it. It seemed a good buy at the time, clinker-built, Shetland-style, wide-beamed and pointed at both ends. It looked lovely, but in fact it was a disaster. The keel was so deep that the mooring bay had to be excavated before it would float. It also wobbled and couped furiously if you moved a finger.

The end came when I had a woman out with me who had never fished before and, after that experience, probably never will again. We were hit by a sudden gale and I decided to get off the loch as quickly as possible. White waves, as white as my fishing partner's face, were sloshing onboard and she was but a moment from blind panic. Me too. As we hurtled down the loch I knew that I would never be able to row the hulk over the sand bar and into the safety of the mooring bay.

There was only one thing for it. I would have to leap out and haul the boat and my passenger to safety. Luckily, I knew the loch intimately, having waded every corner, but my companion was unaware of this and was convinced that I was going to my doom. At the crucial moment, I threw myself overboard and manfully heaved the boat ashore. I then stepped into the mooring bay and immediately found myself in six feet of water, having forgotten that the bay had been deepened.

I helped the woman onto the landing stage. "Well," she said, "that was interesting. Is it always like this when you go fishing, Bruce?" I proffered my hip flask, which she grabbed and emptied in one swallow. She then announced, "And now I think that I would like a cigarette."

"I thought you had quit smoking?"

She looked at me for a moment. "Bruce," she said, "just shut up and hand one over."

33.
When All Else Fails

When all else fails, give them the "turning flee". This technique is best practised whilst seated comfortably in the stern of a loch boat – the blunt end to those of you not accustomed to the nuances of nautical phraseology. Whilst the boat is rowed forward at normal pace, the angler casts at right angles to the moving vessel.

Cast as long a line as you can comfortably manage. When the flies land on the water, feather-light, of course, bring the tip of your rod down until it is parallel to the surface, about two feet above the waves. Keep the rod at right angles to the boat. Do not retrieve the flies. Let them be.

Fish will rise to the flies almost as soon as they touch the water or, and more often, at the precise moment when the flies begin to "turn" – compelled to do so by the forward motion of the boat. There is no need to strike. The fish hook themselves. Watch the flies constantly and be ready to take control the moment a trout grabs.

I was introduced to this technique many years ago by a wonderful Ayrshire gillie who also introduced me to a splendid variation of one of Scotland's most popular trout flies, the Black Pennell. His version was tied with a yellow tail, rather than with the traditional golden pheasant tippets and it has been a good friend to me ever since.

Less comfortable was the gillie's habit of setting the boat into a drift and then, a moment or two after my companion and I had started fishing, restarting the outboard motor. At least, that is what it sounded like to me and it took a few such experiences to get used to the fact that he was only having his early morning heavy-smoker's cough. But it sounded exactly like an old Seagull engine trying to splutter into life.

The turning flee technique works well in virtually all weather conditions, including that angler's curse, a dead-flat calm. I once had splendid sport on a hot summer day on Sweethope Lough near Otterburn in Northumberland, fishing the turning flee. This was in the days before it was developed into a commercial fishery. Within the space of an hour, I took half a dozen nice trout whilst most of the other boats returned "blank".

When Clan Sandison lived in Caithness, I often caught my first trout of the season whilst fishing the turning flee on Loch Watten, in early May, at about 7.30pm, as my son, Blair, rowed me past the broken fence post at the south-east end of Factor's Bay. Blair constantly reminds me about this, claiming that it was only his ability on the oars, rather than my casting skills, that brought about the desired result. The lies that some anglers tell.

But like everything else in our sport, nothing is certain. I remember fishing Loch Caladail, one of the famous limestone lochs near Durness in North West Sutherland, when, because my companion was not allowed to row due to doctor's orders and a congenitally "bad back", I was on the oars, all day. To take as much advantage as possible of the time I spent rowing back up the loch, into the wind, I tutored my friend in the art of fishing the turning flee.

Fishing conditions were difficult, with a near gale-force wind watered by frequent showers but by close of play my partner had caught four splendid trout, each weighing between 2lb and 2lb 8oz and all caught on the turning flee. As he hooked, played and landed fish after fish, I found it hard to keep a fixed grin of supportive pleasure in place.

Consequently, a few months later, when I had my annual outing with a young fishing friend from the village, a mere stripling of forty summers, I hobbled about a bit on the way down to the boat. "What's up, Bruce?" he inquired solicitously.

"Oh, nothing really, just a bad back this morning."

"No problem," he replied courteously, "I'll row." At last, I thought, I would be able to show off my turning flee prowess.

When the boat was drifting and we fished traditionally, casting in front of the boat, he rose and caught trout whilst I remained stubbornly fishless. When he rowed back up to the start of another drift, I lashed away at the turning flee, but to no avail. By the end of the day I had little need to invent a sore back. Mine was on fire, my neck was blazing, my bum was sore and my heart ached. If I had caught just two more trout I might have had a brace.

34.
Two Caithness Gems

Loch Toftingall lies a few miles south from the village of Watten in Caithness. It was one of the first Caithness lochs that Ann and I fished when we arrived in the county. It covers an area of some 150 acres and is shallow. Indeed, it is possible to wade from one side to the other without danger. The landscape has changed radically over the years due to conifer planting and the loch is now surrounded by commercial conifers.

But Toftingall rests on a gravel base and has a pH of approximately 7.5 so it hosts an excellent wild brown trout population of pink-fleshed, hard fighting fish that average 10oz in weight. On our first visit we tramped round the shore to the south end to gain shelter from the strong wind – wind is not an infrequent occurrence in these airts – and were rewarded with two splendid trout, each weighing over 2lb.

We used to visit Toftingall frequently, not only to fish, but to delight in the wide variety of bird life that called the loch home. During winter months, hundreds of greylag geese might roost on Toftingall. They come from the Arctic to winter in Caithness, as do flights of whooper swans from Iceland. One year, in June, we found a pair of swans still at Toftingall. They should have flown north in March and the graceful pair brightened many a summer evening.

The moorlands also used to be a larder for great raptors: hen harrier and short-eared owl, quartering the heather in endless search of prey. I once watched an osprey fishing the loch. I had spent four hours catching nothing and he simply swooped down and lifted a trout of at least 2lb from under my nose. My only consolation was that, much to my astonishment, the bird dropped the fish. So I wasn't the only duffer around after all.

Another frequent visitor was a black-throated diver. Unlike their more common cousins, the red-throated diver, these birds require larger expanses of water upon which to take off and land, a clear flight path, but they are invariably curious and often drift close to the boat.

In windy conditions, Toftingall becomes impossible to fish because the bottom is churned up, clouding the water. A few days later, when things settle back to normal, sport is generally excellent. An average day sent us safely home with half a dozen good, modest-sized trout, with the occasional larger fish of up to 3lb.

On a hot summer day, Toftingall is a super place for a splash and my golden retriever, Breac, the Gaelic name for trout, used to spend hours in the loch, unlike Ann's Yorkshire terrier, who hated water. Sometimes, when the little dog had been sitting near the side of the boat, an ill-considered back cast could send him flying into the water and it was often a close-run thing before I could get the landing net under his sodden frame. The last time, I just managed to catch a glimpse of his black eyes, going down for the third time, before I netted him.

The principal Caithness lochs have not been affected by forestry and visiting anglers will find splendid sport on outstanding waters such as Watten, St John's and Heilen, all readily available at modest cost. The pH of these excellent lochs is in the order of 8+ and trout are of exceptional quality.

My favourite is Heilen, near Castletown, an expert's loch if ever there was one. I can count the number of trout that I have taken from this lovely loch on the fingers of one hand and blank days are the rule, but I keep going back for more. Heilen is very shallow and weedy. Indeed, after July there are few weed-free areas and a good knowledge of the loch is required to find suitable areas to fish.

The average weight of Heilen trout is 2lb 8oz and to take fish of lesser weight is a crime. Specimen trout of up to and over 10lb have been caught in recent years and my best fish weighed 4lb 8oz. Heilen trout are, in my opinion, some of the most beautiful wild brown trout in Scotland and they fight more furiously than you can ever imagine. I preferred launching my attack from the bank, rather than from the boat, and even in high winds, when most of the loch is churned up, clear patches of water may be found along the lee shore.

When angler friends visit, I always try to persuade them to fish Heilen and, invariably, suffer in consequence: "Bruce, you are quite mad. There isn't a single trout in that loch. I swear it. We fished all day without seeing the smallest ripple, fin or splash." My credibility plummets. One wild evening, however, when the wind was howling and rain lashing, I persuaded a friend to join me on Loch Heilen. "Look at the weather," he complained. "Couldn't we just go along to the pub and have a drink and talk about fishing?" he pleaded.

We assembled our rods in the shelter of the old boathouse and I strode purposefully to the loch, almost as a matter of principle I estimated that perhaps fifteen minutes' fishing would salve my honour and, not expecting to catch anything, I let the wind flag my flies out over the surface.

The tail fly, a size 14 Silver Butcher, grazed the surface and immediately the water erupted. A superb trout hooked itself and, during a breathtaking few minutes, gave a spectacular display and a wonderful fight. I landed the fish, which weighed 3lb, and turned to show it to my companion.

His place by the boathouse was empty. Twenty yards away, through the storm, I glimpsed his figure, furiously lashing away as though his last fishing moment had come. I wandered down. "I think that you are right, Peter, this is madness. Shall we head for the pub?" But of answer came there none.

35.
UK's Fastest Flowing River

My first glimpse of the River Spey was from the back of a furniture removal van in . . . well, not yesterday. Thirty boys were crowded aboard, Scouts, en route from the railway station at Newtonmore to camp by the banks of the stream near Creagdhubh Lodge. I remember it rained a lot, but boys are designed not to mind such minor inconveniences.

We spent two glorious weeks, mostly damp, exploring the countryside, swimming in peat-stained lochs, building bridges and generally creating semi-organised havoc. Since these days I have returned often to the Spey, to walk amidst the old Scots Pines which people the banks of the river and to fish in its cold, clear waters for salmon, sea-trout and trout.

Few Scottish rivers have a more dramatic beginning. The Spey rises from the heart of a magnificent wilderness, gathering together waters from 1,150 square miles of mountains and moorlands, guarded over by the peaks of Corrieyairack, Glenshirra, Aberarder and Braeroy. Tiny feeder streams tumble down from Creag a'Chail and Creag a'Bhanain to join Loch Spey. A further fan of burns bustles in from Cam Leac as the river hurries eastwards past Sherramore to Spey Dam near the famous Pictish hillfort in the Black Wood of Craig.

This is the land of Clan Macphearson and when we camped there, we climbed Creag Dubh, "the black hill", to search for "Cluny's Cave". In 1746, after the rout of Bonnie Prince Charlie's army at Culloden, Ewen Macphearson, the clan chief, hid in the cave from official wrath for the part he played in the rebellion. With a price of £1,000 on his head, he remained there for eight years.

It was common knowledge amongst local people that he was there but they never gave him up. Eventually, Cluny escaped to France where he died at Dunkirk in 1756. Whilst in exile, the rents due to him were assiduously paid by his tenants and dispatched to him. The location of Cluny's Cave evaded us as successfully as it had evaded detection by his hunters so many years before.

As the Spey settles into Badenoch by Kingussie, it enters a fine, fertile strath bordered by good agricultural land, kept well-watered by the river. The Spey is notorious for flooding; indeed, Badenoch means "the drowned lands". This is good news for wildlife. The Insh Marshes, on the flood plain through which the river wends its way, are managed by the Royal Society for the Protection of Birds and are a nature reserve, loud with the cry of curlew, redshank, lapwing and the "drum" of snipe. The marshes also host an amazing array of wildflowers, including such gems as mountain pansy, melancholy thistle, greater bladderwort and marsh valerian.

The river now enters Loch Insh, which also plays host to a wide variety of human species: anglers, windsurfers, water-ski enthusiasts, dinghy sailors and canoeists. From time to time there are sharp conflicts of interests but, by and large, people have learned to respect the legitimate rights of their neighbours. Downstream from Loch Insh, between Speybank and the Moor of Feshie, is Lochan Geal, "the white loch".

For many years, people used to talk about the strange trout caught in the loch. Apparently, they were covered with hair. I have fished many of Scotland's "white lochs" but never, ever, have I seen or caught a hairy trout. It is alleged, though, that the trout had tiny hairs on their scales, which, "in certain conditions of light", made them appear hairy. Remember, you read it here first.

The Spey is the fastest flowing river in the UK and it is also one of the finest salmon streams in Europe. Much of the best angling is very expensive and, even then, finding a vacant rod is almost as hard as finding the money to pay for it. But there is excellent access to many parts of the river through local angling associations.

Begin your Spey adventure at Grant Mortimer's tackle shop in Grantown (tel: 01479 872684). Grant's knowledge of the river is second to none. Whether beginner or expert, you will be found fishing which suits both your ability and purse. Tackle hire is also available and, given advance notice, Grant will arrange an expert gillie to guide your efforts to the best advantage.

The season opens for salmon, grilse and sea-trout on 11 February and closes on 30 September. Brown trout fishing is from 15 March until the end of September. The Association has some forty miles of fishing, on the Spey and on its tributary, the River Dulnain. The Spey section has thirty-five named pools, the Dulnain, thirty.

This includes access to Upper Castle Grant Beat, which is strictly fly-only. This first-class beat extends for one-and-a-quarter miles below the New Road

Bridge at Grantown and includes a marvellous pool below the old bridge. My first night-time sea-trout fishing expedition was in Bridge Pool. My wife and I "researched" the location during the day and, as soon as the first bats flicked by, we were in position, cosseted from a cold wind by a hip-flask full of cherry brandy.

Apart from producing approximately 9,000–10,000 salmon and grilse each season, the River Spey is a stunning sea-trout fishery, particularly on the Association water. Up to and over 3,000 sea-trout can be taken during a season. June and July are the prime months for sport with sea-trout and the Spey is probably the most productive sea-trout fishery in Europe.

Numbers alone, however, are only part of the story. The sheer beauty of the river is an almost physical presence. The banks are blessed with splendid woodlands containing magnificent Scots pines, some of which are several hundred years old. Spring is enlivened by clumps of huge, bright yellow daffodils and there are myriad hatches of march browns. Dipper, grey and pied wagtail watch as you cast. The Cairngorm mountains crowd the horizon. Don't waste a moment, go there now.

36.
Loch St Johns

We drifted silently across Loch St John's in a gentle breeze. A great skua winged by, pirating the shores in search of prey. Curlew called hauntingly. A golden finger of sunlight suddenly sparkled through the clouds sending myriad colours, reds and blues, shimmering over the smooth waters. I looked at my watch. Nearly midnight, but still time for a few more casts. Midsummer in Caithness is like that. Always time for a few more casts.

It may be a long way north to the land of John O' Groats but every mile is a mile nearer to some of the finest game fishing in Scotland. Sea-liced salmon, fresh from their ice-cold Greenland feeding grounds, in Thurso, Forss and Wick rivers. Sparkling, acrobatic sea-trout and a vast abundance of wonderful, pink-fleshed, hard-fighting wild brown trout from such famous lochs as Watten,

Heilen, St John's and Clader, all waiting for your well-presented fly.

Loch St John's is a very special place, not only for anglers but also for those who appreciate its remarkable variety of wildlife: roe deer, fox and otter and a wide range of birds, including curlew, oystercatcher, snipe and occasional visits from one of nature's most successful anglers, the graceful osprey. The surrounding moors and fields are rich in wildflowers, including, on the cliff tops, bright blue spring squill, sea pink and wild thyme, and that most iconic of all Caithness flowers, *primula scotica*, the unique, deep blue, Scottish primrose.

It is also the most northerly trout loch on mainland Britain and for hundreds of years its waters have been known to have curative powers. In days gone by, invalids were carried to the loch to drink the water. St John's is also supposed to be able to cure anyone who is feeling depressed or sad in spirit: walk once round the loch and then leave, without looking back, and all cares instantly vanish.

But above all, the loch is one of Scotland's most exciting and best managed trout fisheries. It is in the care of the Loch St John's Improvement Association, founded in the 1960s and as vibrant today as when it was first formed. The association stocks the loch with native fish reared in its own hatchery. These are introduced when they reach a few ounces in weight, however, because of the quality of feeding in the loch, by the following year these little fish have grown to 12oz.

More years ago than I care to admit, when we lived in Caithness, your correspondent was a committee member of the association and as I enjoyed a cup of coffee with Neil Macdonald, the current association Secretary, we talked, as anglers do, about the ones that got away and the few that didn't, about favourite flies, memorable days in the hills and about absent friends now fishing that great trout loch in the sky.

St John's covers an area of approximately 175 acres and has an average depth of six feet. Consequently, trout may be caught from the margins to the middle. They are of exceptional quality and average 1lb in weight with fish of up to and over 3lb taken most seasons. The water is crystal clear and best results come from boat fishing, although bank fishing can be just as productive. Apart from a small area at the north-east corner of the loch, the rest of the shoreline is open to anglers. So, when the wind blows hard, don't hesitate to bank fish.

Loch St John's also has the UK's most northerly mayfly hatch, which peaks in June. This is when specimen trout can be taken, although the loch fishes equally well from opening day on 1 April right through to the end of the season in September. Find the loch on OS Map 12, Thurso, Wick and the surrounding area, Scale 1:50,000 at Gd ref: 225725. The boat-mooring bay is at Gd ref: 222718, to the north of the village Dunnet. Visitors are most welcome and the association has excellent lochside facilities. A road has been built down to the mooring bay, with plenty of space for parking cars. The harbour is first class and it is possible to step almost straight from the car and into your boat. Even better, and most unusual for a Highland loch, it is possible to get afloat without bursting a blood vessel in heaving the boat over rocky shallows.

As always, the choice of flies is very much a matter of personal preference. Most anglers fish a team of three wet flies in the traditional fashion, in front of the drifting boat, short line and quick recovery. However, and particularly during the mayfly hatch and on calm evenings, dry fly patterns can be very effective and, when the wind blows hard, dapping will also produce the desired results. My choice of wet fly patterns would include the following old friends: Ke-He, Soldier Palmer, Black Pennell, March Brown, Greenwell's Glory, Grouse & Claret, Silver Butcher, Dunkeld and Silver Invicta.

Further information about the loch can be had from Neil MacDonald (tel: 01847 896956). Neil is also an expert fly-tyer, so do ask about his favourite patterns for the loch. Visitor permits can be obtained at Dunnett Bay Caravan Site (tel: 01847 821319), just outside the village of Dunnett on the main road to Thurso. If you intend to fish the mayfly hatch in June, early booking is advised.

37.
Bringing Up Anglers

Having children seriously damaged my fishing health. Not that I had them, physically, of course – my wife, Ann, bore that burden – but the patter of tiny feet certainly altered our angling attitudes. Dashing river-wards at the drop of a Greenwell's Glory or the first whisper of a soft south-west breeze was not as simple as it was in childless days of yore.

So we taught them fly-fishing. It seemed to be the obvious thing to do. Our brood, four in number, grew up brainwashed into the belief that angling was an integral part of existence, as natural an aspect of living as breathing, walking, talking, squabbling and nicking father's fishing gear.

Unfortunately, however, everything had to be multiplied by six, rather than by two: rods, reels, lines, flies, waders, fishing bags and landing nets. A single-bedroom, inexpensive holiday cottage for two became a small mansion – they invariably "needed" to take a friend – and the Clan Sandison bank balance suffered dreadfully in consequence.

Whilst Ann spent her time feeding the horde, glued to sink and cooker rather than to a fishing rod, I became a mechanical cast-tying machine and galley slave: referee, instructor, retriever of lost oars, abandoned boats and "Dad I left my camera at the mooring bay and will you get it for me because I don't know the way". It was good training. As a result I can still tie a full blood-knot, blindfolded, behind my back, in half a minute.

In spite of what I may pretend, however, I wouldn't change it, not for all the trout and salmon in the world, regardless of size. These times were precious, unforgettable, irreplaceable moments of supreme joy. I remember the ones that got away and the few that didn't. I remember tears and laughter. I remember them catching their first fish. Happy memories in the dream bank of the mind.

Many families must face similar problems today, not only of funding a family fishing expedition, but also of finding a suitable location where good sport may be had without breaking the bank balance in the process. Providing something for every member of your party, beginner and expert alike, requires careful planning if the holiday is not to end in disaster.

Hotels control a deal of Scottish fishing but not everyone can afford present-day hotel prices, least of all when it might require a minibus to transport your tribe to the scene of action. Equally, the regimen imposed by some angling hotels is not conducive to the exuberance of burgeoning youth or, indeed, to the sanity of other guests.

Therefore, self-catering is often the best option. Come and go as you please, eat, sleep, fish, fight and play to suit yourself in the privacy of your own abode. Given some persuasion and organisation, cooking and interior economy tasks can be fairly apportioned to ensure leisure and pleasure for all – the best of both worlds, with plenty of time to fish.

Finding such a location is not as difficult as you might imagine, least of all in the north of Scotland. The far north is one of the most welcoming and exciting angling locations on planet Earth. Fly-fishers will find outstanding sport with wonderful wild brown trout and the chance of an occasional salmon or sea-trout. Nor will you need a second mortgage to pay for it. Value-for-money angling abounds.

Caithness comes high on my list of venues, particularly with regard to loch fishing for brown trout. Sport with sea-trout is available on Loch of Wester, excellent in September and October, as well as good salmon fishing in the Wick River, given decent water levels. During a week's holiday, concentrate your efforts on Loch Watten, St John's Loch, Loch Heilen and Loch Calder. For a day out in the hills, try Loch Ruard, a forty-minute walk west from Achavanich on the A9 Latheron/Thurso road.

Apart from Loch Calder, most Caithness lochs are shallow. Watten has an average depth of eight feet, Heilen four feet. These waters are lime rich and contain magnificent brown trout. St John's, approximately 170 acres in extent, is perhaps the busiest, particularly in June when there is a mayfly hatch. Watten, which is more than three miles long, has plenty of room for all.

Because these lochs are shallow, fish with confidence, from the margins to the middle. Although everyone has their favourite drift, the truth is that trout rise and may be taken everywhere. My personal pleasure on Loch Watten is to fish out of Factor's Bay, off the fence that runs down to the shore here on the north bank, then in the vicinity of the small island. But the largest trout I ever landed was caught near Oldhall, at the north end, a couple of yards out from the shore – when I was looking the other way.

Loch Calder, the Caithness water supply, is over 100 feet deep at the north end. Trout here are "traditional" Highland fish, generally small, averaging perhaps 8oz in weight, and there are Arctic charr as well. Calder can be seriously wild. You must use an outboard when boat fishing. The bank shelves quickly into deeper water in many places, so be careful when landing. With the bow on the shore, I once stepped out of the stern into six feet of water. Beware when bank fishing. Fluctuating water levels have created soft margins.

However, I am pretty sure that Calder contains some huge fish, including that aquatic "wolf" from the Ice Age, ferox trout. Ferox feed primarily on Arctic charr and can grow to more than 20lb in weight in the space of a few years. If you are looking for that elusive "one for the glass case", you could find it in Loch Calder. To do so, use the old Scottish fishing method of trolling a lure or bait behind a slowly moving boat. Fish it deep, down to thirty feet. Crossing the fingers will probably help as well.

To help you find your dream cottage and the fishing of your dreams, contact Hugo Ross, "Mr Caithness Angling" (tel: 01955 604200). There are few finer places to introduce little ones to fly-fishing than Caithness and I speak from extensive personal experience, times four.

38.
Finding Salmon Fishing

Salmon fishing success has more to do with luck than with skill. Some may disagree, but when it comes to the removal of salmon from their natural habitat, I believe that the all-important factor is simply being in the right place at the right time: when water level, air temperature and weather conditions and whatever other gods that rule the salmon angler's fate encourage the fickle beasts to grab an artificial fly.

Regardless of how much money you pay for your fishing, if conditions are not right then you might just as well go fly a kite for all the good you are likely to do. I have seen salmon anglers on some of the finest beats in Scotland, beats which cost up to and over £300 a day to fish, flog fruitlessly for a whole week without getting an offer. On other occasions, when the water level is right and salmon are moving, even the most incompetent novice will catch fish.

Therefore, if you are to have the best opportunity of sport, it is often advisable to wait until the river is in condition before making a booking. Given that most salmon fishing is reserved well in advance, this might seem foolhardy advice, but there are a number of locations in Scotland where an instant booking is possible, particularly in the north where the price of a day's fishing will not cost you an arm and a leg or engender serious disagreement with your bank manager.

The Town Water of the River Ness at Inverness is readily available to visiting anglers on a day-ticket basis and the beat can produce upwards of 400 salmon each season. Salmon average 10lb in weight but fish of over 20lb are not entirely uncommon. More than 300 sea-trout are also taken, in the river and in the Moray Firth at Clachnaharry and at North Kessock. Contact: Grahams, 37/39 Castle Street, Inverness, tel: 01463 233178 for details.

Loch Ness itself can also offer great sport with salmon, although most fish are taken by trolling rather than by fly-fishing. Approximately 300–400 salmon can be taken each season and the largest fish of recent years weighed 35lb and was caught in 1994 by David Livingston. Unless you know the loch, it is essential that you seek the services of a gillie, not only to guide you to where the fish lie, but also, and as important, to keep you safe; Loch Ness can often be as rough and wild as the sea. For bookings and information go to Grahams tackle shop in Castle Street (see above).

The rivers Nairn and Lossie can give great sport particularly after heavy rain. The Nairn has produced nearly 1,000 salmon in recent seasons. Contact: P. Fraser, 41 High Street, Nairn, Inverness-shire, tel: 01667 453038. Elgin & District Angling club has fishing on the River Lossie, where they take about 100 salmon a year and 400 sea-trout. Most sea-trout are caught in the tidal reaches. Contact: The Angling Centre, Moss Street, Elgin, Moray, tel: 01343 547615.

The River Beauly, to the north of Inverness, is rarely available to casual visitors and is very expensive, but the lower reaches of the river may be fished on a day-ticket basis. The beat extends from below Lovat Bridge on the A9 Inverness/Wick road downstream to Wester Lovat and has some good pools: Below the Bridge, Teawig Pool and Malloch Pool. Contact: Messrs Morison, Ironmongers, West End, Beauly, Inverness-shire, tel: 01463 782213. Fishing on Thursday and Saturday is reserved for Beauly Angling Club members.

In Sutherland, the Association Water of the Naver and the Helmsdale is available on a day-ticket basis. The Helmsdale can produce some 300 salmon, the Naver about the same. These Highland streams are amongst the most famous and exclusive salmon fisheries in the land and access to the main beats is rarely available; nevertheless, the Association Waters can often be every bit as good as the main beats, particularly in low water conditions. For the Naver, contact: The Store, Bettyhill, tel: 01641 521207. For the Helmsdale, contact: River Helmsdale Fishing Tackle, tel: 01431 821372.

Also in the far north, the River Wick in Caithness offers day-tickets to visitors. The river is very much a spate stream, but in good years it is capable of producing upwards of 800 salmon in a season. Late season sea-trout fishing is also available on Loch of Wester. For bookings and details, contact Hugo Ross, The Tackle Shop, 56 High Street, Wick, tel: 01955 604200.

But perhaps above all, the River Spey offers the most readily accessible salmon and sea-trout fishing for all comers. The place to begin your adventure is at Grant Mortimer's tackle shop at 3 High Street in Grantown-on-Spey, tel: 01479 872684. Apart from offering you the chance of a salmon, the Spey is Scotland's finest sea-trout fishery, more than 3,000 fish being taken most seasons. Wherever you decide to go, have a splendid time and best of luck in all your efforts. Cross your fingers and pray for rain!

39.
Making an Angling Dream Come True

Anglers dream of discovering a loch so beautiful that they will never want to leave. A loch full of wild brown trout that rise readily to the well-presented fly almost regardless of weather conditions. A loch where boat and bank fishing bring equally excellent results. A loch that is for their exclusive use and where the only companions will be red deer, golden eagle and otter. A loch guarded by majestic mountains amidst moorlands scattered with an astonishing array of wild flowers. A loch where they will find peace, solitude and splendid sport.

I have found such a loch and it more that adequately fulfills all of these angling dreams: Loch Haluim, on the south-west slopes of Ben Loyal (765m), the Queen of Scottish Mountains, in North Sutherland. The loch lies like a silver and blue butterfly on the moor and gathers in the flow from an area of more than two square miles. It is ninety-six acres in extent, three-quarters of a mile long and up to half a mile wide. The average depth is eight feet and the shoreline meanders in and out around a wonderful succession bays and points and fishy corners for a distance of nearly three miles.

Apart from Haluim, there are a further five, smaller, named lochs, centred on Creag nan Eulachon (244m), all of which also contain wild brown trout: Loch a'Mhadaidh-ruaidh, Loch an Aon-bhric, Loch nan Ealachan, An Caol-loch and Loch Sgeireach. These waters have their own satellites, unnamed lochans, eight in number, and there is more than enough fishing here to keep you busy and happy for a lifetime, let alone for a few days.

Do not expect to catch one-for-the-glass-case on Haluim. The trout average 8oz/10oz in weight and I have only once taken a trout of over 1lb. But these fish fight magnificently and you will think that you have hooked a trout of double the average size. However, there are seriously large fish in some of the surrounding waters, although they are a lot harder to tempt than the trout in Haluim. Apart from Haluim, all the other lochs and lochans are fished from the bank and they will test your skill and patience to the uttermost before giving up their treasures.

I first discovered Loch Haluim in the 1980s when staying at the Altnaharra Hotel. The loch was not generally available to fishing guests, being mainly preserved by the owner, but Ann and I obtained permission to fish it and instantly fell in love with Haluim. The walk out is "invigorating", a distance of approximately three miles from Inchkinloch at the south end of Loch Loyal on the A838 Lairg/Tongue road. We tramped west along the north shore of Loch Coulside before turning north-west over rising ground to head directly for the loch.

Find Loch Haluim on OS Map 10 at Gd reference: 557456. The boat is moored half way up the east shore and this bay is perhaps one of the most productive fishing areas on the loch. Begin by rowing to the north end of the bay, to the left of the inlet stream, and set up a drift back to the mooring bay. You will encounter fish all the way, particularly in the middle of the bay. Remember, the loch is shallow, so cast with confidence. The trout are there. The deepest part of the loch (thirty feet) is in the south bay and when fishing there you should keep the boat closer to the shore.

There is one substantial island in the loch and the narrow channel that leads to it from the east bay is known as Blue Zulu Channel because that famous pattern always produces results in this area. Keep a note of salient points as you progress round the loch. It is such a scatter of bays and corners that it is easy to get lost. Most standard patterns of Scottish loch flies work well on Loch Haluim but, personally, I invariably fish a bushy pattern – Ke-He, Soldier Palmer, Blue or Black Zulu – on the "bob", Woodcock & Hare-lug, Greenwell's Glory or Invicta in the middle, and a Silver Butcher, Dunkeld or Silver Invicta on the tail.

But in all honesty, the trout are not fussy eaters and I think that the size and shape of the fly and how it is fished, rather than the specific pattern, is the key element in persuading the trout to rise. All of which makes Loch Haluim the ideal place to introduce a beginner to the art of fly-fishing. It is almost assured that they will catch trout and, in doing so, will themselves be hooked for life on our well-loved pastime. We have had some glorious days on Haluim with members of Clan Sandison, young and not quite so young – memorable picnics when we cooked the trout that we had caught on a lochside fire and enjoyed a family day out together.

For further details about fishing Loch Haluim and other waters on the Loyal Estate contact: Altnaharra Hotel, Altnaharra, Sutherland, tel: 01549 411222. The estate can also arrange to take you out to the loch by Argocat and pick you up again at the end of the day. For me, the jewel in this angling crown will always be Loch Haluim. On a warm June afternoon, with an eagle soaring overhead, there is nowhere else on Planet Earth that I would rather be.

40.
A Wry Look at the Sporting Scene

It is that time of year again in the Highlands of Scotland. Invasion time, when our southern neighbours arrive in hot pursuit of hunting, shooting and fishing. The moment they set foot in the city of Inverness, they start shouting at each other. They bray loudly as they march down the railway platform to the Station Hotel. They shout at each other over morning coffee in the hotel lounge. They roar at each other in supermarkets where they stock up with mountains of food for their cottages: "Do you think the LODGE will have a garlic press, Wupert?"

I listen to them shopping in disbelief. They clack over cases of wine and bottles of spirits and for some unknown and uncertain reason they always seem to buy vast quantities of oranges, porridge oats, mustard and mint sauce. The check-out point is jammed solid as they argue over who should pay and who has the cheque book: "You don't mind an English cheque, do you?" they haw, haw to all and sundry.

Even if they were mute, they would be impossible to miss because of the clothes they wear, which are more akin to an official uniform: chunky sweaters, plus fours, brogues and stocking tabs for the men, britches or voluminous baggy skirts for the ladies, and even the occasional Inverness Cape. I suppose it is to make sure that any friends they might bump into at Heathrow know immediately that they are about to do the "Highland Holiday" thing.

As they await the arrival of their baggage, they shout at each other and at any unfortunate who has been detailed to meet them. "Lots of fish being caught, Hamish? What's the water like? Make sure you get the rods, look there they are – grab them. Is Wupert here – oh, look, there he is! Hello old man, how is dear Lucinda?" The same pantomime is enacted as they pack themselves and their belongings into the statutory Range Rover. Every living soul for miles around is left in no doubt that they have arrived.

I really have no truck with Scots who denigrate their southern neighbours. I think that those who do so are intrinsically narrow-minded. But I suppose it really depends upon how you define being English. For instance, a Home Counties born-and-bred, public-school-educated, ex-guards officer might not care to be lumped together in the same class as an out-of-work Tyneside ship-builder. A Yorkshireman would be horrified to be called a Lancastrian. In truth, as a race, the English are as diverse in their personalities as are we Scots.

I lived and worked for eleven years in the north of England in the heart of what was then the Durham coalfield, Easington Colliery, Shotton, Peterlee and Hordon, and in rural Northumberland at Bardon Mill on the banks of the Tyne near Mr Hadrian's famous wall. In all of that time I never, ever, experienced anything other than kindness, courtesy and consideration from local people. Even when I wore the kilt.

What I find hard to thole, however, is the southern Englishman and his wife abroad. They are invariably from the Shire Counties, the salubrious, wealthy, gin-and-tonic belt which envelops London. For ease of reference I shall call them SEPs (Southern English Persons). For all I known, they could be from Planet Mars, indeed some of them they may even be so, but the moment I hear their cantankerous cackle I feel my hackles rise. I never experience this when I hear the gentle burr of a Durham or Northumberland accent.

On holiday, those people are just about bearable. At least you know that eventually they will go away. The worst kind, however, are the ones who have bought themselves a bit of Scotland: "My dear, it was an absolute bargain – 5,000 acres and a lovely little six-bedroom house. Wupert couldn't resist it. He adores fishing and shooting and that sort of thing and I have a lovely time with the children on the beach. All our friends come to stay and we have lovely evenings round the peat fire. Do come, you will love it, and the locals are so quaint."

For a greater part of the summer months the estates these "lairds" own are let out to paying guests, people of their own kind of course, but at the end of July, the start of the "Highland Season", the owners descend on Scotland's remote glens and moors in droves. Estate factors, keepers and gillies burnish up their boots and dance attendance on their masters. Local people, quaint or otherwise, keep their heads down and try to continue as normal.

To be honest, their antics do give, unintentionally, a lot of pleasure to residents; the constant name-dropping, the bombast about the schools their children go to, the horses they own, their stocks and shares, clubs and parties, skiing holidays and Caribbean jaunts. Best of all is when romance is in the air. Voice volume rises by at least ten decibels. The male haw-haws inordinately, a lot, to attract his intended's attention, whilst the mating call of the female SEP is unmistakable – a sort of throaty gargle which sounds like: "Aga-Aga-Aga."

Still, bless 'em, I suppose they mean no harm and they do bring in a lot of money to rural areas. Perhaps, given time, they will begin to understand that Scotland is far more than just a cute holiday destination, that it is not simply a place where land and influence may be bought and sold by any Wupert, Dick or Harry on the strength of his bank balance. Perhaps once year, when they arrive, they will notice that we are a people in our own right? I would have no complaint if they did, provided that they just left their loud voices at home.

41.
Highland River

Neil Gunn's book, *Highland River*, opens with an account of the capture of a huge salmon. Not by the nose, but by the hands of a small boy walking the banks of Dunbeath Water in Caithness. It is one of the finest pieces of angling writing that I have read and I suspect that the story was based upon Gunn's own childhood experiences.

Neil Gunn was born in Dunbeath and he was my kind of angler – wandering the moors, exploring the silent places, hills, glens and lochs of the far north. His descriptive writing about the land he loved and the people who inhabited it is an enduring memorial and record of Highland life during the first half of the twentieth century.

Our northern streams are, however, spate rivers: no water, no fish. Some owners try to moderate the flow. The Helmsdale is fed from Loch Badanloch, Loch nan Clar and Loch Rimsdale and from Scotland's less well-known Bannock Burn. These headwater lochs act as a reservoir so that in low water conditions, fresh water can be released into the river. The Thurso operates a similar system from Loch More. The Naver benefits from the lochs to the south of Ben Klibreck, Choire and a'Bhealaich and Loch Naver.

Nevertheless, by and large, northern salmon fishing success depends upon rain and being in the right place at the right time – a state that we anglers dream of, constantly, but all too infrequently achieve. Our inevitable lot is to be greeted with the cry of: "You should have been here last week!" or to see dark rain clouds gathering just as we are about to leave.

It is possible to reduce the odds by fishing when it is most certain that there will be an adequate flow: the spring months, from early January until the end of April. Every angler will agree that catching one spring salmon is worth as much as catching ten autumn fish, but it is invariably savage entertainment trying to do so and seriously cold, hard work.

Part of the problem, in recent years, is that spring salmon have been largely noticeable by their absence; coastal and estuary netting, high-seas netting and, quite simply, man's greed have dangerously depleted migratory fish stocks.

There are indications that this decline, at least in east coast and south-west rivers, has been halted. This is largely due to the efforts of Icelander Orri Vigfusson, whose North Atlantic Salmon Fund has been successful in negotiating the buy-out of interceptory netting stations; in particular, the monstrous English North East Drift net fishery that preyed upon salmon returning to Scotland's east coast rivers.

In the meantime, however, one small Highland stream, the River Borgie, often has outstanding spring sport. From March until the end April, more than fifty salmon may be caught – wonderful, steel-strong, bars-of-silver fish, almost too beautiful to contemplate. Their average weight is generally in the order of 7–8lb, but quite a few double-figure fish are also taken. Indeed, the Borgie sometimes out-performs its more illustrious Sutherland and Caithness neighbours during the early months of the season.

The Borgie springs to life in the flow country south of Ben Loyal, tumbling down Allt Dionach-caraidh burn into Loch Coulside, close by the A836 Lairg/Tongue road. At Inchkinloch the stream enters Loch Loyal and exits four-and-a-half miles later through lochs Craggie and Sliam to form the main river: a seven-mile series of fifty pools that eventually empties into the sea through the golden sands of the beach at Torrisdale.

This is salmon-stalking country, often with a single-handed rod. Wading is not required and even in low water conditions there are deep holding pools where salmon lie. The most infuriating of these pools is below the swing bridge on Beat 3. I often see fish jumping in this pool but I have never managed to persuade one to "take", no matter what I offer.

Perhaps the most dramatic of the pools is Falls Pool, also on Beat 3. It acts as a temperature pool, holding the fish in the main river until May. There are two sets of falls overlooked by a fishing hut. They are not easy to fish and it is difficult to disguise evil intent from the fish because the angler, of necessity, is so close to where the salmon lie.

When fishing the rest of the river, to have the best chance of sport, keep away from the bank, below the skyline. Wherever possible, lengthen your line to cover the lies, rather than tramping down the riverside. The water is generally crystal-clear and the slightest error will spook the fish. Watch and wait. Don't chuck and chance it.

The Borgie is let with a splendid lodge close to the river by Mather Jamie & Partners and early booking is essential. Day tickets are sometimes available on the lower beat, the Association Water, which is great fun to fish and often as productive as the upstream beats, particularly in low water conditions.

Borgie Lodge Hotel is a comfortable and welcoming place to stay and is also close to the river, and the hotel can often arrange fishing on other nearby salmon streams – Halladale, Forss and Thurso, and on Loch Hope which is now Scotland's premier sea-trout water. Dunbeath Water was Neil Gunn's best-loved Highland River, the little Borgie is mine.

Further information from: Martin Ward, Mather Jamie & Partners, tel: 01509 233433.

42.
Go Wild for Real Salmon

As a Scot, I have watched in horror the devastation factory fish-farming has caused in the West Highlands and Islands since the first fish farm was opened there in 1967 at Loch Ailort on the Road to the Isles.

More than a thousand years ago my Pictish ancestors revered wild salmon and considered them to be a symbol of wisdom. The Picts carved images of salmon on their monumental symbol stones and wild salmon have survived in Scottish waters since the end of the last Ice Age.

The fish farmers would have you believe that there is little difference between the objects they produce in their cages and call "salmon", and the real thing, wild salmon. Nothing could be further from the truth, be it either standard factory farm fish or factory salmon from so-called organic farms.

A wild salmon is born where its parents were born, in the same place, in the same stream. When eggs hatch, the little fish live in their freshwater environment for up to three years until ready to go to sea. At this stage of their life they are known as smolts. They weigh a few ounces each and are about six inches in length.

Smolts migrate to the sea where they feed before setting off on a miracle journey to richer feeding grounds in the North Atlantic. Five years after their birth, when they have reached a weight of around 6lb, they set off back to the river where they were born, a journey of hundreds of miles, to begin the cycle of life again.

In contrast, farm salmon are born from the eggs and sperm taken from brood-stock fish, salmon selected for their breeding ability and kept in cages to be "milked" for the whole of their useful lives. The eggs are reared in a hatchery and treated with chemicals to protect them from disease. When the young fish emerge, they are also treated to prevent disease, and then transferred to freshwater rearing cages to be fattened up to smolt size.

The smolts are taken to sea in tubs on the back of a lorry, in bags hung from helicopters or by boats designed for the purpose. They are packed into cages approximately seventy-five metres in diameter. Each cage on a standard farm can contain up to 70,000 fish. On one site, there is generally up to twenty cages, thus upwards of one million fish can be crowded into a small area of coastal water.

Less than two years later, and after feeding the captive fish on a diet high in fat and oil to make them grow as quickly as possible to slaughter weight (5–6lb), most farm salmon are killed, processed and transferred to the supermarket shelf. At this time, a wild salmon is still living in its natal stream.

Cage-packed farm salmon are attacked by billions of sea lice that, in effect, eat them alive. The caged fish have to be treated with a range of chemicals to keep them free from lice until they can be slaughtered. Hundreds of thousands of caged salmon die because of other diseases, probably associated with high stocking densities.

Hundreds of thousands of farm salmon also escape into the wild when cages become torn or damaged. They compete there with diminishing numbers of wild fish for a finite food and breeding resource. They interbreed with wild fish, diluting the unique genetic integrity of wild fish and they can eventually completely displace them.

Scotland produces more than 100,000 tonnes of factory-reared fake salmon per annum. Sea lice from these farms have virtually wiped out many distinct populations of wild salmonids in the West Highlands and Islands as they pass by cages on their migratory routes, going to sea as smolts and returning as adults to spawn. Rivers and lochs that once teamed with wild salmon are now virtually devoid of these fish.

Prior to the expansion of fishing farming in the late 1980s, there was not a single recorded instance of toxic algal blooms in the areas occupied by these farms. They are now a year-round occurrence, exacerbated by the 11,000 tonnes of untreated ammonia dumped into our coastal waters each year by the fish farmers. It is estimated that effluent from West Highland and Island fish farms is equivalent to the untreated waste discharged from a human population of ten million people.

The fish farmers also allege that by farming salmon they are reducing the pressure on wild fish and providing the public with a cheap and nutritious substitute. Cheap it certainly is, but rather than relieving the pressure of wild fisheries it is doing the reverse.

It can take three tonnes of wild fish, such as sandeels, to produce one tonne of factory-farmed salmon. In Chile, the conversion ratio is even higher; a recent study there suggests that eight to nine tonnes of Pacific anchovies are required to produce one tonne of Chilean farmed salmon. Thus, the salmon farmers are playing their part in attacking the base of the food chain and endangering other species of fish that rely upon these small fish for their survival.

The Salmon Farm Protest Group was founded by me to bring these matters to the attention of the public. You can find out more about how the Group worked by visiting its archive website: www.salmonfarmmonitor.org.

43.
Scotland's Aquatic 'Wolf' from the Ice Age

One fine summer day a few years ago, I was fishing Loch Laidon for brown trout. This dramatic loch lies at the heart of Scotland where it silver-ribbons Rannoch Moor for five-and-a-half narrow miles. Off Eilean Iubhair, "the island of the yew tree", the boat bobbed gently over the waves in an accommodating breeze. Small trout rose to my flies, Black Pennell, March Brown and Silver Butcher. My fishing partner and I were well content, at peace with the world and all that it contained.

A moment later we were becalmed. The wind fell and fish stopped rising. Not a dimple stippled the mirror-like surface. Resigned, but content just to be there, we reeled in and opened a flask of coffee. A suicidal bluebottle buzzed impotently on the water a few yards from the boat. As I watched it struggle for flight, from out of the depths, in slow motion, a huge trout appeared and leisurely head-and-tailed over the doomed insect.

This was my first encounter with Scotland's legendary ferox trout, described by Ron Greer, fishery biologist and environmentalist, in his book of that name as "the Aquatic 'Wolf' from the Ice Age". The moment was heart-stopping, the image indelibly stamped in my mind. I can still see every mark on the body of that trout as clearly as I see the words I now write. I still feel the same sense of privilege and awe I felt then at being so close to such a completely wild, magnificent creature.

Ferox trout have survived in Scottish lochs for more than 10,000 years. They are special because they have retained their genetic integrity. Until recently, little was known about their lifestyle and habits other than the fact that they appear to subsist virtually entirely upon Arctic charr; although, as voracious hunters, ferox seem quite happy to snap up other morsels that come their way, including the odd unfortunate bluebottle.

In Norway, remains of lemmings have been found in ferox stomachs, in Scotland, small rodents. However, Arctic charr are the preferred diet and the number of ferox in any given loch depends upon the health of the local charr population. The size of ferox is also governed by the size of the prey species. Ferox eat fish which are generally one third of their own length. Therefore, if the charr population consists of small fish, this will restrict the ultimate size of the ferox which feed upon them. The ideal scenario for ferox is to live in a loch with a large population of modest-sized fish, like Loch Laidon. In such circumstance, ferox grow rapidly and can attain weights of up to and over 20lb in the space of six years.

The reason more is known about ferox today is largely due to an initiative undertaken by Scottish whisky distillers, Ballantine & Co. In 1985, the company invited a number of anglers to take part in a week-long fishing expedition, the objective of which was to catch a record-breaking brown trout. The venue chosen for the attempt was Loch Quoich at the head of Glen Garry in Inverness-shire, a deep, dour body of water, impounded in the 1950s as part of a hydro-electric generating scheme.

A deal of whisky was consumed during the exercise and several double-figure-weight ferox were caught, but the record remained intact. However, the experience fired the imagination of some of the participants who subsequently formed the Ferox 85 Group, fishery scientists such as Andy Walker, Alistair Thorne, Ron Greer and others. Thereafter, they devoted much of their energy and time to the study of these great fish.

In doing so, they are following in illustrious footsteps, not the least of which are those of Osgood Mackenzie, creator of the famous gardens at Inverewe in Wester Ross and author of the book, *A Hundred Years of Sport in the Highlands*. In his book, Mackenzie recalls a basket of ferox trout taken from Fionn Loch, the white loch, to the north of Loch Maree:

How perfectly do I remember one evening in April 1851 (when I was just nine years old), Sir Alexander Gordon Cumming of Altyre sending down a message to us at Pool House, asking my mother and me to come up to the inn and witness the weighing of the fish brought back that day, in case his own statement might be doubted in future years. There were four beauties lying side by side on the table of the small drinking room, and they turned the scales at 51lb. The total weight of the twelve fish caught that 12 April by trolling was 87lb 12oz.

Sir Gordon Cumming's friend and neighbour, Charles St John (1809–56) also recalls trolling for ferox: "I was crossing Loch Ness alone one evening with my rod at the stern of the boat, with my trolling-tackle on it trailing behind. Suddenly a large trout seized it, and before I could do anything but take hold of my rod he had run out eighty yards of line and bent my stiff trolling rod like a willow." St John lost the fish.

The magazine *The Field*, on 13 November 1880, also carried a report on ferox by Sir John Colquhoun of Luss: "The largest feroxes taken in Scotland, not even excepting Loch Awe, have been taken out of Loch Rannoch . . . At Loch Rannoch, in twenty-eight years, three of twenty-three, twenty-two and twenty pounds' weight have been taken."

There is no doubt in my mind that much larger ferox lurk in the depths of Scotland's lochs. The world record rod-caught ferox, landed in Sweden, weighed 37lb 6oz. The climatic similarities between Scotland and Scandinavia suggest that ferox of these weights are also present in Scottish waters. The biggest ferox ever taken on rod and line was a fish caught in Loch Awe, Argyll, in 1866 by W. C. Muir. It is reputed to have weighed 39lb 8oz, although its weight was never authenticated.

Ferox may be caught throughout the fishing season (15 March–6 October), although knowledgeable pundits would agree that April and May can be the most productive months. Unfortunately, here in the Highlands of Scotland, in April and May, the weather can be appalling. I have found myself fishing for trout in a white-out blizzard even towards the end of May. To be properly clad, therefore, is a first priority of ferox fishing. One more layer of clothing is rarely too much. After all, if the sun does shine, you can always take it off.

As to tackle and technique, the best advice I can give is to get a copy of Ron Greer's book. Make it your bible. Trolling a lure, live bait, dead bait, artificial minnow, Devon, spoon or Rapala can all bring results. Use a strong rod, a salmon spinning rod would do fine. Set up your tackle to ensure the line neither kinks nor twists whilst being towed behind the boat. Learn as much as you can about your chosen destination before setting out: depths, where the shallows are, where the loch shelves into deeper water and known ferox lie.

The best places to break both your heart and your tackle in pursuit of ferox are the same today as they were in the days of Osgood Mackenzie, Charles St John and Sir John Colquhoun. Happily, they are readily accessible and, mostly, boats are available for hire. In the Southern Highlands, consider a visit to Lochs Lomond, Awe, Tay, Rannoch, Laidon, Garry and Laggan. Further north, try your luck on Lochs Ness, Lochy, Arkaig, Garry, Quoich, Morar, Sionascaig, Loyal and Calder.

All that now remains to be done is to construct that glass case for above the mantelpiece. When you do so, think big. Given dedication to duty, perseverance, sheer cussedness, determination and grit, you could, one day, fill it with the fish of your angling dreams, the Aquatic 'Wolf' from the Ice Age, Scotland's most noble freshwater fish.

Ferox Trout & Arctic Charr, by Ron Greer, Swan Hill Press, 1995 (ISBN-10: 1 85310 486 8)

44.

Summer Sun

It seems to come round more quickly every year. No, not Christmas, not yet another birthday, nor even the end of the fishing season. I mean the dreaded August holiday. You have hardly recovered from the bank-balance-shattering cost of last year's jaunt, when bang, you're deluged with enticing offers for the next.

You can spend the whole twelve months in a state of near financial ruin and future holiday trepidation. I imagine tour operators plan it that way and they seem to be highly successful in doing so. In spite of the fact that the country is supposedly going down the drain quicker than Niagara Falls and everyone is scratching about for a bare living, holiday firms are booming.

Whatever, the "Great White Flying Birds" in the sky whisk huge chunks of the population off to the sun in ever-increasing loads. Every airport clamours for more space, staff, facilities and flights. Mountains of barely edible food are shoved before dazed travellers, both on the ground and in the air. Middle-aged men with beads and funny hats, followed by brood-clucking mums, single-file on board and hurtle off sun-wards.

Long may it continue, if you like that sort of thing, but, being an angler, I do not. For one thing, packing a rod is a bit of a problem and I would require a whole aeroplane just to accommodate the essentials that our lot needed for a fishing holiday. I remember once meeting two friends at Glasgow Airport. They had gone for a week's fishing in Southern Ireland and, as they came across the tarmac, looked it.

"Had a good trip then?" I asked politely. They stood, speechless, so I waved my hand backwards and forwards in front of their faces. "Hello, it's Bruce, me, come to collect you as promised, remember? Had a good trip then?" This time louder.

In perfect unison they began to undo the top fasteners of their trousers. Good grief, I thought, what on earth had happened to them? I cast an anxious glance round for the nearest exit and for any sign of men in white-and-blue checked hats. "Ah, that's better," they sighed, removing their thigh waders.

"Why are you wearing waders under you trousers?" I asked incredulously.

"It's the excess baggage charge, you see," came the response, "the excess baggage charge." Two cramped hours at 30,000 feet in waders, drinking Guinness? I don't think so.

Summer holidays, as you have no doubt noticed, happen in the summer. Trouble is that it also happens to be the middle of the fishing season. If we are to get any decent weather, then that's when it arrives. What possible point can there be in hurtling through the stratosphere to some overcrowded, baked beach when you could be catching trout in a remote Highland Loch?

Regrettably, when our brood were young, this occasionally resulted in serious family friction. Indeed, my position as Clan Chief was from time to time threatened, like the time I suggested Finland, rather than Crete, for a holiday. I only just escaped with my life. Having said which, the family all enjoy trout fishing. I had made sure of that from an early age.

Ever since the children were little it was accepted practice that we had two summer weeks' fishing somewhere in the Highlands or in the Hebrides. I should have known it couldn't last and, of course, it didn't. I blamed the adverts and glossy magazines for this, and also fifth columnists masquerading as school friends who returned for the winter term with skin the shade of brown boot polish.

My daughter, Lewis-Ann, was first to revolt. At the age of sixteen, she simply announced that if we thought she was going to spend another two precious weeks of her life standing in the pouring rain by the side of some midge-ridden loch in Sutherland, then we were living on another planet.

"That's only because you can't catch fish Lewis-Ann," said her big brother Blair, not helping one bit.

"Mind your own business. I catch more than you and I don't have to resort to worms to do so."

"What a lie! I have never fished with worms in my life!" shouted Blair.

I tried reason. "Now listen Lewis, you always say that. Each year it is the same, but you know you enjoy it once you're there."

"No I won't!" hotly from Lewis.

"But you can't say that, Darling," this from my Ann, my reasonable wife. "You don't know until you have been."

"Yes I do," Lewis snapped back, "because I'm not going and that's that. Why can't we act like normal people . . ."

"Not a hope with you," from Blair.

"Be quiet Blair, that's rude," I said.

". . . and go to a beach in the sun. All my friends do," continued Lewis.

I looked to Ann for support and finding none, capitulated.

Therefore, the following August saw me stretched out in the sun on a quiet beach in south Brittany, and very nice it was too. My rebellious daughter, with the logic only possessed by burgeoning womanhood, complained from start to finish about the heat and there being nothing to do. She sat, hugely sulking, fully attired, under the shade of a multi-coloured umbrella and refused to come out.

To be truthful, I really enjoyed that holiday but still begrudged giving up good fishing time. Two whole weeks is a lot to lose. It was whilst pondering these matters that I struck upon a cunning plan whereby I could enjoy the best of both worlds and save money. Were we to go for off-peak summer sun, in October, for instance, that would leave the fishing season uninterrupted. It worked and kept us happy and content until, eventually, the "brood" flew the nest.

45.
A Competitive Edge

My first and last fling with "performance enhancing substances" happened at my local swimming baths when I was a boy. Prior to an important gala, I was persuaded to take concentrated glucose tablets and, just to get the full benefit of the substance, and to mak sicker, I overdid on the recommended dose. I swallowed three tablets, not one. My performance was consequently less than enhanced, my stomach ached for days and I never touched the stuff again.

All sporting activities now seem to be plagued by the problem. Hardly a major event passes without scandal. Athletes working at the cutting edge of international competition are accused of using illegal substances to increase their chances of winning and officialdom goes to extraordinary lengths to smell out the culprits. Claims and counter-claims rage, reputations are destroyed and lives ruined.

I think that the problem is compounded by the commercialisation of sport. How you play the game no longer matters, winning and not losing is all-important. Amateurism is dead and buried. Sport has become a multi-billion pound international industry driven primarily by profit and business interests. No matter which sport you care to name, all have had their fair share of reports about unfair practices and I believe that this demeans us individually and as a nation.

Except for angling. Competition angling, so far, seems to have escaped the blight, but I wonder for how long? Substantial money prizes are now the rule rather than the exception in competition angling and I suppose, sooner rather than later, somebody is going to try and gain a competitive edge by indulging in some unfair, performance-enhancing activity.

The substance which immediately comes to mind and is most readily identified with anglers is hardly appropriate because it tends to have the opposite effect. In extreme cases an overdose can make you fall into the water and even a modest inducement seriously impairs casting ability, as I know to my cost and to the severe damage of my right ear.

Nevertheless, commercialism increasingly dominates my favourite pastime and the desire to win can be a powerful fishing partner. The additional prospect of a few hundred pounds could lead some anglers astray.

Inevitably, this will mean more rules and regulations, more snap inspections and more officials more closely monitoring competition fishing events. I have attended two competitions, as an observer, and was horrified at the list of rules read out prior to the contestants getting afloat. Watches were synchronised, a whistle blew and an armada of boats, bristling with rods, sped off into the distance. The whole affair reminded me of a military briefing prior to going into battle.

I don't know what they did to the fish but they sure as hell scared me. If this is what the future of angling holds, then I will hang up my rod, happily, for I want no part of it. I had the very strong impression that most of the participants would have been just as content fishing in the local swimming pool, providing that it was well stocked with hatchery-reared trout.

But they were a supremely happy bunch, laughing and joking, clearly delighted with each others' company and no matter what I might think about competition fishing, there is obviously a demand for these events. They undoubtedly give a lot of pleasure, if not to the fish, then at least to participating anglers.

A few years ago, the competition circus reached the gentle island of Islay where the European Fly-Fishing Championships were held. One of the lochs the teams fished was Finlaggan, famous not as a trout fishery, but rather as being the administrative base of Clan Macdonald since the fifth century. Its other claim to fame is the fact that the only salmon ever caught on the loch was taken in 1930 by the comedian Sir Harry Lauder. Poor Sir Harry must have been birling in his grave at this rude invasion of his privacy.

What concerns me, however, is the strong probability that, as cash prizes grow in size and as more money pours in to sponsor competition fishing, irreversible damage might be done to stocks of wild fish. National fishing competitions are now being held on such precious waters as Loch Watten in Caithness and I think that this is reprehensible. Even more reprehensible, in my view, is that many of these events are promoted by the Scottish Anglers' National Association – a body that should be at the forefront of protecting our wild fisheries, not engaged in stripping them bare.

Club competitions, between friends, might be acceptable, and I know that when I am fishing with my son there is always an element of competitiveness, but highly organised, heavily promoted and sponsored fishing competitions for cash prizes will only damage our sport and damage the image of angling in the eyes of the public. If we must have competitions, let them be confined to locations which exclude wild fisheries.

In the world of coarse fishing, the money-men have already moved in. The company Matchroom Sport promotes an annual fishing competition, "Fish 'O' Mania", which offers huge cash prizes to the winner and a day out for all the family: all the fun of the fair, sideshows, swings and roundabouts, beer tents and a computerised score board.

Will Matchroom turn their attention to game fishing? Could they find support for a similar competition in Scotland? I sincerely hope not and am prepared to indulge in whatever performance-enhancing substance that is required to help avert such a catastrophe – glucose tablets included.

46.
Fishing by the Short Loch

I know a place where even on a bad day you will almost certainly catch fish and where the rawest of recruits to our gentle art will find sport. This anglers' paradise lies around Gairloch, which means "the short loch" in Gaelic, in Wester Ross. A wilderness land crowded between Loch Maree to the south and the long arm of Loch Broom by Ullapool in the north, it is an area of 180 square miles enfolding thirty-five mountains, eighteen of which are Munros (more than 3,000 feet high).

Gairloch is a bustling tourist centre. Visitors flock to Inverewe Gardens, begun by Osgood Mackenzie in 1865 and now owned by the National Trust. The gardens contain 2,500 species of plants gathered worldwide. Children bucket-and-spade on shining sands or splash in waters warmed by the Gulf Stream. There are excellent restaurants, hotels, museums and craft centres and, for the more energetic, golf courses, pony trekking, sail-boarding and wildlife safaris.

For the visiting angler, Gairloch offers a vast array of first-class game fishing, not only in the lochs of the Fisherfield Forest, but also in dozens of other waters, both easily accessible and remote.

The Gairloch Angling Association has fishing on more than twenty hill lochs lying between Loch Maree and the sea. Getting to the best of them involves some hard tramping, but the effort is well worthwhile. For you will be rewarded with some of the grandest views in Scotland and, if you are fortunate, some of the country's grandest wild brown trout.

The Association also has fishing on Loch Bad an Sgalaig, to the south of the A832. This water contains some very large pike, introduced in Victorian times. However, it also contains good brown trout, with fish of over 4lb in weight not uncommon. A few years ago, a German visitor caught a 20lb pike one day and a 3.5lb brown trout the next.

The National Trust for Scotland manages a number of lochs in the Poolewe area which are available to visiting anglers. The largest, Loch Kernsary, is joined to Loch Maree and used to, in pre-fish farming days, hold sea-trout, particularly during the autumn. Cross the River Ewe at Poolewe and follow the road east.

There is a forest gate over the outlet stream and as you climb past natural woodlands, the loch comes into view, sparkling below. When Ann and I passed recently, a graceful hind drank from the outlet stream, belly-deep in yellow flag and meadow grass, surrounded by clumps of purple heather and backed by the vivid silver-blue of the loch. An unforgettable and precious moment.

To the south of Gairloch, where the B8056 turns west towards Red Point and the lonely moorlands of Maol Ruadh (the Red Headland), there are a series of lochs managed by Shieldaig Lodge Hotel, one of the best fishing hotels in the north. They offer splendid sport, particularly on the little waters known as the Fairy Lochs: Spectacles, Diamond, Aeroplane and Fairy.

But of all the splendid waters in this beautiful area, my favourite is Loch na h-Oidhche (the Loch of the Night), sheltered by Beinn an Eoin (the Mountain of the Birds) and Baosbheinn (the Wizard's Mountain). At the south end of this mile-long loch stands Poca Buidhe, "the Yellow Stone", a huge granite boulder which provided overnight shelter for anglers in days gone by.

The walk out to the Loch of the Night takes about two hours and best fishing times are either early morning or late evening. So, to have a good chance of sport, anglers used to camp below the stone, watching the loch and awaiting the right moment to launch their attack. The trout here are stunning and they all weigh about 12oz, perfectly matched and very pretty.

Today, there is a bothy by the loch, simply furnished and an ideal base for spending a few days out in the wilds. Southwards lie Beinn Alligin (the Mountain of Beauty), Sgurr Mhor (the Great Rocky Peak), Beinn Dearag (the Red Mountain) and Cam na Feola (the Hill of the Flesh).

South from Loch na h-Oidhche lie Gorm Loch Fada and Gorm Loch na Beinne. They contain excellent trout, with fish to over 3lb sometimes taken. Na Beinne is my favourite, with promontories, fishy corners, sandy bays and interesting weedbeds. These lochs fish best during the day, so the ideal plan is to fish them in the daylight hours and return to Loch na h-Oidhche for the evening.

But the most startling aspect of fishing here is the sudden, dramatic impact of your first sight of Ruadh-stac Mor (1,009m) and the famous Triple Buttress of A'Choinneach Mhor. Be assured, however, while you gaze with mouth wide in astonishment at these magnificent peaks, that that will be the moment when the 3lb trout grabs. It did for me. Although I lost the fish, I will never lose the memory of that view.

47.

Granddad

In a small loch near Scourie in North West Sutherland, there once lived a large, circumspect brown trout of great age and wisdom. His deepwater lair was amongst a tangle of sunken roots, shaded by rowan, hazel and alder. Insects

fluttered down from the branches of these trees and moths were blown from the surrounding heather to land above his nose. With the minimum of effort, he fed regularly and never knew hunger.

When a marauding otter disturbed his peace, he retreated into the darkness of his den, remaining motionless until the danger had passed. Sometimes, strange flies, attached to translucent threads, dragged over the surface close to where he lay. Struggling, half-drowned worms were sometimes curiously suspended in front of him. Brightly-coloured, foreign fish would twitch past jerkily before his gaze against the proper motion of the current of the loch. All these were resolutely ignored.

At midday, throughout the warm summer months, the great fish would leave his lair and cruise off to inspect his domain. Close to the ragged shoreline, he foraged amidst tangled weeds, parting them in his stately progress. The only evidence of his passage was a trail of ripples. Casual observers would never guess that so large a trout could cause such little disturbance going about its natural business. After a circuit of the loch, the fish returned to his lair below the trees to await the next morsel of provenance dropped into his jaws.

One morning, however, the watcher on the shore was no casual observer. An old man crouched in the shelter of a moss-covered rock, surveying the loch with keen, knowing eyes. Earlier, when dawn, with grey-flecked fingers, touched the eastern sky, the man had parked his car, drawn on walking boots, gathered together his fishing tackle and set off up the hill. He covered the ground with ease, as one accustomed to walking in the broken moorlands of the far north. Wind tugged gently at the wisps of white hair that straggled from beneath the hood of his jacket.

A wildcat, ears laid back, flattened to the ground on hearing him approach. The man's feet passed inches from its furious, green-eyed scowl. Spiders, amber and black, centred silver-damp webs. High above, circling in the thermals round Arkel and Foinaven, a golden eagle curiously marked the man's progress over the hill.

Now, his limbs cramped with crouching, the man changed position. A stag, grazing on the far bank, spotted the movement and its head jerked up, staring intently in his direction. As the slow morning grew towards midday, a light breeze sent wavelets dancing. Beneath the trees, the trout stirred and,

with a lazy swish of its vast tail, moved off round the loch. As it passed through a patch of weeds, close to where the watcher crouched, the tip of its tail momentarily broke the surface.

His body tense, every nerve tingling, the old man slowly raised himself to his knees and carefully noted every twist and turn of the trout's progress: past the shingle bank, through the tangled weeds, by the tumble and splash of the inlet burn, round the rocky promontory. The ripples stopped directly below the scrabble of trees on the high bank across from where he knelt.

He sat down slowly, his hand reaching behind him to grasp his fishing rod, still in its faded canvas bag. He crept back from the water's edge and, at a distance of a dozen or so yards, stood upright. Shouldering his fishing bag, he set off back down the hill. His step was jaunty and there was just the hint of a smile on his weather-beaten face. Below the trees, in the cool green depths of the loch, the great fish drowsed through the stillness of the warm summer day and into the quiet night, unsuspecting.

The next day, the circling eagle saw the old man first, crossing the moor, carefully picking his way over the heather, stopping by the high bank and the clump of trees. The wildcat heard the clack of his reel as line was passed through rod rings. The red deer saw the flash from the fly box, as a pattern was selected and attached to a delicate taper of nylon. Then the old man rested his back against a heather tussock and closed his eyes as though in sleep.

The sun climbed through a cloudless sky and reached its zenith. The great trout left its lair and swam off round the loch, telltale ripples flowing behind. Urgently, the old man inched forward and watched the progress of his quarry. When the trout was furthermost from its lair, the man stripped off line from the reel and, lying on his side in the heather, cast the fly towards the trees. With consummate skill, the tiny Greenwell's Glory he had selected snaked in under the branches and settled, gossamer-like on the surface, directly above the trout's lair.

With agonizing care, the man moved slowly backwards, away from the water's edge, gathering loose line into his hand. The huge trout passed the inlet burn, rounded the promontory and swam slowly towards its lair. It sipped in a struggling daddy-long-legs and then settled comfortable beneath the trees. Directly above its head, from whence all good things came, the trout saw the fly and rose quietly and sucked it in. The old man waited for a second, then stood clear and struck. The hook dug deep and held.

Later that same evening, fellow-anglers gathered round to admire the magnificent trout as it lay on the cool marble slab in the front porch of the hotel. The old man was bombarded with questions – where was the trout caught, which fly had he used, how long had it taken to land the fish? But to all enquiries he simply replied, modestly, with a twinkle in his eye, "Oh, really, it was just a bit of luck, you know, just a bit of luck."

48.
The Best of Scotland

For anglers, the best that Scotland has to offer lies in the hills, fishing for wild brown trout. And the best places to do so are in Wester Ross and North West Sutherland – from Inverpolly in the south, north through Assynt and Scourie to Cape Wrath. At the heart of the Inverpolly National Nature Reserve, surrounded by Suilven (731m), Cul Mor (849m), Cul Beag (769m) and ragged Stac Pollaidh (613m), lies lovely Loch Sionascaig.

Sionascaig is a deep loch, dropping to over sixty metres close to the largest island, Eilean Mor. Deer swim over to graze on the island and black-throated divers nest along the seventeen-crooked-mile shoreline that bounds the loch. Trout of up to 15lb have been trolled from the depths and hard-fighting fish of between half and three-quarters of a pound rise voraciously to the well-presented fly. Most seasons also see fish of up to 8lb being caught.

In the immediate vicinity of Sionascaig are many other good trout lochs. The Polly Lochs, Loch Doire na h-Airbhe, Loch an Doire Dhuibh, Na Tri Lochan and Loch a Ghille all lie close by, whilst a few miles distant are such lovely waters as Cam Loch (the crooked Loch), the long ribbon of Loch Veyatie, roadside Loch Borralan and trout-filled Loch Urigill, over the hill from Altnacealgach at Ledmore Junction on A837.

Out in the hills are more. Nestling between Suilven and the grey shoulder of Cansip (846 m), are three first-class trout lochs where good baskets are the rule rather than the exception: Loch a'Chroisg, Lochan Fada and Loch na Gainimh. Reaching them involves a vigorous walk, but you will not be disappointed on arrival. A solitary stag may mark your progress over the moor or an otter cast a quizzical glance, but you will see little of other human beings.

Over the mountains from Loch Sionascaig lies vast and windy Loch Assynt. There are ferox trout here that reach double figures in weight and a large population of wild brown trout that weigh in the order of a few ounces up to more than 3lb. There is also the possibility of an occasional salmon. The fish enter Assynt via the River Inver.

To the north of Loch Assynt, amidst the corries of Glas Bheinn (776m), lie three small lochs: Loch a'Choire Dherig (the Black Loch), Lochan a'Choire Ghuirm (the Red Loch) and Loch Bealach a'Bhuirich (the Green Loch). They are dour, but hold some wonderful trout.

Travel north now, past the magnificent towers of Quinag (808m) to Scourie, where more than 300 hill lochs await your attention. The mountain ridges of Foinaven (908m), Arkle (787m), Creagan Meall Horn (771m) and Ben Stack (721m) enclose and embrace a seemingly endless array of trout waters. Be prepared for some serious compass and map work, and to walk about five or more miles during your day out in the hills in search of sport.

The last part of this journey takes you north again past Rhiconich and over the hill to Durness. As you descend from Gualin, the landscape changes. Instead of broken, boulder-strewn moorlands, you are greeted by fertile, well-ordered green fields created by a limestone outcrop. This limestone enhances the lochs here and they have a high pH and a similarly high quality of trout.

The classic waters are Caladail, Borralie, Croispol and Lanish. They are fished from the Keoldale Sheep Club and hold some of the finest brown trout to be found anywhere in the world – splendidly shaped and marked fish that fight furiously. Catching them, however, is an altogether different matter and this is no place for beginners. The water is crystal clear and the slightest mistake or ill-judged cast alerts the residents to your evil intent.

Caladail is the most popular loch and it is best fished from the boat. The trout average nearly 2lb in weight and fish of 4lb will not raise too many eyebrows at the end of the day. The most productive area of the loch, relatively speaking, is in the middle, about 100 yards north of the small island at the south end; although, in truth, trout can be taken from all round the loch. Fish fine and far off, and don't be afraid to use dry fly on calm evenings.

Croispol contains fish of more modest size and is also fished from the boat. But they are very pretty trout and there are large fish as well. Off the east shore there is a forty-feet-deep hole and the largest trout taken from the loch, which weighed over 4lb, was caught here some years ago by Edinburgh angler, the late Professor Norman Simmonds.

Borralie is deep, 100 feet at the north end, but it holds some veritable monsters. Bank fishing can be excellent, particularly from the west shore at dusk. Trout come up from the depths to feed in the shallower water close to the bank. Do not wade, stay back and cast a short line to tempt them.

My favourite Durness loch is, however, little Loch Lanlish. In years past, trout of up to 14lb have been taken from Lanlish and even today fish of 8lb are not uncommon. Lanlish is fished from the bank and trout can be caught all round the loch – if you are very skillful or, like me, sometimes lucky. If I were forced to choose one area in Scotland to fish, then it would have to be the area described above, my angling paradise.

49.
Beginning

"It's a wrist action. Keep your elbow tucked in . . . pause on the back cast . . . let the line straighten out behind you . . . no, not like that . . . stand perfectly still . . . wait a minute, I'll get it out. Now, aim about six feet above the surface and drive the butt of the rod forward! That's more like it!"

We were standing on the banks of Tweed, fishing the stretch of water above Innerleithen known as the Red Yetts. The day was warm, not too bright. There was the promise of a good evening rise. My companion had never handled a trout rod before, but as he gained confidence, I introduced more complicated matters: the circular motion of the tip of the rod in the twelve-o'clock position, making line, false casting.

Out of the corner of my eye, I noticed a particularly promising rise towards the far bank, under the branches of a beautiful beech tree. The best fish always rise in places like that, don't they? Muttering suitable words of encouragement to my companion, I edged downstream and made a few false casts to get the distance.

Under the beech, the water swirled and I caught a glimpse of an enormous tail. I cast sideways, the rod parallel to the water. As the size 16 Greenwell sneaked in below the branches, I raised my wrist and drew back slightly. The Greenwell stopped and jerked upwards. The light breeze did the rest. Floating perfectly, the fly approached the largest trout I had covered for years. I could hardly breathe, every muscle and nerve tensed and poised for action.

Suddenly, an ear-splitting scream rent the air. My head turned, the fish rose and I struck. Too late. There was a brief turmoil on the surface and the monster was gone. That's life. I waded back to see what had befallen my friend. He was sitting in the middle of the river, line wrapped round his neck, clutching the rod as though his very life depended upon it. Gently, I helped him to his feet. We reeled in. Attached to the first dropper was one of the smallest trout that I had ever seen.

"My! What a beauty!" he exclaimed.

Over the years, I have introduced several friends and acquaintances to the gentle art. All of them have become adherents. Perhaps we have been lucky, but in most cases success was almost instant. I remember taking a Londoner out onto Derwent Reservoir on the Northumberland/Durham border. The closest he had ever come to fishing was Billingsgate Market, but with typical Cockney confidence he ignored my proffered advice, thrashing away, making it impossible for anyone else to raise a rod, let alone cast.

I sat watching in speechless amazement. Flies were whistling backwards, landing with an almighty splash, and then hurtling forwards with demonic fury, crashing into the water two feet from the bow of the boat. As a particularly violent back-cast hit the water, a trout rose. It managed to grab the tail fly a fraction of a second before the line lashed forwards again. Why the rod didn't break I shall never know.

With studied indifference, my friend turned to face the action. The trout had set off for the horizon, jumping spectacularly on the way. He started to reel in and didn't stop until the fish was stuck, half drowned, with its snout hard against the top ring of the rod. "What do I do now?" he asked.

"Well," I answered, "why don't you just climb up the rod and stab the poor thing to death?"

Somehow, I managed to net the fish, a trout about 1lb 8oz in weight. "There you are," he announced, lighting a cigar. "Nothing to it."

Most anglers would agree that a lot of talking and fishing do not go well together. I remember Lew Gardner, another friend I introduced to fly-fishing many years ago. Lew was a mighty talker. A "media man", he operated on the fringes of great affairs and was fond of such phrases as "£4,000-a-year baby Maoists". On our first visit to the water's edge he was in full flood. Loch Awe on a sunny spring day is a joy to behold, but he was too busy talking to notice. The water sparkled. There was the feeling that fish were on the move again after the long, cold winter months.

After some rudimentary guidance from me, Lew entered the water and began waving the rod about. I retreated to a safe distance. During the few pauses he took for breath, I interjected hints on technique. It was so much wasted breath. I was regaled with gripping accounts of Biafra, Vietnam, what Moshe Dayan said the last time they met and so on. My attention wandered and I fell asleep in the warm sunshine.

I was awakened by a cold, wet feeling on my face and I looked up straight into the eyes of half a dozen fine trout, all in the order of 8oz to 10oz in weight. "Come on," said Lew, "I've caught them all. The bar's open." Oh well, who knows why fish take anyway?

All things considered, I think it's been worth it. The hours spent explaining the intricacies of the blood knot, the dangers of wading, when to strike, how much water to put in the whisky and other essential matters. My friends all caught fish. None of us forget that first fish, so to be able to introduce someone to this magic world is reward enough.

But, alas, as facilities for expert tuition expand and become more readily available, so no doubt will the demand for my services diminish. So be it. Let those better equipped to do so than me carry on the good work. Perhaps then I'll be able to really concentrate on that ever-elusive one for the glass case.

50.
Arkaig Treasure

The Battle of Culloden was over in about half an hour. By midday on Wednesday, 16 April 1746, more than 2,000 men of Prince Charles Edward Stuart's army lay dead or dying on Drumossie Moor near Inverness. The rest, including their "Bonnie" commander, were flying in disarray or lying helpless, waiting for Cumberland's eager bayonets to end their misery.

The brutality with which government forces acted that day, slaughtering the wounded, is a stain on our nation's history and long after the Young Pretender had escaped to France, Butcher Cumberland's brigades continued to ravage the north, burning castle and croft, raping women and, for their barbaric amusement, murdering young and old alike.

Soon after the battle, government troops paid a call on Cameron of Clunes whose house stood by the banks of the River Arkaig near Fort William. As Cameron hid in the hills, he watched them strip his wife and his servants naked and ransack his home, "depriving them of all means of subsistence except for five milk goats".

Rebel or not, to be a Highlander was enough. The innocent and the guilty were, without discrimination, to feel the full wrath of a badly frightened British parliament: "The people must perish by sword and famine." The clan system and the dignity of the Highland way of life were to be destroyed.

The only battles that rage today along the road to Loch Arkaig are between angler and fish, but I never pass this way without remembering the aftermath of the 1745 Jacobite Rebellion. Perhaps if Charles Edward Stuart had arrived in the Highlands in search of fishing, rather than a throne, many innocent heads might have remained more firmly attached to their owners' shoulders and much bloodshed averted.

Loch Arkaig is one of Scotland's most popular fisheries. It is approximately twelve miles long by up to three-quarters of a mile wide. It contains good stocks of wild brown trout, which average in the order of 8oz, ferox trout, which can grow to an enormous size, and, of course, the species upon which ferox prey, Arctic charr. The loch also offers the possibility of sea-trout and salmon, which enter via the River Lochy and the River Arkaig, but, because of the impact of fish farming, few are ever caught.

The building of the Caledonian Canal in the nineteenth century, the more recent hydro-electric power developments of the 1950s and fish farming have substantially altered the character of this lovely loch and the quality of its fishing. Nevertheless, good sport may still be had, particularly towards the shallower west end where two perfect streams, the River Dessarry and the River Pean, feed into Loch Arkaig.

An old track leads west up Glen Dessarry, climbing between Sgurr na h-Aide (867m) to the south and Sgurr na Ciche (1040m) to the north before dropping down to the ruined croft buildings at Finiskaig on the shores of sea-Loch Nevis. This track passes Lochan a'Mhaim and its adjacent, unnamed neighbour, both of which hold wild trout which average 6oz, but, unless you plan to camp out at Finiskaig, it is a long way to hike for breakfast. All the lochs noted above are fished from the bank.

On Loch Arkaig, best results come from boat fishing, although bank fishing can be productive in the vicinity of many burn mouths. However, avoid wading since the water often deepens quickly close to the shore. There are no boats for hire, so if you wish to get afloat you must provide your own. There is a small hill loch to the south of Loch Arkaig which is worth a cast, Loch Briobaig, reached after a stiff climb north from Inver Mallie.

To the north of Loch Arkaig are two further, excellent waters. Tackle them from Caonich. Climb north-west from the road for one mile to reach the first and largest, Loch Blair, three-quarters of a mile north/south by up to a quarter of a mile wide. A step further north from Loch Blair will bring you to its more modest neighbour, Lochan Dubh. A circular tour, visiting both lochs, makes a splendid day out and should send you home with supper.

Loch Arkaig's other claim to fame again concerns Bonnie Prince Charlie's rebellion. Whilst the Prince was being hunted throughout the Highlands, a French vessel was sent to rescue him at the west end of the loch. Twenty thousand pounds in gold coins was taken to the meeting place. But when they failed to find the Prince, the money was buried nearby – where it remains, allegedly, to this day. My view, however, is that if it was buried anywhere, then it was most likely in the pockets of the local lairds, rather than in a hole in the ground by the loch.

Most standard patterns of Scottish loch flies work well on Arkaig, including Ke-He, Black Pennell, Soldier Palmer, Greenwell's Glory, March Brown, Silver Butcher, Kingfisher Butcher and Silver Invicta. Loch Arkaig is covered by a Protection Order so it is illegal to fish without written permission. Obtain this from Bidwells Property Consultants, 33 High Street, Fort William, Inverness-shire, tel: 01397 702433. The Rod and Gun Shop (tel: 01397 702656) also issue permits.

51.
The Morning Rise

Dawn breaks. First birds sing as fox and badger slink to the safety of their lairs. A gentle breeze ruffles the surface of the stream. There is a sudden movement in the forest. A green-clad figure steals stealthily from cover and crawls silently towards the riverbank. Weak sunlight glints off the dull metal of a landing net.

An angler inches forward, making use of every scrap of cover to obscure his progress from the fish in the river. He freezes at the sound of a splash. A late owl blinks and flaps homewards, ghost-like through the gloom. The angler's right hand feels for the cork handle of his fishing rod. In a single, well-practised move, the thin wand bends then whips forward. The tiny dimple of his fly appears on the water. The moment of truth.

Catapulted into the ever-increasing chatter of the burgeoning day comes a mighty crash as the river erupts in a shower of sparkling spray. The angler rises to his feet, rod firmly grasped, reel screaming. The fish runs for the tail of the pool and leaps. It "bores" on the bottom. The trout runs and leaps again and again. Finally, the angler nets a huge fish, removes the fly and kills the trout. It is done, finished.

Pretty gripping stuff, you will agree, and I am sure you recognised the angler? Yup, that's right, it was me and I like to think I played the part pretty well. Eat your heart out, Robert Redford and *A River Runs Through It*. Not everyone has either the skill or patience to be up at sparrow-fart to hook and land a 4lb wild trout in a narrow, tree-lined stream. It takes dedication to duty and an intimate knowledge of your quarry. But, I suppose, after all, someone has to show the way?

But it is just fancy – a story, a figment of my imagination, an unattainable dream. How I like to think of myself, up at the crack of whatsit and down to the river before bat bedtime. The reality is that I could no more get out of bed in time to greet the morning rise than I could play Beethoven's Fifth Piano Concerto to ecstatic applause on stage in Edinburgh's Usher Hall. Even as a child, the advent of morning filled me with such horror that it took the combined efforts of the whole family to prise me out of my pit.

At weekends, they didn't bother to try. I would happily have spent the whole day in bed had it not been for the lure of the Saturday matinee show at the Ritz Cinema in Rodney Street. At the age of twelve, I was marched off to our medical practitioner, Dr Henderson, to try to discover what was wrong with me. The assurances my long-suffering mother received did nothing to alter my habits. I continued to behave as though I was infected with some rare form of Scottish sleeping sickness.

Service in the Army, you might be excused for thinking, should have cured me. It didn't, I simply altered my sleeping habits. When I learned that, in the Middle East, HM Queen's finest worked only from 7.30am until lunchtime I immediately volunteered for duty in southern Arabia. This was the highlight of my military career. Come noon, I indulged in a positive orgy of mind-bending, relaxing, undisturbed sleep. It wasn't until I returned to civilian life and the necessity of earning a crust that I reluctantly began to rise at a reasonably respectable hour.

So I do have a problem with the dawn rise. The spirit may be willing but, alas, the habits of a lifetime are hard to break. Before getting hitched, like most sensible men, I made sure that my intended partner was as devoted to angling as she claimed to be devoted to me, and it was largely due to her influence that "things" began to change in the early-bird stakes. She talked knowingly about the dawn rise, which fascinated me because, of course, I have never actually seen one. I wondered if it really was as exciting as people said.

Several serious expeditions were therefore launched in hot pursuit of the phenomenon. In 1965 (I think?) we missed the dawn rise when we arrived two hours late on the banks of Derwent Reservoir on the Northumberland/Durham border. We then moved to a haunted house in the South Tyne Valley a couple of minutes' walk from the river. In spite of the proximity of the stream, I never managed to hit it at first light. By the time I had done with the week's work and rampaged through the garden, I was good for nothing other than sleep. At least that is what I claimed.

When we moved to the far north, there was so much wonderful trout fishing available during civilised daylight hours that it never occurred to me to leap loch-wards in the middle of the night. But my better half is made of sterner stuff and, eventually, I succumbed. She devised a fail-safe plan to ensure that even I could not be late. We would hike out to a remote loch the evening before, sleep in a convenient shore-side fishing hut and thus be in place come the first blink of the new day.

It was mid-May and we set off after work on the Friday evening full of hope and steely resolve. Ah! Spring in the Highlands! It began to snow at about 9.30pm and by 10pm the wind had reached gale force. Spray from the loch lashed the side of the hut as we shivered inside, crouched over a single-burner stove. After supper, we huddled on the hard floor in damp sleeping bags, listening to the storm raging about our ears.

It was impossible to sleep. My back ached. I felt as though I was trapped in Caliban's riven oak tree. Out of sheer exhaustion, we eventually dropped off. As you will no doubt have guessed by this time, we slept right through the dawn rise. Dispirited and fishless, we retired home stunned and hurt. Dawn rise? What dawn rise? I don't believe such a thing exists.

However, this year I intend to make a special effort to be in the right place at the right time, come what may – well, June really. It never gets dark up here in June. My cunning ploy is to start fishing at midnight and then simply wait for dawn to come to me, rather than the other way round. I am much better at staying up late than getting up early, so I can't fail to be there when first light breaks; must get into training with a short nap, right now. Close the door quietly please, when you leave?

52.
A Cunning Plan

It is never too early to start planning for the new trout fishing season. Here are nine of my favourite destinations where even the world's worst anglers, including yours truly, will catch more than their fair share.

These are wild brown trout lochs set amidst magnificent scenery and yet easily accessible. There is something here for everyone – beginner and expert alike – and they are the ideal locations for introducing a newcomer to the gentle art of fly-fishing and for a happy family fishing expedition.

Loch Rangag lies adjacent to the A9 Latheron/Thurso road in Caithness. The brown trout average 6oz in weight and fussy eaters they are not. Fish rise to all patterns of artificial fly, no matter how expertly or inexpertly they are offered. This makes Rangag ideal for little ones. I introduced my four-year-old grandson, Brodie Telford Macgregor Sandison, to fly-fishing on Rangag, where his second cast produced his first wild brown trout.

My late father-in-law, a sceptical Yorkshireman who had never cast a fly in his life, also broke his duck on Loch Rangag. He lost count of the number of fish he caught and ever after considered himself to be an expert piscator. There used to be a small boat on the loch but, honestly, it is far less bother to bank fish.

Loch Stemster is just across the road from Rangag, where the wild brown trout are generally accommodating. The great attraction of Stemster lies as much in the beauty of its surroundings as it does in its circular shape. No matter from which direction the wind blows, there is always a sheltered area of bank from which to fish.

The loch contains excellent quality, pink-fleshed trout that average 8–10oz in weight. Clan Sandison has had great sport here, sometimes with a brace of 1lb fish caught on the same cast. There is a boat available, but I prefer bank fishing. A track leads to the north-west corner were there is a parking and picnic area.

The south shore is pin-pricked with finger-like promontories along which it is possible to safely wade out a considerable distance, allowing you to cover a vast area. Otherwise, stay back from the bank, casting your flies into the shallow water close to the shore. Stemster fishes well throughout the season, particularly in the early months. Offer them: Ke-He, Greenwell Glory, Silver Butcher.

Loch Meadie is on the right of the main road, a few miles from Westerdale, before you reach the forestry track. The loch is one mile long by up to 300 yards wide and full of brown trout that average 8oz and rise readily to almost any pattern of fly. Bank fishing can be productive, but the shoreline is rocky and wading uncomfortable. Launch your assault in the boat. Begin by drifting from the mooring bay down the west shore, about ten yards out from the bank.

Loch Gaineimh is accessed from the forest track. The loch is approximately half a mile long by up to 500 yards wide and it never sends visitors home without at least something for supper. The fish are not large but they are plentiful and fight well. Gaineimh is best fished from the bank and there are splendid little beaches where you can rest from piscatorial effort and enjoy a picnic.

Another Loch Meadie, near Altnaharra in Sutherland, is one of my favourite lochs. The south bay, where the boats are moored, is reached from the narrow, winding road from Altnaharra to Loch Hope. At first glance, Meadie looks a modest affair but, in fact, the loch extends north from the south bay for a distance of more than three miles and a boat is essential to properly explore the loch. On a bad fishing day, Meadie produces baskets of twenty to thirty trout. On a good day it is even nicer. The fish are small, but they fight well and give great sport.

A tree and scrub-covered island guards the narrows between the south bay and the northern section of Loch Meadie. The flora on the island has largely escaped the ungentle administration of the local sheep and deer population. Hence, the vegetation exemplifies what much of the North Highlands of Scotland must have looked like 1,000 years ago.

Loch Haluim, to the east of Meadie, is another beginner's paradise. However, reaching Haluim is a serious trudge over rough ground, but you can arrange to travel there in relative comfort by Argocat. The loch lies like a blue butterfly on the golden moor and there is a boat to help you explore all its nooks and corners.

Quite apart from fishing, Haluim offers a practical lesson in natural history. It is almost certain that during the day you will see golden eagle, buzzard, peregrine and raven. The hill abounds with deer, and red-throated diver, greenshank and curlew call hauntingly. Wildflowers grow in profusion: bog asphodel, butterwort, lousewort, milkwort, cotton grass, tormential, marsh violet, bogbean and many more. Haluim offers all these and some of Scotland's most exciting wild brown trout fishing.

Loch Beannach, "the loch of the hillocks", lies to the north of the A837 Bonar Bridge/Lochinver road and is one of Assynt's most prolific wild brown trout fisheries. Beannach is, quite simply, also one of the loveliest lochs in Scotland, surrounded by dramatic Assynt mountains, Suilven and Canisp to the south, the long ridge of Quinag to the east.

A well-tramped track reaches the loch from the road after any easy hike of thirty minutes. At the end of the track, you will find an amazingly beautiful water, a wild straggle of bays, promontories and fishy corners dotted with more than a dozen small islands. Beannach trout are not large but they rise readily to most patterns of fly and give a good account of themselves.

Every angler is an expert here, and you should have a cast or three in the adjacent lochs, Loch Uidh na Greadaig, "the grilse loch", and Loch Bad nan Aighean, "the loch of the grove of the hinds", on the way out to Beannach. The unnamed lochans to the north of Beannach should also be explored. The lochs here are an angler's dream come true.

Loch Urigill is another angling dream where wild brown trout will rise with dash and spirit to your flies. There are sandy beaches, ideal for picnics and splashing. The loch is generally shallow, three-quarters of a mile long by up to half a mile wide.

In June, there is often a mayfly hatch producing exciting dry fly-fishing and Urigill is best fished from a boat, although bank fishing can be just as rewarding. There are abundant stocks of 6–8oz trout with the occasional fish of up to 2lb in weight. However, the largest trout taken in recent years weighed 8lb, so be prepared.

A favourite drift is in the south-west corner of the loch, near the two small islands, where the principal feeder stream enters. Most anglers fish a traditional team of three wet flies and you should start proceedings with Black Pennell,

March Brown and Silver Invicta. Dapping can also produce excellent results. Accommodating trout and splendid scenery make Urigill the perfect location for a family fishing expedition and this loch will delight anglers of all ages.

Loch Laidon: I was once accosted by an angry angler at a game fair. "The information in your fishing book about Loch Laidon is wrong," he exclaimed without preamble. Mortified, I asked him to explain. "You told me to expect a basket of thirty to forty trout on an average day. In fact, I caught more than fifty."

Laidon is like that and is one Scotland's most productive and exciting wild brown trout lochs, where angling success is guaranteed. The loch lies on Rannoch Moor in the heart of Scotland, 1,000 feet above sea level. It is 140 feet deep, six miles long by up to half a mile wide – two miles if you include the finger-like north-west arm.

If you enjoy geographical tricks, at the end of the north-west arm of Laidon, as noted above, you may stand with a foot in Perthshire, Inverness-shire and Argyllshire at the same time – provided, of course, that you are possessed of three legs.

Easiest access to Laidon is from the east, from Moor of Rannoch Station. A good track, on the line of an old cattle drover's road through to Glencoe, margins the north shore. There are a number of secluded, sandy bays, perfect for bank fishing and lazy picnics along the way.

Laidon trout average 6–8oz in weight and they are not particular about what they eat. For starters, offer Black Pennell, Grouse & Claret and Silver Invicta. Be aware, nevertheless, that Laidon also contains much larger fish as well as legions of their smaller brethren. The largest trout was caught in 1999 and weighed 9lb 8oz, and a fish of over 8lb was taken in 2004.

WHAT YOU NEED TO KNOW

Loch Rangag and Loch Stemster: Location: OS Map 11, Thurso & Dunbeath, Scale 1:50,000. Grid references: Loch Rangag 177415, Loch Stemster 190424. Contact: Hugo Ross, Fishing Tackle Shop, 56 High Street, Wick, Caithness, tel: 01955 604200.

Loch Meadie and Loch Gaineimh: Location: OS Map 11, Thurso & Dunbeath, Scale 1:50,000. Grid references: Loch Meadie 091480, Loch Gaineimh 051470. Contact: Ulbster Arms Hotel, Bridge Street, Halkirk, Caithness, tel: 01847 831641, fax: 01847 831206

Loch Meadie and Loch Haluim: Location: OS Map 16, Lairg & Loch Shin, Scale 1:50,000. Grid references: Loch Meadie 496398, Loch Haluim 555456. Contact: Keepers Cottage, Ben Loyal Estate, Tongue, by Lairg, Sutherland, tel: 01847 611216.

Loch Beannach and Loch Urigill: Location: OS Map 15, Loch Assynt, Scale 1:50,000. Grid references: Loch Beannach 135264, Loch Urigill 244100. Further information from S. McClelland, tel: 01571 844377; see also www.assyntangling.co.uk. Permission from the Assynt Angling Club, c/o Caberfeidh Restaurant, Lochinver, tel: 01571 844321; Lochinver Fish Selling Co, Culag Square, Lochinver, tel: 01571 844228. Accommodation: Cathel Macleod, Polcraig Guest House, Lochinver, tel: 01571 844429. Cathel Macleod caters specifically for anglers.

Loch Laidon: Location: OS Map 41, Ben Nevis, Scale 1:50,000. Grid reference: 390555. Easiest access is from Rannoch Station, which lies at the end of the B846 road, which runs west along the north shore of Loch Rannoch. For permission to fish and further information, contact the gamekeeper on tel: 01882 633246. Bank fishing but a boat may also be available.

53.
The Rough Bounds

The small boat was busy and its decks crowded with passengers. Once clear of the harbour, the Sound of Sleat greeted us with sparkling, blue-bright waves and I thrilled to the feeling of adventure that comes only with the salt scent of sea spray. Ahead lay our destination, the tiny hamlet of Inverie on the Knoydart Peninsula, forty minutes from Mallaig at the end of the Road to the Isles.

Knoydart is one of Scotland's last great wilderness areas. It enfolds 55,000 acres and lies to the west of Fort William between "heaven and hell" – the names given to the two fjord-like sea lochs, Nevis to the south and Hourn in the north, that guard it.

Apart from by boat, the only way in is on foot from Strathan at the end of the public road at the head of Loch Arkaig, a taxing sixteen-mile trek. The path climbs through Glen Dessary, amidst the ragged mountains where Bonnie Prince Charlie hid after his defeat at Culloden, to the ruins of Finiskaig on the shores of Loch Nevis. The route then winds past Camusrory and Carnoch before climbing steeply through Gleann Meadail and down to the River Inverie.

My accommodation in Inverie was a cottage and in the early evening I wandered out to see what I could see. The bay was mirror calm and several yachts lay peacefully at anchor. The smell of peat smoke filled the air and I watched as the crews of the yachts bundled themselves into tiny dinghies and rowed ashore. Most of the occupants seemed to be heading for The Old Forge Inn, so I followed them.

Steeping through the door, it was as though I had been transported into an entirely new world. The long bar was thronged with people who were clearly enjoying themselves enormously. Two musicians, guitar and violin, were playing and singing lustily, with the rest of the assembled company joining in. At the end of each piece, loud cheers echoed round the room.

The Old Forge Inn is owned and run by the remarkable Ian and Jacqui Robertson and it is the "hub" of social life in Inverie. Ian told me that most of the 4,000+ visitors who come to Knoydart each year pass through his doors and the pub has attracted an astonishing number of accolades and awards, including the "Highlands and Islands Best Visitor Experience" in 2007.

The following morning, I met Drew Harris, the manager of the Kilchoan Estate, the western part of the old Knoydart Estate, which is now run as a sporting and recreational enterprise. I wanted to have a closer look at what the estate had to offer people afflicted with angling and, perhaps, remove a few brown trout from their natural habitat.

[131]

Drew is one of those people who does not understand the meaning of the word "impossible" and showed it through his boundless enthusiasm and obvious love for the land he looked after. Under Drew's guidance, I fished remote Loch an Dubh-Lochain for wild brown trout and the delightful little Inverie River for salmon and sea-trout. Loch an Dubh-Lochain lies at the heart of the Rough Bounds of Knoydart and can be found at Gd ref: 820005 on OS Map 33, Loch Alsh & Glen Shiel, Scale 1:50,000.

The loch is deep, dropping to a depth of almost 100 feet, and is one mile long by up to 400 yards wide. Look out for pretty wild brown trout that average 8–10oz in weight. But there are much larger specimens as well, including ferox trout – the aquatic 'wolf' that is descended from species that have inhabited the loch since the end of the last Ice Age – along with their attendant population of Arctic charr.

Loch an Dubh-Lochain is the headwater loch of the River Inverie, a notable salmon and sea-trout fishery that is recovering from the less than welcome impact of the fish farms in Loch Nevis. Drew Harris of Kilchoan Estate is conducting a re-stocking programme which is beginning to produce encouraging results. In spite of low water levels during my visit, several sea-trout of up to and over 4lb in weight had been caught and released, and salmon parr were abundant.

There are two other trout lochs on the hill to the south of Kilchoan, Loch Bhraomisaig at Gd ref: 785973 and its unnamed satellite lochan to the west on the slopes of Lagan Loisgte. Bhraomisaig lies at about 350 metres and it might test your lungs a bit getting there but it holds some excellent trout, which can exceed 4lb in weight. Neither Bhraomisaig nor its satellite surrender their residents easily but, be assured, they are there, waiting for your carefully-presented fly.

Offer them Kate McLaren, Black Pennell, Ke-He, Solder Palmer, Loch Ordie, Greenwell's Glory, March Brown, Woodcock and Hare-lug, Invicta, Silver Invicta, Silver Butcher and Alexandra. For permission to do so, contact Drew Harris on tel: 01687 462724, email: drewhkilchoan@onetel.com. The estate has excellent accommodation for visitors, including a bunkhouse and self-catering cottages.

But the estate is not only about stalking and fishing. It encourages hillwalkers and provides first-class bunkhouse facilities to accommodate them.

There are whale-watching sea trips and visits to remote, uninhabited islands. You may stalk red deer with a camera and watch otters at play in the river and along the shores of Loch Nevis. Or simply relax in the outstanding comfort of the estate's self-catering cottages.

It was hard to leave Inverie but at 11.00am on a Monday morning, I found myself back on the pier awaiting the arrival of the ferry. As we headed out across Loch Nevis towards Mallaig, I watched the village fade and merge into the backdrop of blue-grey mountains. But I was quite certain that I would be back.

54.
Keep Your Hair On

Single strands of horsehair are invisible in water, particularly running water. It is the perfect material for making the perfect cast, guaranteed to fool the most circumspect trout. All you need to do is to find an accommodating cuddie. Proffer a carrot at the front end whilst discreetly snipping off a few strands from the rear.

The strands are a lot thicker than you might think and are naturally tapered. Wet the hairs and join them together with dexterous blood knots. Be gentle. With patience, you should end up with a cast of about eight feet to nine feet in length, constructed from three or four strands, depending upon the size of the horse's tail.

If at first you don't succeed, like Bob the Bruce, try, try and try again. It is worth persevering because horsehair makes the most lethal cast I have ever used. The trouble involved in preparing one is well worth the effort of doing so. Honest.

I have caught trout of up to 1lb 8oz using horsehair casts, on the River Tweed near Innerleithen, with a size 18 Greenwell's Glory. Provided you maintain a constant strain, avoid slack line and keep in touch with the fish, horsehair is amazingly strong. But with an ill-considered snatch, jerk or a moment's inattention, it breaks like worn thread.

Prior to action, test the cast. I attached a fly to my first horsehair cast and hooked it up to a wire fence. I then pretended that I had risen a fish. I struck and the cast snapped. I tried again, but this time I only raised the point of the rod firmly, rather than striking. The cast held. Even when I simulated a trout stripping line from the reel, the cast remained intact.

My proudest moment came one evening when my late father and I arrived at the river to find Tweed in spate – a black torrent, flooding seawards loaded with chunks of trees and broken branches. Dad moaned about the weather, I, being young then, set off for my favourite part of the stream with my horsehair cast and the small dry fly.

I fished the fly downstream, close to the bank, carefully searching back eddies and quiet places beneath overhanging boughs. Wading was quite impossible, so I knelt and, on occasion, lay full length on the ground in order to guide my fly into inviting, fishy corners. Within an hour, I returned triumphant and showed dad the four fine trout that I had caught.

Fishing a horsehair cast is a delicate art and it requires the use of an appropriate rod. I used a wonderfully supple, seven-foot greenheart rod, a dear friend that now decorates the wall above where I write. It was eventually pensioned off in favour of a split cane rod and new-fangled, modern, monofilament nylon.

Since then, my well-loved pastime has become a multi-million-pound, world-wide business, commercially driven by tackle manufacturers and advertisement-hungry angling magazines. Hardly a month passes without the introduction of some new technological innovation: lighter rods, thinner cast material, automatic reels, lines for all seasons – fast sink, slow sink, intermediate, "slime", cellular, floating, double taper, single taper, weight forward – dished up in all the colours of the rainbow.

Artificial fly patterns have also undergone dramatic changes and fishing magazines are packed with detail about how to tie up the "fly of the moment". These concoctions generally catch more anglers than they do fish, but it keeps everyone busy and cash registers ringing.

It takes all sorts to make an angler and no one person holds any single truth. Neither have I a right to pontificate about how others should enjoy their fishing. But I regret the passing of more simple times, more rustic, intuitive angling, and I worry about where our sport is heading. Are we becoming just a race of fish-killers, less aware of the pleasure of being on river or loch? Have we lost our angling innocence?

Whatever, our brave new, technologically advanced, angling world has brought some advantages, at least for beginners to the gentle art. Setting up in business is far less expensive than it was when I started fly-fishing. My first trout rod cost the equivalent of a month's wages. Today, excellent rods are available for less than the average day's pay. This also applies to reels, lines, flies, landing nets et al, and it is possible for the embryonic Walton to get him or herself well-kitted-out for £100.

What is not on sale anywhere, however, is an angling philosophy and that, perhaps, is the saddest aspect to me about fishing today. Anglers seem to care less and less about the trout they fish for or, indeed, where they go to fish for them. Stocked fisheries, commercial put-and-take ponds, provide for the needs of these people – so-called "stockie-bashers".

Competitive fishing is also becoming big business, with ever-larger cash prizes for the winners. Tackle manufacturers have spotted the chance of productive advertising and sponsor these events. We now have national and international teams, dedicated to catching more fish than their rivals.

But true sport fishing is not about catching more fish than your neighbour, bigger fish or, indeed, any fish – as I know all too well from personal experience. Fishing has a much deeper significance: the ability to free the mind from everyday care, to understand our proper place in God's "braw, bright, birling world".

Those who degrade this truth by engaging in cash-for-killing fishing competitions do angling a great disservice. They promote the production of fake, hatchery-reared fish that all too often escape into the wild and damage native fish populations.

In my view, there is no place in Scotland for put-and-take fisheries, least of all in the Highlands. They devalue the reputation of Scotland as being the finest place in the world to fish. In the meantime, I'm off to filch a carrot from the kitchen. Our neighbour down the hill has a splendid Clydesdale named Napoleon and I think that it's about time I paid him a visit. Now, where did I put the scissors?

55.
Ducked in the Don

If someone else, particularly a member of my own family, had done anything so stupid, I would have been furious. As it was, I had only myself to blame for coming so close to such an unplanned and unannounced meeting with my maker. The incident happened when I was fishing Dam Pool on the River Don and I barely escaped with my life.

Tall reeds fringed the south bank and they had been cut but not removed. The reeds had "hinged" through ninety degrees and lay, raft-like, on top of the water. Peering into the depths, I followed my cast of three wet flies as they swam in the current just below the surface. My heart almost stopped when I saw the trout of my dreams, a huge fish, at least 6lb in weight, shoot out from under the rock ledge in the middle of the stream and make for my tail fly.

It grabbed, and in the heat of the moment, I put a foot onto the reeds and did a neat forward-somersault into the deep pool. Those who have been in a similar situation recount that the whole of their life passes before their eyes, as though in slow motion, even although they are fighting for survival. Believe me, it's true. As I lay on the bottom, scenes from my childhood flashed upon my inner senses.

I remember thinking, "So this is what it is like to drown – not so bad, really." I was, however, still clutching the rod, in a reflex action, and the trout was still hooked. I was fully clothed, wearing thigh waders, with a heavy fishing bag round my shoulders. Somehow, I managed to remove the bag and struggle to my feet. My head was barely above the surface. Had the river been a few inches higher I would have been a goner. I laboriously reached the bank and lived to tell the tale. So did the trout but I will never forget that fish.

Dam Pool is on the Castle Forbes Estate, nine miles of double-bank fishing from Bandley downstream to Glenton. Apart from excellent trout fishing, there are more than thirty named salmon pools. Downstream, Monymusk Estate fishing extends for a further fifteen miles and also offers a wide variety of sport with both salmon and brown trout.

Indeed, this is one of the principal attractions of fishing this part of the

River Don; no matter what the water conditions might be, there is always the chance of sport, if not with salmon, then most definitely with magnificent brown trout. There are eleven beats on Monymusk, all of which are fished from the Grant Arms Hotel.

The Don is, in my opinion, the finest brown trout stream in Europe. It contains wonderful fish. In recent years, the river has produced remarkable, specimen trout, fish of up to and over 7lb in weight and brown trout of 4lb are caught most seasons, particularly during the early months, in April and May. The average weight of Don trout is in the order of 1lb 4oz, but most anglers return all fish under 2lb.

Upstream from Monymusk, the Don runs through Paradise Wood, a magical wonderland of mature deciduous trees planted in 1719 by the then local laird, Lord Cullen. The stream here offers outstanding dry-fly water fishing that has no peer anywhere in Britain, and I include famous English chalk streams such as the Itchen and the Test.

One of the most exciting trout I have ever taken was caught on the Monymusk Water on a blisteringly hot summer day in Island Pool, near the superbly restored edifice of Pitfichie Castle. An island divides the river flow and, in low water, the north channel is easily reached. A shingle bank projects into the pool and I waded the loose gravel as far as I could safely manage but, the deeper I went, the more difficult it became to retain my balance.

Just beyond the very limit of my casting range (not great at the best of times and even less so with trees and bushes behind) was a particularly inviting lie: shadowed by a willow, deep, dark, shaded and exactly the place where, if I were a trout, I would hide from the midday sun. One more step and I would cover the lie. As I made the final cast, the gravel beneath my feet began to give way and I felt myself slipping – which is exactly when the trout struck, almost pulling the rod from my hand in its first wild rush.

More by luck than by any skill on my part, I managed to inch backwards onto firmer ground, by this time wet to the waist. But the trout was still hooked, careering round the pool, leaping and splashing in the sunlight, sending crystal droplets dancing, rainbow-like, in the still air. I never should have caught that fish but when he eventually came to the net he weighed 2lb 8oz, so I didn't argue.

The start of the Colquhonnie Hotel water is one mile south from Cock

Bridge, in Strathdon, where the river passes under the road at Luib, a wonderful nine miles of outstanding fishing all of which is double bank apart from a three-quarter-mile stretch in front of the hotel. The great attraction of fishing here is, again, the quality of sport with brown trout.

So why not start your 2003 fishing season with a visit to the glorious River Don? Provided you don't take an ungovernable plunge into the stream, I promise that you will not be disappointed.

Castle Forbes water tel: 01975 562524; Grant Arms Hotel tel: 01467 651226; Colquhonnie Hotel tel: 01975 651210.

56.
Ladies First

One woman angler is more effective than any ten male anglers. Chauvinists can grouse and girn all they like but this is a fact, at least it is as far as I am concerned. From that notorious day in 1922 when Georgina Ballantine landed her record-breaking 64lb salmon on the River Tay to the present time, it has been so.

Those who disagree probably don't fish with female companions and consequently know little better. I do, all too well, and throughout my angling life I have struggled to understand the successful-female-angler syndrome. How is it that they always seem to manage to catch the brutes whilst we poor males remain fishless?

Diana Huntingdon, fishing the River Awe in 1927, landed a 55lb salmon, and another of 51lb in 1930; Mrs Morrison took her 61lb salmon from the River Deveron in October 1924; Pauline Kirkbride's 29lb Dee fish from the Woodend Beat; Lady Burnett's 45lb Tweed salmon. There are plenty more.

This also includes the late Mrs Kelly of Edinburgh, one of the most proficient trout anglers I ever knew. Mrs Kelly fished Loch Leven in the 1950s and I have seen her catch more trout to her own rod than the combined total for the whole of the Kinross Angling Club. If there were fish moving, Mrs Kelly caught them.

My daughter, Lewis-Ann, is perpetually lucky or, as she points out, skilful.

Even as a child, on her first fishing trip in the hills to the south of Scourie, Lewis-Ann caught fish whilst the rest of Clan Sandison thrashed fruitlessly. Regardless of the weather, Lewis-Ann always catches fish.

Ann, my long-suffering better half, is just as useful in matters piscatorial. One day, fishing a series of lochans between Glutt and Dalnawillan in Caithness, I left her to her own devices and stamped off to do business in more promising waters. I returned fishless whilst she caught three, each over 1lb 8oz in weight.

Even worse than being fishless was the fact that I had hooked and lost one of the largest wild brown trout that I have ever encountered, a specimen fish of, I estimated, around 7lb in weight. My landing net refused to open and in trying to force it to do so I snagged the top dropper in its folds. When the fish set off for the middle of the loch, the cast broke.

My worst nightmare, however, occurred while boat fishing with Ann on Loch Seilge in Strath Halladale. She was in the stern, I was in the bow. We were using identical patterns of artificial flies: Ke-He on the "bob", March Brown in the middle, Silver Butcher on the tail. Ann took eight trout. If I had caught two more, I would have had a brace.

I remember also the Loch of Lintrathen lesson. I had been invited to have a day there with an angler who had fished for Scotland. I got the impression that he was not entirely happy when Ann joined us in the boat but, ever courteous, he grinned bravely and said nothing.

"Are you going to start fishing, Ann?" he asked after a few moments. She had been fishing, with her customary short line. He just hadn't noticed, being otherwise engaged, standing in the stern, casting to the far horizon.

When Ann caught her first trout, he was fulsome in his praise. When the second fish came to her net, he still managed to keep smiling. But after the third trout, he reeled in and said, "That's a very interesting technique you are using, does it usually work so well?"

"It does for me," Ann replied, neatly hooking another fish.

The secret of their success, I am convinced, is two-fold. Firstly, women are persistent. Lady Burnett used to fish every minute, right up to close of play. "What's the time Jimmy?" she would ask her gillie. "Five minutes to go, Madam," he would reply. "Right, long enough for another dozen casts." During which time she invariable hooked a fish.

Secondly, there is technique. Macho males lash out miles of line and, in doing so, often lose contact with their flies. The ladies fish near and dear, dancing out their cast barely a couple of rod lengths' distance from the boat. Mrs Kelly sat on the bottom of the boat, at the bow, flicking a short line over the gunnel. It was deadly.

Over the years, I have come to accept the fact that, invariably, Ann is going to catch more fish than I do. I may not enjoy it, but there is little I can do. At times, however, it is hard to keep the fixed grin in place as she lands yet another trout to my none.

Hazel Pirie is another. I once saw her deliver a drubbing to her two male companions whilst sea-trout fishing on Loch Dionard in Sutherland. Both the men were experienced rods, Mark Bowler, editor of the magazine *Fly-Fishing and Fly-Tying*, and Adrian Latimer, who has been fishing for more than twenty-five years.

Hazel was a novice. At the end of the day, she had three sea-trout, the men none. On their second visit to the loch, the men suggested, less than tactfully I thought, that Hazel should bank fish, thus giving them more space in the boat to properly attack. "Keep your rotten boat, then," Hazel exclaimed. "See if I care." She caught two fish from the shore. Mark and Adrian? Nothing.

On these facts I rest my case: one woman angler is far more effective and efficient than any ten men. If this be error and upon me proved, I will eat my landing net.

57.
The Happy Strath

Strath Halladale is a happy place, unlike neighbouring Strathnaver to the west, where memories of the Sutherland Clearances overshadow every stick and stone. In the early years of the nineteenth century, 2,000 people were ruthlessly evicted from Strathnaver to make way for sheep. The River Naver may be a more illustrious salmon fishery than the Halladale but I always think of the Naver as being a river of a thousand tears. In my mind's eye I see flames enveloping the thatch-roofed township houses and hear the sound of women and children weeping, the harsh commands of the factor and his officers destroying a centuries-old way of life, distraught families trekking north to an uncertain future.

The River Halladale rises from the heights of Cnoc nam Bo Riabhach (373m) to the south of Forsinard and flows due north for twenty-two miles to reach the sea through the golden sands of Melvich Beach. Access to the river is easy, the whole length being bordered by the A897 Helmsdale to Melvich road. The most productive part of the river is the lower eight miles, divided into four beats which rotate daily, each fishing three rods when the water is suitable.

Beats are numbered south to north: Beat 1 from above the road bridge at Bunahoun to Harper's Pool at Craigtown; Beat 2 from MacBeath's Pool downstream to Lady Bighouse Pool at Achlemore. Beat 3 from Munro's Pool to Connagill; Beat 4 is from Connagill through the canal section to above Halladale Bridge on the A836 Thurso/Bettyhill road.

The season is from 12 January until 30 September and salmon average 10lb, grilse 6lb. However, much heavier fish are frequently taken and the heaviest salmon of recent years weighed 23lb. Although few fish are taken in January, the Halladale can provide excellent spring sport. These fish give a splendid account of themselves in this narrow stream and are a joy to catch. My first Halladale spring salmon came from the Weedy Pool on Beat 4 in 1979 and although it weighed only 5lb I can still feel the ache in my arms from playing it. Even nicer was the fact that I hooked it a moment before my son arrived on the riverbank and he was thus able to land it for his "aged parent".

When water levels are low in the river, I head in a different direction, to the surrounding hills with their superb wild brown trout lochs. There are a number in the heart of the Flow Country, Sletill, Leir, Lochan nan Clach Geala and Talaheel, but these waters, for me at least, have been forever ruined by factory tree-farming. However, to the north of the strath, in the hills on the east side of the river, there are three first-class lochs which are always worth a visit when salmon action is slow. They are Loch na Caorach and its neighbour, Loch na Seilge (pronounced "Shalag"), and little Loch Akran.

The first two hold splendid trout which average 14oz in weight. The latter,

Loch Akran, is a beginners' paradise, packed with bright little red-spotted fish which take virtually any fly on request. On the west side lie two other lochs which are rarely fished and which can offer outstanding sport: Loch na h-Eaglaise Mor and Loch na h-Eaglaise Beag. Don't miss them.

But when conditions are right on the river, there are few finer places to fish in all of Scotland. There are fifty principal pools, but in high water the runs in between can all hold salmon. The river is highly user-friendly and wading is not really required. A ten- to twelve-foot rod will cope with most eventualities and the river is strictly fly only. The patterns of fly which do most damage include: Garry Dog, Willie Gunn, Stoat's Tail, Silver Stoat's Tail, Black Doctor, Hairy Mary, Shrimp patterns and Waddingtons-various.

Size will depend upon water height and a floating line is the most useful means of presenting them. Everyone has their favourite pools and mine include the Bridge Pool at Birchwood, the falls at Forsil Pool by Culfern and the pools in the rocky, high-sided gorge by Achlemore: Gorkill, Upper Hut, Lower Hut and Lady Bighouse.

Finally, if you are "blessed" with non-fishing companions, they will find plenty in Strath Halladale and its airts to keep them thoroughly amused whilst you fish. The yellow sands of Melvich Bay are ideal for the bucket-and-spade brigade. Reay Golf Course, a fine, traditional Scottish links course, is a few minutes' drive east beyond the Split Stane into Caithness.

The Split Stane stands on the north side of the main road to Thurso, cleaved by the Devil's sword as he chased a young woman. This stone marks the old boundary between Caithness and Sutherland. South down Strath Halladale to Helmsdale will bring your non-piscators to the delights of the award-winning Timespan Heritage Centre, which tells the story of these lands, including details of the great Kildonan gold rush of the nineteenth century.

But for me, the real treasure here lies in the clear waters of the River Halladale, in its silver salmon and sea-trout, and in the golden trout which inhabit the moorland lochs and lochans. Early booking is advised and there are well-furnished properties available for rental with or without fishing: the Netstore, a two-minute walk from Melvich Beach and accommodating six adults and two children; the Fishery Cottage, also close to Melvich Beach, which sleeps four; and Riversdie Cottage at Forsinain.

Charges for both accommodation and fishing are reasonable and for details you should contact Ms Audrey Imlach, Bunahoun, Forsinard, Strath Halladale, Sutherland, tel: 01641 571271. I guarantee that ten minutes after your arrival you will agree with me – Strath Halladale is a happy place.

58.
Leap Before You Look

Scotsmen easily jump vast distances. Our ankles are like coiled springs, the result of centuries of practice avoiding our enemies, and we wear the kilt because it gives our shanks freedom of movement in dangerous situations. Unlike loin-strangling breeches, the free-flowing kilt allows us to hurl ourselves unhindered over cavernous ravines. As our pursuers gape helplessly in awe at the sight of our manly nether regions in full flight, we escape by leaping the void.

The most famous "leaps" are tourist attractions: Randolph's Leap over the Findhorn near Relugas in Morayshire; the Soldier's Leap across the River Garry at Killiecrankie to the north of Pitlochry; and Macgregor's Leap over the River Lyon in Glen Lyon, a mile up the glen from the village of Fortingall, "the fort of the strangers". Visiting these chasms, I am astonished that anyone should have dared to jump them. But I suppose it's amazing what being pursued by a bayonet can make one do.

My wife Ann and I pondered these matters a few years ago as we stood on the edge of Macgregor's Leap, wisped by damp spray from the peat-stained river. "Listen," I said, "why don't you have a go? I will get down to the water's edge, count to three, then you jump and I will take a photograph. It will make a great shot." Of answer came there none, but I clambered down anyway. From below, the leap looked even more daunting – an empty space arched over a raging torrent. Clearly an invitation to disaster.

Find the River Lyon on OS Map 51, Loch Tay, second series, Scale 1:50,000. Macgregor's Leap is at Gd ref: 727476. There is no signpost but the location is obvious. Park off the road on the grass verge and follow the sound of the stream to find the north side of the Leap.

Glen Lyon is the heartland of Clan Gregor and they were known as "the children of the mist"; so-called because of their astonishing ability to nip out of said mist to remove anything not securely nailed down and then disappear back faster than anyone could mutter "mayhem".

In 1603, James VI, safely ensconced on the throne of England, decided to sort out his misty children once and for all. An Act was passed authorising "the extermination of that wicked, unhappy race of lawless lymmaris, callit the MacGregor". The clan was hunted like animals – men summarily shot, women branded and their children sold off as slaves and cattle boys to Lowland and Irish farmers.

In the fourteenth century, the inhabitants of Glen Lyon were even less fortunate: the Black Death, bubonic plague, killed them all. They lie buried at Fortingall where a tall stone in a field marks their resting place. Close by, in the churchyard, is the 3,000-year-old yew tree, reputed to be the most ancient tree in Europe, alive and well when Pontius Pilate was allegedly born at Fortingall.

The River Lyon is born as the Alit Mhic Bhaidein burn on the west shoulder of Creag Mhor (1032m) to the north of Tyndrum in Argyll. The headwaters of the stream have been impounded for hydro-electric power generation purposes, thus forming Loch Lyon. After leaving Loch Lyon, the river flows east down Glen Lyon for a distance of some thirty miles before joining the Tay, two miles downstream from the village of Kenmore.

Fewer salmon are taken now than in pre-hydro-electric days, but the river can still produce salmon of up to and over 20lb in weight. The Lyon is also noted as a brown trout fishery. The best of the salmon fishing is in the first six miles of the stream. Fish are held in the lower river by the steep-sided, wooded gorge above Fortingall, which acts as a temperature pool. Salmon rarely reach the upper beats until April and, depending upon the severity of the winter, sometimes not until May.

There are sixty pools on the river and many of them named by Peter Dewar (of Dewar's Whisky) who fished the river during the middle years of the last century. Some of the most productive pools are: Junction Pool, Limekilns, Suspension Bridge Pool, Peter's Pool, Weaver's Pool (near Macgregor's Leap), Rock Pool, Invervar Bridge Pool, Still Waters, Roro Bridge Pool, Lower Wall and Wall Pool.

The river can be comfortably fished from the bank. When fishing Platform Pool it is helpful to have a fellow angler "spot" the fish for you from the opposite bank. The wooden platform that gives the pool its name is unsafe and should be avoided. The upper river, Chesthill, Invervar, Innerwick and Meggerine, is easily covered using a twelve-foot rod and in low water conditions, a trout rod would be more appropriate.

The river was in full spate when we visited and the peat-stained flood reminded me of the golden glow that radiates from a glass sparkling with uisge beatha, the water of life, and of a famous story about Tommy Dewar when visiting America to promote the Dewar brand. At a prestigious gathering of the great and good, Tommy was introduced to "Mrs Porter-Porter, with a hyphen", to which he responded, "And my name is Dewar Dewar, with a siphon."

As we turned to leave Macgregor's Leap and the white-foamed river, Ann stopped and said to me: "If you are so keen to see someone perform that long-jump, why don't you do it? Not scared are we?"

"Not at all," I lied. "Under other circumstances, I would not hesitate."

"So why not today then?" she asked.

"I should have thought that was obvious," I retorted, "I am not wearing the kilt."

59.
New Year's Day

This is the time of year to be resolute. Time to dredge up our deep-rooted sins for their annual inspection. Each year I stolidly resolve to give up the same things: smoking, strong drink and eating too much. Each year I seriously resolve to start doing the same things: brisk walking, home improvements, gardening and being nice to Ann's animals – Hareton, her dastardly Yorkshire terrier with the hideous white-toothed grin, and her demanding, clawing cats, Sam, Nelson and Archie.

I picture myself, after a few months of strict resolve, fleet of foot, bright of eye, lithe and lightsome, springing sprightly up some sheer-faced mountainside without a cough or a splutter. I see the smile on the face of my better half as I hurtle daily down the hill to collect the mail and the papers from the village post office; a regularly washed, shining-bright car; fresh wallpaper in the lounge. I share her joy as the nimble fingers of my left hand wrestle with garden weeds whilst my right hand applies a dripping paintbrush to our cottage wall.

Sadly, however, my thoughts invariably speak a whole lot louder than my deeds, in spite of all good intent. Come February, or maybe in a good year March, I am back to the old, dissolute ways. I light up, drink up, eat up, slouch about and, when she is not looking, shout at the animals. I try to console myself with the assurance that the really important thing is to try to be aware of one's little foibles and that it truly is the thought that counts. But it doesn't work.

I also invariably resolve to be much kinder to my fishing tackle. Refurbish rods, strip the lines from my reels and carefully dry, polish and oil them. Mend the hole in the landing net and weed out all the rusty, featherless hooks from my fly boxes. Remove that Willie Gunn which has been deeply embedded in the back of my fishing jacket for the past three seasons. Life is, after all, simply a question of priorities and, as every angler will confirm, our precious tackle comes before all else. Well, it should.

I also resolve to be tidy. Rather than just dumping everything in a corner of the garage when I return from a fishing expedition, this year I will be the soul of neatness. Waders unwrinkled and properly suspended. Wet jacket and hat hung up to dry. The remains of the picnic dumped in the bin and not left to rot in my fishing bag. Bits of nylon and tangled casts safely destroyed. A place for everything and everything in its place. I might even construct that rod rack I have been planning to build for at least a decade.

In days past I used to blame the children for the disaster area that is generally known as my fishing tackle. All four of them fished and frequently with my tackle. I was convinced that they were the most untidy, inconsiderate bunch of humans ever to fankle flies. They, not I, were responsible for the mess. I reasoned that once they had gone, "things" would be a whole lot different. Well they have gone and "things" are a whole lot different. If anything they are worse.

My most dangerous habit – well one of them, as anyone who has had the misfortune to borrow my fishing jacket will confirm – is biting off flies from the cast and simply stuffing them into the first available pocket. By the end of the season my fly boxes are near empty and my pockets full. Pulling out a hankie can shower people for miles around with killer patterns, other than the dozen or so stuck into their fingers.

When my children visit us, they stand and stare at the heap in the garage shaking their heads in disbelief, poking about among the broken Thermos flasks, rusted reels and sopping boots, half-eaten sandwiches and squashed, dripping beer cans. "How do you do it, dad?" they inquire with undisguised awe. "Are you not ashamed? You are supposed to set us an example. How can you find anything in that junk-yard?"

"Everything is essential," I plead.

"Yeah," they reply, "like half a ham sandwich, six empty nylon spools, a bottle of Mucelin circa 1969, rusty pliers, ten yards of binder twine, a mouse-gnawed chocolate biscuit, and, look at this, dad, your driving licence!" I wondered where it had gone.

Therefore, and before the New Year is a day older, I resolve to sort it all out and to keep it neat and tidy for ever and ever amen. Never again will anybody be able to criticise. This will be the "Year of the Vastly Improved Sandison": tidy, fastidious, organised and in complete control. I might even become smug about it, conducting parties round the garage to marvel at my orderliness, modestly pretending that it has always been thus.

I will write out my resolutions on a clean sheet of white paper and put it by my desk. Every time I sit down to work, there it will be, to remind me of all the benefits that will accrue through my strict compliance to the injunctions on the list. In no time at all, I will be the man that I have always wanted to be: upright, sober, conscientious, supremely fit in body and mind.

The only trouble is that it is snowing just now and a howling Arctic gale is battering our cottage. And there is no heating in the garage. And I have a cold. Otherwise, you understand, I would not hesitate for a moment. I would be out there and in among that pile of tackle in the corner of the garage quicker than you could mutter Ke-He. Honest?

60.
Big Alisdair's Loch

Lochindorb lies seven miles north-east from Grantown-on-Spey astride desolate Dava Moor, glowered over by the mighty Cairngorm mountains, unseen from the busy A939 Grantown/Nairn road. The name means "loch of trouble". But not for anglers, because Lochindorb is the ideal place to introduce beginners to the gentle art of fly-fishing, or to restore one's own angling self-confidence.

Lochindorb gained the "troublesome" reputation because of its association with the great and mighty. Or rather, great and nasty, dependent upon your historical point of view. An important castle stood on the small man-made island at the north end and, in Scotland, where there is a castle, there was invariably trouble. Edward I, the "Hammer of the Scots", paid Lochindornb a social call in 1303 whilst quelling yet another rebellion of his unwilling, surrogate subjects. After spreading death and disaster over a wide area of Moray, he relaxed at Lochindorb, no doubt doing a bit of fishing whilst enjoying the view. Before he left, he gave instructions for the original keep to be enlarged to the status of a castle.

In due course, the castle on the island became the property of one of Scotland's most unprincipled villains, Alasdair Mor Mac an Righ, or "Big Alasdair" to his friends. He is better remembered in history as the Wolf of Badenoch, the natural son of King Robert II. His peers regarded big Alasdair as a monster – which was saying something in lawless, fourteenth-century Scotland, when anything not firmly nailed down was considered fair game by all. Going to bed safely at night then was no guarantee of a safe awakening the following morning.

Having married the Countess of Ross for her rich lands, rather than for her beauty, Alasdair deserted her when he discovered that the lady's family had excluded said rich lands from the marriage agreement. The Countess appealed to the Bishop of Moray for redress and that unhappy prelate made the mistake of finding in the Countess's favour. The Wolf responded by stealing large chunks of the Bishop's property and was immediately excommunicated by the outraged prelate. Big Alasdair therefore decided to "re-educate" the Bishop.

The Wolf paid a late-night call on the towns of Forres and Elgin, doing what he did best, burning, rape and pillage, including the destruction of one of the most beautiful places of worship in Europe, Elgin Cathedral. The affair eventually ended with the Wolf on his knees doing public penance before the Scottish court, which had been assembled for that purpose at the front door of the Church of the Blackfriars in Perth. But the Countess never got a single penny and Badenoch continued to live with his mistress who bore him five lusty sons. Big Alasdair died, not much mourned, in 1405, it is said after losing a game of chess with the Devil at another of his "lairs", Ruthven Castle on the banks of the River Spey.

It would be a poor day indeed if this lovely Highland water sent you home empty-handed. Even the biggest duffers in the world, and I include myself in that luckless brigade, should catch their fair share. The loch is full of small, brightly-marked brown trout which average just under 8oz in weight. They give great sport and you should manage at least a brace or two. Perfect for breakfast, dressed in oatmeal and fried – the trout that is, not the piscator.

There are larger fish in Lochindorb, so treat every rise with caution and respect. Trout of over 6lb have been caught here in the recent past. Fish rise and are taken all over the loch and no one place is essentially better than another. The loch is generally shallow, two miles in length by up to half a mile wide. A minor road margins the east bank and the west bank may be accessed by a track leading round the north shore to Terriemore Farm. Boat fishing brings the best results and my favourite drift is down the east shore past Lochindorb Lodge, but the west bank, south from Terriemore Farm to the first promontory, where a feeder burn enters from Carn Bad Churaich (409m), can also give excellent results.

The ruins of Lochindorb Castle, with its infamous water dungeon, can still be seen on the small island, entangled in bramble and birch trees. Those consigned to the dungeon swam and sank; the pit was filled with sufficient water to ensure that the occupant could not sit down. I never cast a fly by the shore of the island without thinking of the self-seeking wild Wolf, sitting in the great hall, plotting his revenge on his unfortunate wife and the hapless Bishop of Moray.

Plotting the downfall of the loch's trout is less taxing and damaging, at least to human life and limb. Or should be. One autumn day, Ann and I were fishing Lochindorb when the wind rose suddenly to gale force. Flinging both fishing rods to Ann, I grabbed the oars and began to struggle back, across the wind, to the mooring bay. As we neared safety, two fish grabbed our flies, which had been left trailing behind the boat, one trout on each cast. In a flurry of lines and hot cursing, anxious not to lose the fish, rods were passed from hand to hand and, in the heat of the moment, the boat grounded in the shallows and tilted sideways.

I slid out, in slow motion, and found myself sitting up to the waist in the cold waters of the loch. Wet is wet, so I dragged the boat ashore and, dripping, reeled in. Firmly attached to a size 14 Silver Butcher was a good trout of 1lb. The other fish had long since gone. "Thank you, Bruce" said Ann, leaping nimbly ashore. "Let me have the rod and I will land it." I considered, momentarily, open rebellion, but wisely did as told. In these circumstances, even Big Alasdair himself would never have dared to argue with Ann.

Boats are no longer available on the loch, but the bank fishing is still as good and it is free – no permit required.

61.
First Loss

I first committed the sin of angling on Tweed and I lost my first salmon in the pool below Coo Ford upstream from Innerleithen. My elder brother and I were staying in a flat in the village, he to study for exams whilst I attended to a boy's proper function in life, the removal of fish from their natural habitat.

Autumn sunlight sparkled as the stream swept through a narrow neck into a slow, deep pool. I was fishing for trout, using a light rod with small flies. When my line stopped I thought that my fly had snagged on an underwater obstruction. I inched forward to retrieve it. Both Wellington boots filled with water. I tugged, tentatively, in order to save the fly. Flies cost money and I could ill afford to lose one.

Peering into the depths, my heart stopped when I saw the shape of a huge salmon, its sail-like tail moving gently from side to side and my fly, a Silver Butcher, firmly attached to its great jaw. As far as I could make out, the fish didn't realise that anything was amiss but I was consumed with fear and excitement. If only I could land the salmon, I thought, I would never complain about anything again for the rest of my life.

The salmon and I were locked together. If I moved forward, it sidled away. My rod was arched in anger, the thin line taught. I applied more pressure. The fish shook its head. I stopped, terrified that the line would break. I decided that my only chance would be to try to "walk" the salmon into shallow water. If I succeeded, I had decided that I would throw myself on it and trust to luck that I could wrestle it ashore.

After my second step, the salmon became aware of danger. With a mighty swish of its tail, it roared upstream. The line burned my fingers as the reel screamed. I saw the fish once more as it leapt from the water, crystal droplets flying from its silver shoulders. My line broke and I tumbled backwards into the shallows. Dragging myself ashore, I wept, tears pouring down my face. My brother had come to look for me and asked what was wrong.

"I've lost a salmon," I replied.

"Is that all?" he said. "Come on, supper's ready."

Tweed, "the Queen of Scottish rivers", has ensnared my soul for as long as I can remember. The scent and sound of the stream comforts me no matter where I go. When I joined the Army, on journeys south from Edinburgh to London, I would bid a sad farewell to the river as the train rumbled over Border Bridge at Berwick. On returning, no matter what time of day or night I passed, I would hang out of the window to catch a glimpse of Tweed. Seeing the river meant that I really had come home.

Now, after so many years of confusion and diminishing numbers of fish, I read with joy and happiness that Tweed salmon are back in force and that the river is returning to its former glory. Tweed is, in my view, not only Scotland's most important river, but also a strategic indicator of the state of the Scottish nation. If Tweed is healthy, then all must be well in the land God gave to Jock Tamson's Bairns.

Tweed is born amongst the barren moorlands surrounding Tweed's Wells, south from Moffat. It flows eastwards for 100 miles through salmon beats synonymous with all that is best in fishing: past the grandeur of Sir Walter Scott's home at Abbotsford; through the Junction Pool where Tweed meets Teviot; by Sprouston where Canon William Greenwell plied his incomparable trout fly, the Greenwell's Glory, tied by Tweed's most famous fly-tyer, James Wright; through the deep pool at Ladykirk where King James IV nearly drowned in 1500; gathering in the waters from almost 2,000 square miles to deliver them to the grey North Sea at Berwick.

I now live and work in North Sutherland, but a part of me will always remain by Tweed. It holds precious memories. My future wife and I fished a tributary of Tweed, Lyne Water, a few miles apart, when we were children, although it was six years before we met and married and started our own fishing club; all our children were introduced to Tweed and fly-fishing almost as soon as they could walk. I have fond thoughts of Mr Fraser, a dour Aberdonian and Tweed bailiff, appearing as if from nowhere on his ancient bike and calling across the river through the gloaming, "Have you got your permit, lad?"

"Yes, Mr Fraser!" I would shout back, although I can't remember him ever holding it in his hands.

But for me, Tweed had always been more about brown trout fishing than chasing *Salmo salar*, the King of Fish. Days spent on the river seemed endless when I was a boy, the space between unbridled happiness and the stern discipline of school; of triumphs, fishing close to the bank after a spate with a cast made up out of single strands of horse hair and a tiny Greenwell's Glory and catching half a dozen trout; singing "He Shall Feed his Flock" from Handel's "Messiah" whilst fishing downstream from Manor Bridge and taking trout as long as I kept on singing; friends met and made on the river bank.

I taught my father to fish. He never did much damage to the fish because he found it hard to take advice. If dad saw a fish rise he would stay, rooted to the spot, casting again and again over it in the firm belief that the fish would eventually surrender and take his fly. It never did. I see him now, in my mind's eye, as light faded, in the middle of the river, completely oblivious to every worldly care and enjoying every moment he spent in the embrace of "My Lady Tweed". Should such a joy as this be a sin, then I have no regrets whatsoever about pleading guilty to committing it.

62.
Relaxing at Rhiconich

Anglers relaxing at the Rhiconich Hotel in North West Sutherland have more than 100 trout lochs and a spate salmon stream awaiting their pleasure. Whilst hotel guests have priority, it is virtually certain that casual visitors will also be found fishing. The nine principal lochs have boats whilst the others are all fished from the bank. Fishing is by fly only and trout average 8–12oz in weight with a few specimens of up to and over 2lb.

Each season produces approximately 1,000 trout, most of which are returned to fight another day. Salmon and sea-trout stocks have been decimated by sea lice from factory salmon farms but a few are still taken most seasons, principally from Loch Gharbet Beag. Productive trout flies include Ke-He, Black Zulu, Blue Zulu, Black Pennell, Grouse & Claret, Greenwell's Glory, March Brown, Soldier Palmer and Silver Butcher. For salmon and sea-trout, use Stoat's Tail, Hairy Mary, Silver Doctor, Black Pennell, Soldier Palmer and Connemara Black.

Clan Sandison first discovered this amazing anglers' paradise during the early 1970s. Since then, we have spent endless, memorable days tramping the moorlands and mountains of North West Sutherland. Everything that makes Scottish trout fishing special can be found here: solitude, peace and serenity; outstanding flora and fauna, and a dramatic landscape that has lain largely unchanged since the end of the last Ice Age 8,000 years ago.

Another irresistible attraction is that there is so much for non-anglers to do and see. Little ones can bucket-and-spade on the Oldshoremore beaches. The most northerly UK mainland golf course is a few miles away at Durness. The nature reserve and bird sanctuary of Handa Island is easily accessible and the long ridge of Foinaven (908m) demands to be climbed.

Narrow Crocach is the largest loch to the west of Rhiconich. It lies like a silver and blue butterfly on the moor, one mile long by up to half a mile wide. Four islands guard the approach to the western arm and the channel between the south shore and these islands is a favourite drift – although, in truth, fish may be caught virtually anywhere throughout the length and breadth of this fine water.

The loch is reached from the Ardmore road. Park at the end of the road and follow the well-made path for ten minutes. A step north brings you to the south end of the loch were the boat is moored. Crocach is best fished from the boat. This makes it a whole lot easier to visit the surrounding lochs, such as Loch a'Phreasan Chailitean, Loch Eileanach and little Lochan na Cloiche.

To the south of the Ardmore road is Loch Skerricha, draining into the head of sea Loch a'Chadh-Fi. This used to be a decent sea-trout water and could still be home to a few salmon. The boat is moored at the east end and you should concentrate your efforts along the high cliff on the south-west shore. The loch becomes weedy as the season advances and is best fished in June and early July. If action is slow on Skerricha, decamp and bank fish the unnamed lochan to the north. It has good brown trout.

Some of the largest fish are taken from Loch na Thull, to the south of Rhiconich where there is also a boat. This water has been spoiled for me by the introduction of smolt-rearing cages at the west end. Far more pleasant and exciting is to wander out to Loch na Claise Carnaich, a place of simply stunning beauty overshadowed by the long grey shoulder of Cean Garbh, the most northerly peak of Foinaven. The tiny lochans surrounding Claise Carnaich also provide sport and you need at least a week to properly explore them all. There is a boat on the main water and on Lochan Cul na Creige, the others are easily fished from the shore.

The last time my wife, Ann, and I passed this way we were en route for the summit of Foinaven and paused for a cup of coffee where the Allt na Claise Carnaich burn tumbles into Claise Carnaich. It was a warm, calm morning and the whole surface of the loch was stippled with the rings of rising trout. It is a tiresome haul up the unrelentingly steep shoulder of Creag na Claise Carnaich and by the time we reached Ceann Garbh we were in the clouds. We continued south to climb the final slope to Gaun Mor, the high point of Foinaven.

The clouds lifted and we were rewarded with a spectacular vista. To the north we looked down into Strath Dionard and the silver ribbon of the River Dionard. Westwards we caught a glimpse of the Heather Isle of Lewis in the Outer Hebrides. South lay the Trotternish Ridge on Skye and the mountains of the Fisherfield Forest in Wester Ross. If you want to appreciate all North West Sutherland has to offer, make the pilgrimage to the top of Gaun Mor, a prize beyond compare.

Also a prize beyond compare is a day out on Loch Gharbet Beag. Walk down to the Rhiconich River from the hotel. There is a good, though muddy, track by the side of the stream. The river can produce sport with migratory fish but only after heavy rain. Gharbet Beag is just over one mile in length, pinched into an hourglass shape by narrows. The loch is generally shallow but, at the narrows, may be ten feet or more deep in high water. This is where most salmon are encountered. Other noted lies are the Minister's Burn and Black Point on the east shore, the Tail of the Loch and Green Point on the west shore.

For further information and details, including the rental of Oldshoremore Lodge (self-catering), contact the Rhiconich Hotel, Sutherland IV27 4NR, tel: 01971 521224, fax: 01971 521732, email: info@rhiconichhotel.co.uk website: www.rhiconichhotel.co.uk.

63.
Somebody's Got to Do It

Work is for poor unfortunates who can't fish. The luckiest of all people are those who manage to combine both. Thomas Tod Stoddart (1810–80), for instance, was a famous Tweed fisherman, poet, traveller and author of *The Art of Angling as Practised in Scotland*. Tom was also a lawyer but he rarely indulged himself in that profession. He was once accosted by a local magistrate who asked him what he was doing with himself these days. Outraged, Tom roared: "Doing, man? What do you mean doing? I'm an angler."

I fall into a similar category. But even though I have been writing for more than twenty years, concerned neighbours still stop my wife, Ann, and inquire:

"Oh, Mrs Sandison, has your man got a job yet or is he still writing?" Worse, I am often congratulated by complete strangers for penning some of the greatest angling fiction ever produced in Scotland – just because my hopeful predictions about what they may or may not catch fail to live up to their expectations. A sad truth about fishermen is that when they are successful, it is all down to their own superlative skill, but when they come home empty-handed, it is their gillies' fault.

Expectation, of course, is what fishing is all about. Expectation and the sure and certain knowledge that by the end of the day we will have caught our fair share, be it but a single small brown trout or a monster to fill that ever-ready glass case above the mantelpiece. At least, that is our firm belief when we first cast in the morning, the motivation that propels us irresistibly through the fishing day. If the fates are unkind and we catch nothing, then we know that there is always tomorrow, or the next day, a time when we will undoubtedly cover ourselves in piscatorial glory. Maybe.

One place is Scotland where angling dreams can come true is Elphin in Sutherland. This is an area of untamed beauty, dominated by magnificent peaks: Ben More Assynt, Conival, Canisp, Suilven, Quinag, Cul Mor, Cul Beag and graceful Stac Pollaidh. The rivers Inver and Kirkaig offer sport with salmon and sea-trout and the surrounding lochs, Assynt, Awe, Cam Veyatie and Sionascaig, offer outstanding action with wild brown trout and monster ferox. A few years ago, Willie Morrison, then owner of the Inchnadamph Hotel, showed me a fine basket of ferox from Loch Assynt: three fish weighing 22lb, the heaviest of which tipped the scales at 10lb 8oz. I also have reports of ferox from Sionascaig that weighed over 17lb.

But for me, the real joy of this area lies not in the dark depths of vast lochs or sparkling rivers, but in the myriad hill lochs which carpet this ancient landscape in a shining array of silver and blue. Virtually all of this fishing is readily available, at very modest cost, to visiting anglers. Thanks to the good offices of the Assynt Estate and the local angling club, you could, if you wish, fish different waters every day for several seasons. All that is required is proper permission, stout walking boots, a compass and map, and a willing spirit. If anybody tells me to "get lost", I instantly head for Assynt, the light of angling battle glinting in my eye.

One water here, Loch Urigill, deserves special mention. It is the ideal place to introduce beginners to the gentle art of fly-fishing. As sure as night follows the other thing and summer spring, they will catch fish; and, having done so, will be embraced forever by the welcoming, comforting arms of the "brotherhood of the angle". Loch Urigill is shallow, just under two miles long by up to about three-quarters of a mile wide, and lies on the northern skirts of the Cromalt Hills.

June and July produce a splendid mayfly hatch and this is the best time to launch your assault. Boat fishing is most productive and blank days are rare. The trout are of modest size, averaging in the order of 10oz, but good numbers of larger specimens are taken most seasons. Dapping works well and the favourite pattern of dapping fly is the Loch Ordie. There are also ferox trout in Urigill and those Ice Age descendants can at times be tempted using the old Scottish angling method of trolling.

There is a lifetime's fishing around Elphin and Assynt. This wonderland has provided me with some of my most enduring angling memories. I have fished in allegedly more exotic locations, from Patagonia to Finland, but the sudden shock of seeing Canisp, Suilven and Assynt as you drive down the hill to Ledmore Junction is, for me, a gateway to paradise. However, spare me a thought as you net another red-speckled trout from Urigill or stride splendidly across grey, scree-scattered slopes. The more I write about fishing, the less time I have to fish. Yes, indeed, work is for poor unfortunates who can't fish.

64.
Caring for the Inner Angler

Cold, curried-beef sandwiches are bad news in a packed lunch. It happened to me one sharp spring day while fishing Loch Awe and ever since I have investigated each slice before the first bite. I suppose it depends upon your attitude towards food; you may be the sort of angler who considers a break for lunch as only so much wasted fishing time. However, I like my nosh, and have a very healthy respect for the needs of the inner man.

Just because one is out in the hills, or in the middle of a loch, is no reason for lowering standards. It is perfectly easy to make the lunch at least as interesting and exciting as the fishing. In this regard, I suppose I'm luckier than most because my wife, Ann, also fishes and applies the same care and attention to the preparation of lunch as she does to casting a neat fly, on a short line, to a rising trout. Over the years we have developed a pattern and have now got it down to a fine art. Lunch is, fishless or otherwise, something that I always look forward to.

For many years we lived close to Tweed. If non-fishing friends visited us, particularly those from south of Mr Hadrian's Wall, we would prepare a special picnic and take them to our favourite spot on the banks of the river. It was in a proper wood, with beech, sycamore and oak, old and majestic, nodding over the stream. The way in was hard to find, as it seemed as though you were driving into a solid wall of hawthorn hedges. But the ground was hard and it was possible to take the car right into the wood.

This little haven was a sheltered garden, full of bluebells, primroses, eyebright and wood sorrel and a warm, sunny day, a gentle breeze and rising trout soon persuaded our guests that fly-fishing was the most rewarding and exciting of all pastimes. Lunch sealed the bargain: melon, game soup, cold chicken, Greek salad, strawberries and cream, washed down with ice-cold Riesling; the sound of the wind in the ancient trees, the murmur of Elgar on an old battery-operated gramophone. Our companions didn't stand a chance – they became anglers.

Before we were married, we used to fish Portmore Loch, south of Edinburgh. It was exceedingly dour and fish were few and far between. But a good bottle of wine and huge, French-style sandwiches encouraged one mightily. At that time we often fished with friends who used to come through from Glasgow for the day and we took turn-about in producing lunch. There was only one rule: that the wine had to cost no more than 15s 6d a bottle.

Our source of all things excellent in wine and food in those days was Messrs Valvona and Corolla, Elm Row, Edinburgh. It was, and still is, an Aladdin's cave of culinary delight where nothing is ever too much trouble and every purchase, regardless of the amount of money involved, is treated with the utmost courtesy, interest and consideration. Producing an interesting picnic or packed lunch is really only a question of pre-planning, which is why my Ann does it. I make grunting, encouraging noises when asked for advice but have long learned that my most useful course is to keep out of the way and attend only to the tackle and transportation, and the drinks. I'm quite good at that.

One of our finest lunches occurred a few years ago when we had taken two friends out for a day's fishing, their first ever such adventure. The loch we proposed to fish involved a stiff walk over the moor in Strath Halladale, Sutherland. Our northern moors are bog-filled and soggy and it was a hot day. When we arrived at the loch, our companions were tired and weary and not persuaded that fishing was all that we had claimed.

We settled upon a grassy bank and, moments later, I handed out their favourite tipple: one large Campari and soda with ice and lemon and a similarly adorned gin and tonic. Instant good humour. Lunch was avocado pears with lumpfish-roe filling, turtle soup with sherry, chicken legs, lamb cutlets, salad, cheese, celery and biscuits and piping-hot coffee. Wines on offer were Chablis and Beaujolais. The day's fishing produced fifteen trout and our guests caught four each. The biggest fish weighed 2lb and it was a perfect day.

I wouldn't like you to get the idea that we always eat like that when we go fishing. We couldn't afford it, for one thing, but we do try to avoid the standard recipe for indigestion so beloved by many of the supposed fishing hotels that snare the eager angler: curled sandwiches, a chocolate biscuit and an apple or orange. There are few things more soul-destroying after a hard morning lashing away in the pouring rain than to be confronted at lunchtime with shrivelled hunks of cheese-filled bread and lukewarm coffee.

Over the years, it has given us just as much pleasure to be able to produce a really first-class picnic, miles from anywhere, as it has given us to see our friends catch their first wild brown trout. Nevertheless, some of the most memorable meals that Ann and I have enjoyed have been prepared from the simplest and most readily available of ingredients. What can compare with the delight of freshly caught trout, cooked in the embers of a lochside fire? When all else fails, that's what we go for.

65.
Leith It to Me

I once met an angler who fished six days a week, April to September. After all, he told me, "What is retirement for if it is not for fishing?" He walks from his home to the river in waders carrying his rod and angling gear. Strictly a dry-fly man, he uses size 20–22 flies and a 7ft 6in split-cane rod.

How much do you think all this fishing costs him? The answer is not a single penny. His river is the Water of Leith in Edinburgh, one of Scotland's best-kept angling secrets, twenty-three miles in length from its source in Pentland Hills to the sea in the Firth of Forth.

Permission to fish the stream is freely given. All you need is a permit. The bag limit is six trout per rod per day and the size limit is eight inches. The upper half of the river is fly only. From Slateford Bridge down to the mouth of the river at Leith Docks, fly or bait fishing is allowed.

I was born and brought up in Auld Reekie, Scotland's capital city, and the Water of Leith was my playground. Even then, in the early 19– . . . well, not yesterday . . . brown trout dimpled the surface of the stream. I used to visit a small garden at Canonmills that overlooked the river and this is where I saw my first ever brown trout rising to a fly.

Bonnington Mill and Powderhall, where the river is sluggish, was also a favourite boyhood haunt of mine. *Chariots of Fire* star runner, Eric Liddell, won major events at Powderhall Stadium in 1922. Me, I nearly drowned there hunting for a coot's nest and dangling bread stuck on a bent pin to try to tempt trout.

My rod was a garden cane, my line a piece of string filched from father's shed. In later years, once I had graduated to a proper rod and could afford to buy a fly, I fished the upper reaches, near Balerno. The Leith is tiny here and considerable skill must be employed if you are to have any hope of catching breakfast.

The late Dr Graham Priestly of the Water of Leith Conservation Trust had long links with the river. He held the position of High Bailiff and until the end of his fishing days was an Honorary Bailiff. The origin of the title High Bailiff is unknown, but Edinburgh City archives include mention of "a Bailie of the Water of Leith" as far back as 1606 and the original Bailiffs may have been employed to collect rents from the mills alongside the stream.

The first mills on the river were established in the twelfth century when King David I granted the canons of Holyrood Abbey the right to build and operate them, hence the name Canonmills. By the end of the nineteenth century, there were more than eighty mills along the course of the river. Mill weirs impeded the progress of salmon and sea-trout whilst effluent from these mills and other sewage from city works effectively killed the water as a migratory fish system.

Since then, the mills have closed and a waste disposal system has been installed which bypasses the river. Consequently, water quality has improved enormously. Indeed, there are recent records of salmon and sea-trout returning to the river, although the weir at Dean Village is at present impassable to them and there are no alternative spawning areas on the lower river for them to use.

If you plan to fish, then the visitor centre at 24 Lanark Road is the best place to start. After obtaining your permit, wander round the exhibition. It might not help you catch trout, but it will certainly improve your enjoyment of the stream as you attempt to do so. Two publications are on sale here, both essential reading: *A Guide to the Water of Leith Walkway*, and *The Water of Leith*, a collection of essays by experts about the river and its environment.

I left the visitor centre and, after waiting an age for a break in the traffic, crossed the busy road. My friend greeted me on the other side, tackled up and anxious to be off. We walked up the right bank, past the site of Redhall Castle, knocked about a bit by Cromwell in 1650. George Inglis laid out the woodlands here during the eighteenth century and they are still splendid today, alive with the sound of birdsong and the scent of wild garlic.

The river is narrow, the banks tree-lined and an angling challenge. A good trout rose under the branches of a willow, as trout always do. I watched as my companion got to work. His casting skill was exemplary. A short line upstream, pinpoint accurate. The small March Brown slipped beneath the branches and covered the lie, but to no avail. Unfazed, he reeled in and we continued to the next pool.

I asked him why he loved the river so much. "It's not just the trout," he replied, "although there are plenty of them if you know where to look and how to catch them. Neither is it just because the river is within walking distance of my front door. It is much more. The river is so beautiful. At times, on a summer evening, the light arches down through the branches of the trees and builds a cathedral-like canopy over the pools. I have seen otters playing in the river. The Water of Leith is a small part of paradise."

For me, in philosophical terms, the Water of Leith divides anglers. I make no apology for using the word philosophical. Angling is not a sport, never has been and never will be, at least in my view. If you have little interest in history, flora and fauna or conservation, the Water of Leith is not for you. If you expect to catch lots of fish, head for a commercial put-and-take fishery.

But if you appreciate all the things I have mentioned, and welcome an angling challenge, the Water of Leith will test you to the utmost. I pondered these matters as I looked at the river in the Dean Village in the centre of Edinburgh. A young man cycled up and parked his bike by the railings. He tackled up and entered the stream: "Got the afternoon off," he said. The moment his fly landed on the water an accommodating trout grabbed.

For more information contact the Water of Leith Conservation Trust, 24 Lanark Road, Slateford, Edinburgh, tel: 0131 455 7367.

66.
Catch and Release

Many Scottish trout anglers are uncomfortable with a "catch and release" policy: once a fish has been caught, the hook is removed and the fish is then returned to the water to fight another day. The concept emanates from America, although some Scottish anglers operate a personal "catch and release" policy throughout much of their fishing lives.

Few American anglers kill the fish they catch, perhaps not as much from personal choice, but more because the USA fishery policy demands that virtually all fish must be returned. The state of Montana was first to introduce the concept and it has spread, not just throughout America, but throughout the world.

The purpose of the American approach is to preserve fish stocks and allow trout to re-establish themselves in waters that have become fishless: industrialisation, chemical farming, pollution, hydro-electric schemes and the predatory greed of man destroyed hundreds of miles of once-pristine trout waters. Many have been restored and America now has outstanding trout fishing.

Chile adopts a similar policy, designed to conserve wild fish stocks. Only three trout per angler may be killed each day and should you break this rule you could find yourself in prison. Argentina is moving in a similar direction, aware of the importance not only of preserving stocks of wild fish, but also of the importance of wild trout fishing to their rural economy.

The story is repeated throughout the world but not in Britain. Here, the pursuit of private profit is God. Having wiped out most of the wild fish in England and in the south of Scotland, owners have been allowed to introduce hatchery-reared, foreign species, particularly the ubiquitous North American rainbow trout. Rather than address over-fishing, the root cause of the problem, government and their fishery advisors have preferred to turn a blind eye.

Consequently, it is not unreasonable to suggest that within a few generations indigenous species of wild trout could entirely disappear from these islands. This is not crying wolf. Already, many of our major fisheries have become little other than sacrificial stew-ponds, often full of mis-shaped, sad trout that are a disgrace to both those who rear them and to those who fish for them.

The River Tweed is stocked with brown trout. Hatchery-reared trout from Kielder Reservoir in Northumberland are transported south to re-stock the famous chalk streams in England. The Lake of Menteith's water is stocked with 1,000 fish each week, bought in from various hatcheries throughout Britain. Loch Leven, once an international byword for quality brown trout, was for many years stocked with rainbow trout.

Put-and-take fisheries have bloomed throughout Scotland in recent years and may now even be found as far north as Bettyhill in Sutherland and near Halkirk in Caithness. It seems to me to be the height of idiocy to introduce stew-ponds to places where wild trout still reign supreme. The only reason for doing it must be commercial gain. But what of the people who patronise these places? Do they really imagine that hooking and landing a 5lb hatchery-reared rainbow trout is angling?

Fishing pressure is partly to blame. There are upwards of four million anglers in the UK and more take up the sport every year, particularly fly-fishing. Neither does the angling press help. Some fishing magazines promote the view that the only measure of piscatorial success lies in the size and weight of fish caught. Competition fishing compounds this problem and increases angling pressure. Therefore, in order to meet demand, waters are stocked.

Fishing has become a highly commercialised, multi-million-pound business and the price we are paying is the loss of native species, not only in connection with brown trout, but increasingly with salmon and sea-trout. As fish farm disease and pollution empty our rivers and lochs of wild fish, riparian owners clamour for permission to restock with hatchery-reared specimens.

It is the responsibility of the Scottish Government to reverse this cycle of decline and to protect and preserve Scotland's wild fish species, either through direct intervention or through the powers they invest in Scottish Natural Heritage, the Scottish Environment Protection Agency and salmon district fishery boards. Sadly, however, none of these bodies seems prepared to act to save our wild brown trout and salmon, generations of which have survived in our waters since the end of the last Ice Age, 8,000 years ago.

When my wife, Ann, and I were in Chile, managing a fishing lodge on Lago Yelcho, about 1,000 miles south from Santiago, most of our guests were Americans and happy with "catch and release". I believe that those who argue that a fish, once hooked and then released, will die anyway are misguided. During two periods of six months, fishing most days and releasing the majority of fish caught, I never once encountered a dead fish floating on the surface of any of our lakes.

The only trouble we had was from an English party, whom I can only describe as "fishmongers", rather than anglers. I explained our fishery policy to them when they arrived: everything goes back to the water other than those fish we need for the table. This news was greeted with less than enthusiasm and I anticipated some difficulty.

Two days later, it duly arrived when the party leader appeared in the kitchen. "Now look here, Ann," he exclaimed crossly, "we like eating fish. Fish for breakfast, lunch and supper, fish cakes, fish pie, poached fish, grilled fish, fricassée fish, fish curry and fish kedgeree. Is that all right with you?" It was all right with Ann, but I organised the fishing and briefed our local guides accordingly. I hope that the English party enjoyed their energy-giving soups and hearty beef and lamb lunches.

67.
Fishing Robinson Crusoe-style

Launching a boat that day was impossible. A summer storm raged across Lago Yelcho, howling out of the north from the ice fields and jagged peaks of the Cordillera de los Andes mountains. I was marooned on my island, Isla Monita, in Chilean Patagonia, 1,000 miles south from Chile's capital, Santiago, just as certainly as Robinson Crusoe had been marooned on his island, Mas a Tierra, 400 miles west from the old city of Valparaiso.

Isla Monita is owned by a group of men who love trout fishing. Which is where I came in. From Inverness on an icy November morning to the blistering heat of Patagonian summer. The owners had invited me to look after their lodge for six months. I flew Scotland's flag and wore my kilt for the journey. Nobody batted an eyelid in Inverness or London. A few smiled in Amsterdam. Sao Paulo in Brazil was an entirely different matter and at 0500hrs in Santiago I thought I was about to be arrested.

Isla Monita is a magical place to be marooned, ". . . full of noises, sounds and sweet airs, that give delight and hurt not". There is only one dwelling on the tree-covered isle and it was built in the 1960s, raised above the ground, timber-peaked with red-painted, overlapping wood tiles. All the construction materials had to be rowed down the 1,000-feet-deep lake from Puerto Cardenas in the north – a wicked, muscle-racking, twenty-two-mile haul, constantly exposed to the vagaries of wind and weather.

I had read Charles Darwin's description of the area in *The Voyage of the Beagle*, but nothing could have prepared me for the sudden shock of seeing for the first time the majestic, impenetrable Patagonia temperate rainforest: thousands of square miles of deciduous and coniferous trees, climbing from sea-level to cover mountain tops more than 7,000 feet in height.

I marvelled at luma, with stilt-like roots and fragrant leaves; the bright green foliage of tica; canelo, the sacred tree of the Mapucho Indians; the red-shredded bark of arryan, summer-covered in delicate white flowers; coigue, the most common forest species, 150 feet tall with a trunk thirteen feet in diameter at the base; the mighty alerce, longest-lived of all Chilean trees, some of which survive for more than 3,000 years.

The lodge surveys these wonders from a plateau carved into a shoulder of the island. Cropped grass bounded by a bamboo fence leads to an orchard full of the scent of apple, cherry and plum trees. Hummingbirds worry banks of scarlet fuchsia; black-necked swans parade gracefully across the bay; reeds rustle in the wind, nodding with crystal droplets. The forest resounds with the call of giant wrens and striped woodpeckers. From the lake comes the haunting call of the Chilean great grebe.

Isla Monita is surrounded by snow-capped peaks. From my bedroom window I looked onto Co el Plomo (2,060m), a miniature Matterhorn enfolding a shining white hanging glacier. Tiny streamlets tumble from the glacier, streaking the forest silver, cascading endlessly over ancient precipices, hurrying ice-melt waters to Lago Yelcho, painting the lake myriad shades of green, yellow and blue.

Lago Yelcho is one of the most productive and exciting fisheries in Chile. The lake contains excellent stocks of brown trout, rainbow trout and brook trout. The best of the fishing is at the southern, shallow end of the lake, close to Isla Monita. The Rio Futaleufu is the principal feeder stream and the island divides the flow of the river into two large bays: Cascada to the east, Huala to the west. Huge trout prowl through the backwaters and eddies where the river enters the lake.

Directly opposite the lodge is Yeco Bay, named after cormorants which use a large tree-stump as a roost. La Cabana stream feeds Yeco Bay with cold waters from Co Moragna (1,848m). Brook trout and large brown trout gather in the river estuary in search of food. Fish of over 7lb have been caught and my best brook trout was a magnificently speckled specimen weighing 4lb 8oz.

I watched, transfixed, as I saw him leave his bank-side lair and rush to take my fly.

The most distant of the Isla Monita fishings involves an exhilarating forty-minute boat trip north to the Bay of the Glacier, giving wonderful views westwards to Ventisquero Glacier and wonderful fishing along two miles of tree-fringed margins. Closer to the lodge, fifteen minutes by fast boat, is another small bay where a spectacular waterfall raises a mist cloud above a deep pool. I have seen trout in the teens of pounds gliding in and out of the pool and cast over them, again and again, but without success.

The lodge has fishing on five other lakes as well as on Lago Yelcho. They are tiny by comparison and vary in size from fifty to 100 acres. But they also contain splendid trout and offer some of the finest fly-fishing to be found anywhere in the world. The average weight of fish caught is around the 3lb mark, but all the small lakes (*lagunas*) hold fish up to and over 10lb in weight. My favourite is Chava, secluded and guarded by the tree-clad slopes of Monte Verde (1,892m).

The lake lies like a silver butterfly amidst dense green forests and it is fed by streams from the snow fields. The water is aquamarine and Chava is scattered with tiny islets and reed-fringed corners where huge emerald and gold insects hover and turn. The air is full of the sound of wren and ibis and the happy splash of rising trout. Chava is fished from the boat and the trout are of exceptional quality. Because the water is so clear it is often possible to see fish rising, ghost-like, from the depths to take your fly or, tantalisingly, to turn away at the last moment and glide slowly back into the darkness.

All of the Isla Monita fishing is by fly only and most guests use barbless hooks. Apart from trout for the table, all fish are returned. Nothing is certain in angling but it is more likely than not that you will catch your biggest-ever trout at Isla Monita. Well, that is what I told an America doctor, "Mad Dog" Molchun, a Vietnam War veteran, as I pushed the boat out one morning on Chava. Two hours later we hadn't seen a fin, let alone had an offer, and Mad Dog turned to me and inquired, quizzically, "Bruce, are you the guy who called the witch doctor a son of a bitch?"

"Sorry, Mad Dog," I replied. "Tomorrow, I will wear my kilt and sing to them. That always works."

68.
Away From It All

The Garvault Hotel is the remotest hotel on mainland Britain; its notepaper says so and the *Guinness Book of Records* confirms this fact. If you are looking for value-for-money trout fishing, simple comfort and good food, then look no further.

The hotel lies on the slopes of Ben Griam Mor (590m) close to the twisting little B871 road from Kinbrace to Strathnaver in Sutherland. Southwards, the mountains of the Ben Armine forest and crags of Coire na Saidhe Duibhe crowd the horizon. Eastwards lie the gentle hills of Borrobol and the headwaters of the Helmsdale River. To the north is the Flow Country.

The Garvault Hotel offers fishing by arrangement with neighbouring estates on a number of lochs to suit all states of physical fitness and ability. Contact Graham Bentham on tel: 01431 831224 for details. Novice or expert, ardent hillwalker or self-confessed sluggard, there is something here for everyone.

The three principal waters are close to the hotel and contain wild brown trout that vary in size from 6oz up to glass-case specimens of 7lb and more. There are also Arctic charr and, from time to time, salmon are encountered.

Collectively known as the Badanloch Waters, they cover an area four-and-a-half miles long by up to one mile wide. Although the three lochs are interlinked, they are fished separately as Lochs Badanloch, Nan Clar and Rimsdale.

Badanloch covers 650 acres and has an average depth of seventeen feet. Large baskets are the rule rather than the exception. The average weight of trout is about 8oz, although most seasons produce larger fish. The most productive area is towards the west end, in the narrows, and in the shallows where the island of Rubha Mor guards the entrance to Loch Nan Clar. The south shore also fishes well, particularly near to the inlet burn from Loch Alltan Fhearna.

Loch nan Clar, 670 acres, is the middle water of the group and has produced trout of over 8lb in weight. However, you are most likely to encounter fish in the order of 8oz. But regardless of size, they rise readily and fight well.

On Nan Clar, concentrate on the area of Rubha Mor at the east end, and the narrow entrance to Loch Rimsdale in the west.

Rimsdale is the last in the series, 723 acres of fine fishing, three miles long by three-quarters of a mile wide. Rimsdale is probably the most productive loch and certainly has the largest trout. Recent baskets have included fish of up to 7lb. Rimsdale is shallow, averaging twelve feet in depth, and the sandy bay at the north, where Rimsdale Burn and Alit Lon a'Chuil burn enter, can be very productive. The trout here are almost golden in colour.

High winds can sometimes make boat fishing difficult, so an outboard motor is essential. You must take your own, or pack a strong young friend who can row. Most anglers use the traditional "in-front-of-the-boat" Scottish style of fishing, with a team of three wet flies. Offer them Black Pennell, Black Spider, Black Zulu, Blue Zulu, Ke-He, Soldier Palmer and Butchers. But when confronted by glassy calm, try a dry fly. It can be deadly.

There is enough trout fishing here to last a lifetime: easily accessible waters like the three named above and many more at the end of an invigorating tramp into the wilderness, such as Coire nam Mang and Druim a'Chliabhain that lie in the flows between Ben Griam Beag and Ben Griam Mor.

One of our most splendid outings started from the hotel. Ann and I followed the Coire nam Mang track but, where it turns east, we continued north for three miles to reach Caol-loch Beag and Caol-loch Mor. After fishing them, we headed south-west for a mile and a half to find Loch Sgeireach. All of these lochs hold wonderful little trout that fight with great dash and spirit.

Apart from the lochs, great sport can also be had in the small burns that flow south to feed the Badanloch waters. I first discovered them when I was a boy. My parents had dropped me off at the bridge over the Allt Lon a'Chuil burn and gone on to fish Loch Rimsdale.

I stalked the burn north to as far as Loch Molach, following its twists and turns with increasing delight and pleasure. There had been heavy rain, so the burn was full. The pools where the flow changed direction produced wonderful brown trout, red-spotted, yellow-bellied fish of up to and over 1lb in weight.

Another unforgettable memory of that first visit to Strath Hemsdale and Strathnaver is of father's car breaking down one night somewhere between

Garvault and Syre. We huddled in the back whilst dad did things under the bonnet, but to no avail. Just as all seemed to be lost, including father's temper, a man appeared out of the gloom on an old bicycle, followed by an old sheepdog.

He stopped and asked if he could be of assistance. He then disappeared under the bonnet and, eventually, called on dad to "give it a turn". The engine sprang to life. I still remember father trying to thank our benefactor, who refused all offers of payment for his help.

"You must be a mechanic," father said.

"Oh no," came the reply, "I am a Mackay from Strathnaver."

69.
I Want a Word With You . . .

My youngest daughter, Jean, was fascinated by the casting clinic at a game fair we visited a few years back. Eventually, she asked me if she could have a lesson. Ignoring the implicit insult that I had been less than satisfactory as her angling mentor, I held my peace and simply agreed. I have learned from bitter experience that arguing with Jean is a fruitless undertaking that almost invariably ends in tears – mine.

The instructor, a good angling friend, soon had Jean under control, which was something I had never achieved. As I watched, I was amazed at the rapid improvement basic instruction from a professional could effect. But, from time to time, I noticed that Jean stopped casting and fell into deep conversation with her tutor.

Eventually, Jean wandered over and smugly announced: "You know all you have been telling me about casting? Well, he says it is a load of rubbish." I spluttered, searching for words with which to defend my reputation. Jean spotted my distress instantly and moved in for the kill. "He says he wants a word with you, now."

Resigned to my fate, head hanging in shame, I shambled over. "What are you trying to do to me?" I pleaded. "She will never let me forget this if I live to be a hundred. You have destroyed my life."

Unperturbed, my friend handed me a rod and a said: "Come on Bruce, let's try to sort something out. We can't have you going around being a danger to yourself, if not to any fish that might come your way."

Most of us imagine that just because we thrash about with a trout rod and, occasionally, stumble onto a kamikaze fish, that we are competent, indeed even expert, anglers. Like the way we drive our cars: the other driver is to blame, never us. But that session at the casting clinic was of great benefit to me and reminded me of the danger of misleading beginners by suggesting we can teach them to cast. Yes, we can show them how to get a fly onto the water but, in doing so, we often infect them with our own faults and casting misdemeanours.

Over the years, I have introduced many embryonic Waltons to the delights of fly-fishing, starting with my own father. Dad was a golfer but one night, kindly driving down to collect me from the River Lyne near Peebles, he made the fatal mistake of saying: "Here, son, give me a shot at that." For the rest of his life, father was an angler and I had the pleasure of being his tutor.

Which was a mixed blessing. Being driven to the river, rather than travelling by bus, was terrific but constant complaints about wrong flies, badly made-up casts and lack of fish were harder to thole. However, there is no doubt in my mind that giving someone a love of fly-fishing is the right thing to do. All my children were so instructed at an early age: Blair, aged five, on Loch Boardhouse in Orkney; Lewis-Ann, seven, on Mrs Little's Loch near Scourie; Charles on Loch Watten in Caithness; and Jean on Loch Mela in deepest Sutherland.

More decades later than I care to remember, they are still all committed fly-fishers and the memory of the times we spent together in pursuit of trout has been an enduring family bond, regardless of who caught what or how many or how large – providing, of course, that it was always me.

One of the joys of trout fishing is its accessibility, particularly in Scotland. There are literally thousands of locations where good sport is available at modest cost, many of which are ideally suited to beginners – lochs where fish almost jump straight into the boat by themselves, which is mightily encouraging to any angler, beginner and expert alike.

One such location is Loch Laidon on Rannoch Moor, that vast, desolate, water wilderness which lies at the very heart of Scotland. Laidon trout average three to the pound and large baskets are the rule, rather than the exception. They rise freely, fight hard and are perfect for breakfast, lunch or tea.

Laidon also contains much larger specimens, of up to and over 10lb in weight, caught using the old Scottish fishing method of trolling: a large bait, sunk to a depth of thirty feet, trailed behind a slowly moving boat. Grim work but a possible way of filling that ever-ready glass case waiting above the mantelpiece.

I love Laidon, not only because it is so user-friendly to anglers, but also because the loch lies amidst such dramatic surroundings, dominated to the west by the mountains of Glencoe. Bank fishing can be highly productive but a boat gives access to dozens of secret bays and fishy corners.

Further north, there are more perfect beginner's lochs: Little Loch Awe near Inchnadamph in Assynt; the hill lochans of the Glencanisp Forest to the east of Lochinver; Fada and the Suilven plateau lochs; Loch Rangag in Caithness, north from Latheron, where my first grandchild, Brodie, caught his first trout; beautiful Loch Hakel, near Tongue, a few minutes distant from my front door.

The wild trout lochs of Scotland, in all their diversity, are a priceless, irreplaceable treasure to be nurtured for the pleasure of present generations and for the pleasure and comfort of generations of anglers yet to come. In spite of my alleged failings as an instructor, I have no regrets whatsoever about introducing beginners to this delight. After all, there is nothing to stop them seeking better, more professional casting advice than I can offer. Just ask Jean. Quicker than it takes you turn this page, she will confirm that it is the right thing to do.

70.
Birds of a Feather

Most anglers have a keen interest in ornithology and many will have been following the long-running debate about controlling the numbers of Scotland's great raptors. As the new fishing season gets under way, here is a guide to help anglers recognise the most pernicious and dangerous of all raptors: *Willies nonscotica.*

These creatures wreak havoc on our fragile Highland environment and also pose specific problems for anglers. Because of their powerful talons, the Willies can easily stop fishermen from gaining access to lochs and rivers. Willies have so over-fished many Scottish waters that there are now very few salmon and trout left. There are also horrifying stories of innocent humans, walking in Scottish hills and glens, being ruthlessly attacked by flocks of Willies.

Carefully study this guide. Make sure that you can properly identify the species. When out in the hills, if you spot a Willie, immediately report the sighting to the nearest police officer:

Habitat: The Willie's preferred habitat is Scottish countryside with grouse moors, or part moorland and deer forest. Willies are particularly widespread in mountainous districts near to salmon rivers and trout lochs in the neighbourhood of stately castles and Victorian mansions in remote glens, but they are also found in any area of Scotland that might attract either British government or European Union grants and subsidies.

Food: Mainly hard cash in the form of public funds (see above) but they will also take adjacent, less wealthy Willies and indigenous species such as crofters, shepherds and small farmers. Much of their food is stored for future use in Guernsey, the Isle of Man, the British Virgin Islands and Zurich banks various.

Characteristics: In their never-ceasing hunt for food, the Willies will often sink to great depths of depravity with scarcely any perceptible signs of embarrassment. In contrast to this, paying out money, especially to employees and to local tradesmen, is slow and frequently accompanied by a rather laboured "sob". The Willies trap much of their prey in and around the Palace of Westminster, the Scottish Parliament building and in Brussels by planting out inducements to attract their quarry. These include sporting holidays, haunches of venison, sides of salmon, a bit of fun on the side and "votes". They hunt with great skill and it is not unusual to see half a dozen at once gathered round these government watering holes.

Appearance: Even at a distance the Willies' call is sufficiently distinctive for easy identification. Their incessant cry for public money sounds like, *"wearethetrueguardiansofthecountrysideandyouoweusaliving"*. This is complemented, when they are aroused, by an additional call sounding like *"getoffmylandyoubloodypeasant"*. Some Willies tend to be morally aware but most have the teeth white with a tight black band round their intellect. Length: about 5ft 2in to 6ft 6in. Beak: bulbous and often tipped rosy-red. Lower jaw: loose and protruding. Forehead: none. Feathers: perpetually ruffled.

Breeding: The Willies reach sexual maturity in their early thirties when they produce 2.4 offspring. Incubation is by both sexes for up to seven years. Young Willies (Boy: Justin; Girl: Julia), when part-formed, are sent to cloning-schools to preserve the genetic integrity of the species. The mating call of the adult female Willie is unmistakable, a high-pitched croak like: *"Aga-Aga-Aga-Aga"* repeated over and over again until she is satisfied. The female differs only marginally from the male in outward appearance and, when on the nest, both Willies adopt a similar dress pattern: tweed skirt or moleskin trousers, blue-serge sweater, flat cap worn at an angle over the right ear.

Nests: The principal nest is in Scotland where the Willies are sheltered by archaic land-ownership laws. The nest is always close to the things the Willies like to kill: golden eagle, hen harrier, peregrine, goshawk, osprey, buzzard, heron, grouse, red deer, wildcat, otter, hare, rabbit, rats, mice, moles, voles, salmon, brown trout and sea-trout; in coastal areas: merganser, cormorant, shag, goosander, annoying seagulls, whales, if they can get them, and all species of seals.

Status and distribution: Some Willies are resident all year round but most are autumn visitors, the bulk of them generally arriving via Inverness from about mid-August to mid-October. There are an estimated 4,000 pairs, most of whom have alternative nests in Edinburgh, Glasgow, London and the English Home Counties. There are several sub-species including: *Willies Guestus*, *Willies Americanus*, *Willies Europeanus* and *Willies Arabicus*. Most prolific, and noisiest, are *Willies Guestus*, who are much given to shouting to each other at the top of their voices in public places.

Recent evidence suggests that the other Willies sub-species are impacting heavily on the indigenous Willies' prerogatives. These new breeds are aggressive and attack at the slightest provocation. They also have sufficient resources to soar much higher in price when it comes to snapping up choice morsels of property. However, at the first sign of communal danger, all of the Willies, regardless of place of birth, form themselves into huge flocks for protection.

Field Research: Ongoing studies indicate that Willies numbers are now seriously out of control; they have increased their influence to such an extent that they are a threat to all other forms of indigenous Scottish life, particularly in connection with the Willie's reluctance to allow anything to impinge upon his hereditary right to do whatsoever he pleases with his nesting site, regardless of the needs of other species living there.

Anglers interested in finding out more about Willies could usefully contact the Royal Society for the Protection of Berks at various offices throughout Scotland.

71.
Hill Loch Fishing at Its Finest

Foinaven (914m), a massive, grey slab of a mountain, towers over the tiny loch. As I fished down the reed-fringed shore, the water shimmered in afternoon sunlight. The moment my flies touched the surface, the water exploded as two good trout grabbed, simultaneously, both of which were in the order of 12oz in weight.

The second, third and fourth casts brought similar results and within half an hour I had caught more than a dozen perfectly-matched fish. They were unusually coloured, with a green tinge, which probably reflected the habitat in which they lived. I kept two for supper and returned the others to fight another day.

This was hill-loch fishing at its finest and well worth the not inconsiderable effort involved in reaching such a distant loch. It lay at an altitude of 200 metres in a small corrie on the south side of the mountain. All that is best in my favourite pastime can be found here, near Scourie, amidst the wilderness lands of North West Sutherland.

Earlier that morning, four eager anglers, including my wife, Ann, my son Blair and his wife, Barbara, and myself, set off from Stack Lodge to explore Beat 7 of the Scourie Hotel fishings. It involves a long walk, about eight miles, there and back, but there are excellent stalkers for most of the way.

As you hike north-east towards Arkle (787m), you might be tempted to stop for a cast in lochs which lie adjacent to the track, Loch a'Cham Alltain, Loch na Nighe Leathaid and Loch Airigh a'Bhaird. Resist the temptation to do so, otherwise there might not be enough time to do proper justice to that which lies ahead.

Make sure that you are well prepared, with compass and map, food and warm clothing, all the essentials for a day out in an area where the weather can be notoriously unpredictable. In our case, that morning, we also packed Ann's macho thug of a Yorkshire terrier, Heathcliff, her inseparable companion.

A few days earlier, the wretched beast had set off in hot pursuit of a mallard and her ducklings and, not having learned to swim properly, had ended up drifting helplessly out into the middle of a cold loch. Blair, acting above and beyond the call of duty, I thought, stripped off and waded out to rescue the brute.

Since the "accident", I had been giving Heathcliff swimming lessons: long piece of binder twine attached to lead, dog in loch, then towed shore-wards, amidst much encouragement and advice on how to do a proper doggy-paddle. You would think that a real dog would instinctively know these things, but then, I suppose one has to make allowances for Yorkshire terriers.

Like all of the Scourie Hotel fishings, Beat 7 consists of not one loch, but more than a dozen or so, spread over a wide area. The principal water here is Loch an Tigh Sheilg, a long straggle of deeps and skerries, corners and inviting bays, and as you round the skirts of Arkel, the loch lies below you to the left of the track.

Blair and Barbara, being much younger and fitter than Ann and I, had decided to walk another two miles to reach one of the most beautiful waters in the area, Loch an Easain Uaine – "the Loch of the Green Waterfall" – reached by leaving the track at the outlet burn from Loch na Tuadh and following the south shore up and into the corrie that enfolds Easain Uaine.

The burn that drains Loch na Tuadh feeds Loch an Tigh Sheilg and Ann and I based ourselves at the small, sandy beach here. This is a substantial burn and, like many similar Sutherland burns, it can hold excellent trout, particularly after heavy rain and towards the end of the season. Where the stream flows into an Tigh Sheilg is also an excellent place to begin.

The bottom here is sandy and even, making wading comfortable and easy. Soon, however, you are forced onto the bank and you should pick your way with care and caution because the water deepens quickly. Fish the south bank, working north towards the end of the loch. You will find great sport all the way with hard-fighting, very pretty trout that average around 8–10oz in weight with a few much larger fish to keep you alert.

At the far end of the loch, where it narrows and flows out in the Uidh an Truim stream, it is possible, with care, to cross to the other side. Having done so, walk eastwards until you pick up the first burn entering an Tigh Sheilg from the slopes of Foinaven. Follow it up the hill for half a mile to find little Loch na Stioma Gile, "the Loch of the Green Trout".

Our day ended with a basket of eleven trout weighing some 9lb, wet feet, tired legs and wind-burnt faces. The hardest part was leaving. Evening sunlight shadowed the grey mountain and curlew and golden plover piped and called to us as we made our way back up to the track. The path led us homewards through the hills, past mirror-calm lochs stippled with the rings of rising trout. A black-throated diver swept by, neck outstretched, calling hauntingly. The perfect end to a perfect day.

See OS Map 9, Cape Wrath, Second Series, Scale 1:50,000. Loch an Tigh Sheilg is at Gd ref: 296496. Further information from the Scourie Hotel, tel: 01971 502396.

72.
A Highland Half-hour

A Highland half-hour does not necessarily mean thirty minutes. On occasions it can mean months, even years. Once, when I asked a local plumber for urgent assistance, he told me that he would be along to sort it out within a half-hour. That was more than twenty years ago and we still await his arrival, which seems increasingly unlikely now that he has been called upon to attend to more celestial plumbing emergencies "upstairs".

In a similar fashion, those not acquainted with Highland manners might believe it when they are told that the loch they wish to fish is "just a step or two beyond the top of that hill". In reality, this generally means a gut-busting hike of Everest proportions. Visitors should also be warned that just because there is a boat on the loch they intend to fish, that does not necessarily mean that it is in the water or, once they have manhandled it to the water, that the boat will float.

These matters are all part of the rich tapestry of trout fishing north of the Great Glen and, in truth, I don't think that I would like it to be any other way. It just takes time to get used to it, and time and patience to adjust to the circumstances you find, if and when you do eventually arrive at the chosen location. Fishing days that began with all the signs of an impending disaster often end up as the most fondly remembered outings.

However, this philosophical view is not shared by many southern anglers. They are accustomed to getting what they paid for, or what they think they paid for: convenient parking, easy access to the waterside, boats waiting and ready, oars and outboards in place, landing net in the bottom of the boat and a minion to help them board and to push them off. Forelock-tugging is not obligatory but it does help to keep them happy.

All of which I should have remembered when two friends of ours, from south of Mr Hadrian's Wall, having invited us out for dinner one evening, asked if there was a Kyle of Tongue trout loch nearby where they could have a couple of hours' sport before dark. There was indeed, a wonderful little water, rarely fished and, really, only "a step or two beyond the top of that hill". I even tied up suitable casts for them.

Eventually, the famous duo appeared for their expedition – in chest waders. As gently as possible, I tried to explain that this was not a good idea. Wading was not required, and chest waders would only make the journey less comfortable. Ann and I could not could persuade them to wear walking boots. They knew better and off they went. We watched them reach the first rise and left them to it. We had done our best and they were responsible adults.

A few months later, I picked up a copy of a fishing magazine and noticed that one of my friends had contributed an article on his recent north of Scotland fishing experience. Apparently, their after-dinner fishing trip had been a complete disaster because they had been ill-advised by someone (me, but unnamed in the article) who should have known a lot better. I read on with growing interest.

They had got lost and, by the time they eventually found the loch, it had begun to get dark. Nothing daunted, they waded in and set about the removal of trout from their natural habitat but, because of the undergrowth behind them, kept getting their flies snagged. One toppled into the loch, soaking himself from head to foot in the process, which convinced them to call it a day – or, rather, as it by was then, night. Pitch black and they were torchless.

They didn't have a clue as to where they were but guessed the route back by following a track that looked as though it might be leading in the right direction. It was but, as they found to their cost, it also ran along the edge of a fairly steep gully, into which they tumbled, head-over-heels, chest waders and all. Still, it's an ill wind because, at the bottom, they recognised where they were and eventually made it safely back to their car.

I telephoned to express my sympathy and, yes, it had been a nightmare, apart from not catching any fish and, yes, at one stage they had thought that they were going to die. However, with the passage of time, they now realised what an amazing adventure they had had and both regularly "dine out" on the story to the great amusement and delight of all and sundry.

In fairness, I should point out that the pair are salmon anglers, rather than trout anglers, and are more accustomed to the orderly drill of fishing for the King of Fish, rather than for its humble cousin, Tammy Troot. They still visit regularly, to fish for salmon, but, strange to relate, they haven't asked me for any more advice about after-dinner trout fishing. Well, at least it introduced them to really wild sport "just a step or two beyond the top of that hill".

73.

Sparing the Rod

I tried to come to terms with my grief and sang a few lines from a song written by London's "Coster Laureate", Albert Chevalier: "We've been together now for forty years, and it don't seem a day too much . . ." But I knew that it had to come. Good things can't go on forever. There had been times when we were parted but it was never for long and the joy of being together again soon blew all cares away.

This time there would be no happy reunion, only bitter-sweet memories of the care-free days that we spent together; of our first meeting on the Roman Wall in Northumberland; of walks into Scotland's wilderness places where our only companions were red deer, otter and wildcat; when golden eagle and greenshank marked our passage; the heart-stopping sound of trout rising on a distant lochan.

I assembled my cane fishing rod for the last time, fitted reel and line, made up a cast and tied on three favourite flies. Nothing but the best would do: Ke-He, Greenwell's Glory and Silver Butcher. All that remained to be done was to find a suitable place on my work room wall from which to hang it. At least, in spirit, we would be together, even although I would no longer fish with my old friend.

Anglers are like that. They become attached to their rods. Physically, of course, when they fish with them, but also, at least in my case, emotionally. The rod was built for me by a Mr Stott who lived in a cottage near the Twice Brewed Inn on the Roman Wall. He had spent most of his life building rods for Hardy's of Alnwick and I asked him for a 9ft 6in split-cane rod with a butt-extension so that I could use it for both trout and sea-trout.

When modern materials, such as carbon fibre, arrived, everybody rushed to embrace the new, lighter, rods. They became status symbols. Anyone who was anyone had to have one; all very nice in their own way but expensive if you were bringing up a family and, as our lot did, they all fished. Apart from that, I liked my cane rod and was more than happy to keep fishing with it, rather than with any of the new boys in town.

Inevitably, over the years, it was damaged. The top section snapped when I was trying to retrieve a fly that had become stuck on an underwater obstruction. The resultant repair reduced the length of the rod by a couple of inches. I took it to Chile with me in the 1990s where it encountered a lot of seriously large brown trout, brook trout and salmon. It was in use every day, six days a week for twelve months.

A complete overhaul helped but by this time, the top section was permanently out of alignment with the rest of the rod. No problem. I just adjusted my casting technique to compensate and got on with it. More serious, however, was the fact that the jointing mechanism between the middle and top section had become loose and, in moments of extreme excitement, when casting over a rising trout, the top section would fly off into the distance, much to the amusement of my fishing companions.

The only time I came near to losing the rod happened one day in the 1980s when I was fishing Loch Watten in Caithness. I had moved forward in the boat to land a very good trout that my companion had caught and, when I turned round to continue fishing, there my rod wasn't. It was a strange moment. I knew that it had been there a moment earlier. What could have happed to it?

The only solution was that I had somehow managed to tip it overboard when I moved. "Come, Bruce," my friend said, "why aren't you fishing?" For the rest of the afternoon, I rowed the boat and cursed inwardly. How could I have done something so stupid?

Three weeks later, Ann, whilst treating a patient, discovered that he was a professional diver. "Ah," she commented, "I think that I know someone who would appreciate a word with you." He agreed to try to find the rod. We took a boat out to the area where the rod had gone overboard and, whilst I rowed up and down over the area, he followed behind the boat, coming up every few minutes to check direction.

Just when I was about to give up, his hand rose Excalibur-like from below the surface, clutching the rod. I wish I could say that a 6lb trout was attached to the tail fly but that would be untrue and, as everybody knows, we anglers never lie. Whatever, I can still remember the feeling of joy I felt as I took the rod into my hands.

As the years advanced, we – my cane rod and I – became figures of fun. When we appeared at mooring bays, knowing glances would be exchanged, tongues wagged and hands raised in failed attempts to stifle ribald laughter. At first, I tried to explain the advantages of cane-built rods over the new-fangled jobs – firmer action, greater accuracy, perhaps not lighter, but much more comfortable and easier to use – but to no avail. So I gave up trying. The rod worked for me. That was all that really mattered.

The end came in 2008 during a gale on Loch Hope. Whilst rowing back to the mooring bay, my angling companion inadvertently sat on the rod. I sent it off to hospital, yet again, but eventually even I had to admit that it was done, finished and deserved nothing other than honourable retirement. As I write these words, it hangs on the wall. When I glance up at it, I remember the good times we had together.

74.
Great Sport

The 2010 salmon season has been one of the best in living memory, particularly up here in the far north of Scotland. Heavy rain brought with it unusually high numbers of fish, returning to their natal rivers to spawn. Even our small streams have enjoyed spectacular sport and, consequently, brought huge smiles to the faces of the anglers fortunate enough to be, for once, in the right place at the right time.

I have been fishing for the "King of Fish" for more years than I care to remember, although, to be entirely truthful, I am much more of a wild brown trout man than a dedicated salmon angler. Nevertheless, when the opportunity arises, I am happy to have a cast or three, more in hope than in the expectation of catching anything. But from time to time my patience is rewarded, and I managed to catch my fair share this summer.

But what is a "fair share"? Given the overall decline in salmon numbers over the past few decades, some would argue that catching and killing just one salmon is one too many. Thus, the "catch and release" principle has become policy on most of Scotland's salmon rivers; by all means, hook, play and land a fish but, having done so, carefully return it to the water to survive and spawn and fight another day.

I have serious problems with this philosophy. Of course, there are many who would claim that the act of catching and playing a fish does not cause the creature pain because, they argue, fish do not feel "pain" in the way that we humans understand it. I disagree. I believe that fish do suffer pain when being caught. So why do I persist in fishing? Is it simply for the adrenalin rush released by the excitement involved? I suppose that has something to do with it but, for me, not ending the process by killing the fish is an even greater act of cruelty.

Which is not to say that I kill all the fish that I am lucky enough to catch; most of them – trout, sea-trout or salmon – are returned. But this is by my own free choice, not by official dictate. If the rule on the river or loch was that all fish were to be returned, then I wouldn't fish there; there are other ways to obtain an "adrenalin rush" than inflicting distress on fish. Watching Scotland trying to play football springs instantly to mind, or listening to pontificating politicians arguing that black is white or white is black.

The vast majority of anglers, or at least the ones that I know, share a similar view and act responsibly. This evidenced by the fact that upwards of 50% of all salmon caught by rod and line anglers in Scotland are now returned. On some rivers, the figure is considerably higher, up to 90% of fish being returned. This is particularly important for our endangered spring salmon, perhaps the most magnificent of all salmon, silver from their North Atlantic feeding grounds and bars of purest steel, entirely beautiful.

Government, in its wisdom (if you will forgive the oxymoron), fully supports the catch and release policy. They argue that in order to ensure the survival of salmonid species, it is essential. Few would disagree but, if they are really committed to this principle, why then do they continue to allow the indiscriminate, interceptory netting of wild salmon in our estuaries and around Scotland's coastline? Whilst rod and line anglers experienced outstanding catches in July, with the vast majority of these fish being returned, the netsmen also had a field day, but killed every single fish that they caught.

Anecdotal evidence tells that Billingsgate Market in London, the traditional destination of most Scottish salmon caught in nets, has made it perfectly clear that it needs no more salmon from Scotland; allegedly, it can't cope with the quantity already received. I have similar reports from the north coast about sea-trout; dozens of boxes of net-caught sea-trout are being shipped south. These comments do not, of course, apply to the West Highlands and Islands where wild salmon numbers have almost completely collapsed anyway because of the impact of factory salmon farming.

But it does seem to me to demonstrate, yet again, that law is indeed an ass. It is a criminal offence in Scotland to either sell or buy rod-and-line-caught salmon, a law enacted with the sole purpose of protecting wild salmonids from commercial exploitation. But it is another "law" for the netsmen who can, legally and with impunity, kill as many salmon as they like. This sounds daft to me, as it does to thousands of my fellow anglers.

Whatever, we live in a daft world and all we can do is to try to make the best of it, that and to voice our concerns. In the meantime, five salmon, three of which were returned, have been added to my lifetime total of fish caught: twenty salmon in near sixty years. I remember them all and, most of all, the wonderful fish that I caught a few weeks ago in a small Highland river that is shortly to become the finest smoked salmon in the world.

75.
Where to Stay?

There are fishing hotels and fishing hotels. Some establishments that claim this distinction couldn't tell the difference between a trout and a doorknocker. Therefore, I advise anglers searching for sport to follow a dictum drummed into me during military service for Queen & Country: "Time spent in reconnaissance is seldom wasted."

Anglers have basic requirements. Top priority is that there must be the chance of a fish or three, be they salmon, trout or sea-trout. We need accurate information about access to fishing and expect our hotel to be able to provide that, and to provide whatever else is needed – sound boats, outboard engines and knowledgeable guides to help us on our way.

We want a rod room and a deep freeze to store the fish we hope to catch, also local patterns of flies and basic fishing tackle to be available in case of emergencies. We expect adequate food, flexible meal times, sensible packed lunches and a well-stocked bar and wine cellar. And, prior to retiring to a warm bed in preparation for further adventure, a place where we can relax and swap stories of ones that got away and ones that didn't.

After more than half a century angling in Scotland, I have been fortunate enough to find four "proper" fishing hotels that meet most of these requirements. They are the Merkister in Orkney (tel: 01856 771366; www.merkister.com), the Ulbster Arms in Caithness (tel: 01847 831641; www.ulbsterarmshotel. co.uk), the Inver Lodge Hotel at Lochinver (tel: 01571 844496; www. inverlodgehotel.co.uk) and the Angler's Retreat on the island of South Uist in the Western Isles (tel: 01870 610325; www.anglersretreat.net).

I first visited Orkney in . . . suffice to say our car was lifted onboard in a spider-web of grappling hooks. Nowadays, it's roll on and roll off in comfort. But the welcome anglers receive at the Merkister Hotel on the shores of Loch of Harray in Orkney remains the same: warm, friendly, supportive and completely designed to meet every whim of the serious piscator. This is a fishing hotel par excellence.

The Merkister Hotel, owned and run by the Macdonald family, is a happy ship and it shows: walls are adorned with glass-case specimen trout that would bring a smile to the face of the most jaded spirit. Apart from Loch of Harray, the principal waters are Swannay, Boardhouse, Hundland and Stenness. Offshore islands – Hoy, Rousay, Sanday, Westray and Eday – have in themselves fishing opportunities enough to last several angling lifetimes. The Merkister Hotel will guide you to the best of this sport with courtesy and kindness.

The Ulbster Arms Hotel in Halkirk, Caithness, is as unpretentious as it is excellent. For decades it has played host to anglers fishing the Thurso River. In these parlous times for *Salmo salar*, when distinct species of fish may have been lost because of the impact of pollution and disease from inefficiently regulated factory salmon farms, the Thurso still manages to produce between 800 and 1,500 fish most seasons.

The hotel is "comfortable" in the best tradition of Highland fishing hotels. The staff are constantly helpful and obliging and the food is outstanding. At the end of the day, in the bar before dinner, the talk is almost exclusively "fishing". Perhaps above all, the presence of Eddie McCarthy – fishery manager and Thurso expert – and his team of gillies gives the hotel a special distinction. If anybody can guide you into a fish, then these are the people to do it. Honest.

For complete angling hedonism, the Inver Lodge Hotel is supreme. Nicholas Gorton, the manager, has achieved the miracle of combining a relaxed, unhurried atmosphere with meticulous, faultless service. In my opinion, no other Highland fishing hotel comes anywhere close to matching the standard of accommodation, food and comfort offered by Inver Lodge.

The hotel offers salmon fishing on the rivers Inver and Kirkaig, as well as trout fishing on several hundred lochs. My joy here, however, is the Kirkaig, particularly the upper beat, which begins at Kirkaig Falls, reached after an invigorating hike of forty-five minutes. The steep climb down to the fishing platform at Falls Pool is but a modest precursor of what is to follow – hours of mountain goat stumbling downstream to fish the other pools. Nobody has the right to call himself or herself "salmon angler" until they have experienced fishing this beat.

For the best and most consistent of all fishing, for salmon, trout or sea-trout, you must cross the broken waters of the Minch to the Outer Hebrides. The Angler's Retreat in South Uist is the essential base for your expedition, a comfortable guest house splendidly run by Billy and Marion Felton, steeped in tradition – warm, welcoming and irresistible.

In fact, I find everything about South Uist irresistible. The amazing softness of the Atlantic air, the spring flourish of wildflowers amidst the fertile machair lands, the call of oystercatcher and curlew on a summer evening, and, of course, the happy sound of rising fish. This is an island for all seasons. June brings thrilling trout fishing on classic lochs such Grogarry and Stilligarry. Summer and autumn usher in sport with sea-trout and salmon on supremely lovely waters, including Kildonan, Fada and Roag.

Billy Felton is one of the island's most experienced anglers and he offers his guests the best possible advice on flies and tactics, based upon years of experience fishing these waters. But be warned, fishing on South Uist could seriously alter your life. Once experienced, you might never want to fish anywhere else again.

I have known the places I have described above for many years. They have never let me down. There have been days when salmon, trout and sea-trout were less than co-operative – after all, that is an essential adjunct of every angler's life – but on these few occasions, at least I have been fishless in comfort. What more could one ask?

76.
The Silver Tay

We slept in the heather beneath an ink-black, star-bright sky. A velvet cloud of pipistrelle bats whisked out into the darkness from nearby ruined croft buildings. A fox barked sharply in the distance. A solemn owl ghosted by on silent wings. Late curlew called hauntingly. Loch water lapped the shores of my dreams and sleep came easy in that warm night.

This resting-place was on the margins of Loch Ordie in Perthshire, high above the River Tay near the old cathedral city of Dunkeld. Our Boy Scout camp was based on the banks of the river at Inver Park and we had set out earlier that morning on an adventure hike into the wilderness crags of Deuchary

Hill (509m). In these few hours, I fell hopelessly in love with the River Tay.

From its source amongst the thread-fingered busy streams of Ben Lui (1,130m) by Tyndrum, to the vast expanse of the Firth of Tay, the river runs for a distance of 120 miles. It draws strength from an area of more than 2,800 square miles. Water from the mountains of Breadalbane and Glen Lednock feed mighty Loch Tay. They flow from the ribbon lochs of Laidon, Rannoch and Tummel and Forest of Atholl tributaries to mingle tighter in the sea-salt tide by the fair city of Perth.

During the Scottish Wars of Independence, Clan MacDougall won a victory over Robert Bruce at Dalrigh in the hills above Killin at the west end of Loch Tay. The clan possessed a magnificent brooch, torn from the plaid of the fleeing King of Scots. In 1529, the Earl of Atholl built a hunting lodge in Glen Tilt for King James V, when 1,000 men were employed to herd deer down from the corries of Beinn a'Ghlo for His Majesty's pleasure. His daughter Mary, Queen of Scots, was similarly entertained in Glen Tilt in 1564 before she herself became the hunted one.

The most famous "hunted" ones of the Tay today are, however, its Atlantic salmon. For hundreds of years, *Salmo salar* has provided sustenance and sport for Tay fishermen. John Richardson described the salmon fishings in 1788:

> The fishings employ between two and three hundred fishers. Six vessels are employed during the season running to and from London which is the principal market. A considerable part are sent fresh in the spring season, and for the past two years the greatest proportion of the fresh salmon has been packed in ice.

Salmon were also abundant in 1922 when Miss Georgina Ballantine caught her famous, record-breaking fish – a salmon weighing 64lb. Over the years, the story of its capture has often been disputed: some claim Georgina was not holding the rod when the great fish took, that her father, who was with her at the time, was a gillie who worked on the estate. The truth of the matter is somewhat different.

Her father, James Ballantine, was a local businessman, parish register and an expert angler. He was the last lessee of the Boat of Caputh beat on the river and had been born in a house on the banks of the Boat Pool, from which the huge salmon was taken. James and his daughter had spent the day trolling the pool using preserved dace as bait. They had already landed several large salmon and their catch for the day was in the order of 140lb.

Georgina was small in stature, barely over five feet tall, and was already showing the signs of the severe arthritis that she increasingly suffered from following her duties as a nurse during most of the period 1914–18. Their boatman had gone home but Georgina's father decided to fish down the pool one last time, with Georgina holding the heavy greenheart rod. The fish took from behind the Bargee stone, which lies near the top of the pool, and was successfully landed after a great struggle.

The salmon was displayed in the window of P. D. Malloch's shop in Perth and Georgina stood at the back of the crowd who had gathered to admire it. Two elderly men were particularly overawed by the size of the salmon and Georgina heard them talking:

> One said to the other, "A woman? Nae woman ever took a fish like that oot of the water, mon. I would need a horse, a block and tackle, tae tak a fish like that oot. A woman – that's a lee anyway." I had a quiet chuckle up my sleeve and ran to catch the bus.

The Tay has always been famous for the quality and size of its salmon and more than twenty fish weighing over 50lb in weight have been taken from the river. A salmon of 71lb was recorded as being hooked and played but not landed in 1868 by Dr Browne, Bishop of Bristol. He was fishing near the mouth of the River Earn, a tributary of the Tay that flows into the Firth of Tay from the south, but after a battle lasting ten hours, the fish broke free.

When the grey finger of dawn inched its way into my sleeping bag, I awoke to find mist shimmering over the calm waters of Loch Ordie. Around me in the heather lay my companions, one by one stirring to greet the coming day. We clattered about, washing in the loch, making breakfast. It was sad to leave, to tramp back down the hill to civilisation. But as we cleared the lower forest, the River Tay lay before me like a silver thread and I felt as though I had returned home.

77.

Auld Lang Syne

In a few hours, it will be midnight, 31 December. Worldwide, people are preparing to welcome in the New Year. Sober or not so sober, happy or not so happy, in their varying conditions, throats are tensing for a cheer. When I was outside earlier this evening, bucketing in additional fuel to stoke up our New Year's Eve fire, I closed the coalhouse door and looked up at the night-black sky.

The Northern Lights, the "merry dancers", fingered the star-splashed canopy, touching the far horizon from Ben Hope in the west to the crenellated ridge of Ben Loyal and the leaden waters of the Kyle of Tongue. A herd of red deer champed the grasses of the field in front of our cottage. The sound of our stream tumbling down the hill from Beinn Bhreac was like the sound of ice cubes clinking in a freshly filled crystal glass. And I found myself thinking about fishing.

I remember my son, aged six, learning to fish on Loch Boardhouse in Orkney; my daughter, thrashing a Scourie hill loch with an eight-foot greenheart rod, whilst we all tried to control our laughter – she caught the only trout of the day; second son, Charles, as an infant, eager and intent – with a stick, a piece of string and a huge Hairy Mary – fishing in the sea; the youngest, Jean, who seemed to have been born with a trout rod in her hand, so effortless and expert is her casting technique.

I remember a day when we rested at Suileag Bothy, below the towering bulk of Suilven near Lochinver in North West Sutherland. A best-bib-and-tuckered dipper bobbed and splashed in the Abhairn an Clach Airigh burn. Loch an Alltain Duibh sparkled in autumn sunlight, its surface stippled with rising trout. Purple heather and red-bedecked rowan brushed its banks. We drank from the stream and rehearsed verses from a poem by Norman MacCaig, who loved this land and fished here for decades:

Its water goes down my throat
with a glassy coldness,
like something suddenly remembered.
I drink its freezing vocabulary
And half understand the purity
of all beginnings.

As evening beckoned, sending long shadows fluttering over the majestic shoulders of Quinaig and Clas Bheinn, we picked our way carefully homewards over the moor. The dogs, weary after the long walk, panted to heel. The white cottage at Little Assynt grew larger as we approached and we could distinguish the outline of our car, parked in the distance. Our day had brought us, as always, the sense of complete happiness that can only be found in mountain and moorland solitude. Apart from a brace of wild brown trout, we had asked for nothing more. As the mystical stream hurried us north, singing its ageless song, we carried with us its burden of joy, "half understanding the purity of all beginnings".

Sorry, I'm rambling. Wait a bit, though. On second thoughts, I'm not sorry. After so many years fishing, surely I am allowed a small ramble? Hang on a moment whilst I pour myself a decent measure of the "water of life" and consider the matter. After all, it is New Year's Eve. During my angling life I must have cast millions of times, so why then do I still keep catching the back of my neck? I must have rowed hundreds of miles up and down lochs large and small in all kinds of weather – well it seems like it – and tied thousands of casts and lost countless numbers of flies.

The first trout I ever caught, which was all of three inches long, was on Lyne Water, a tributary of Tweed. I was fourteen at the time, fishing near Romano Bridge. It came out of the stream on the back cast. When I found it in the undergrowth, it seemed to me to be the most beautiful creature that I had ever seen. Another beautiful "creature", unbeknown to me then, was, at the same time, fishing a mile and a half upstream: my future wife, Ann.

They have been good years and I regret nothing, not even losing that monster trout at Unthank on the South Tyne when we lived near Bardon Mill in Northumberland; nor the Tweed salmon in the Long Pool, upstream from

Innerleithen, when I was sixteen, although I wept at the time; nor the day when Ann and I almost capsized the boat in a howling gale on Gladhouse Reservoir, near Edinburgh. We should never have launched the boat in the first place, but she insisted, in spite of being well-advanced towards the birth of our first daughter, Lewis-Ann.

I used to make up my late father's cast. He has long since departed to that great trout loch in the sky but I always remember his boyish enthusiasm for our well-loved pleasure. I taught dad to fish but to little avail. If father saw a trout rise he would remain rooted to the same spot for hours, convinced that, through sheer perseverance, it would eventually rise again and take his inexpertly offered fly. It never did. Ever-hopeful, dad, and generally fishless. But expectation is what fishing is all about, the sure and certain knowledge that by the end of the day we will have caught our fair share, be it a single salmon or a small brown trout.

Angling has been, and still is, one of the greatest joys of my life. Not just simply catching fish, which I occasionally do, but with the whole bang-shoot of the business of being at one with nature. I adore Scotland and everything it stands for: the smell, the touch and the taste of my native land; its kindly people, lonely moors and distant mountains; its trout-filled lochs and peat-stained streams. Damn all and anyone who dares demean this treasure.

Well, here it comes and welcome, another new year in all its pristine splendour. Another new beginning. Make the most of it. Make it the best year ever. A year of happiness, a year of care, courtesy and consideration for all creatures great and small, human or otherwise. I will begin with a kiss for Ann, my best friend and fishing companion, sitting opposite me by the fire. May there always be love in your life and wild trout in your loch.